P9-CEZ-943

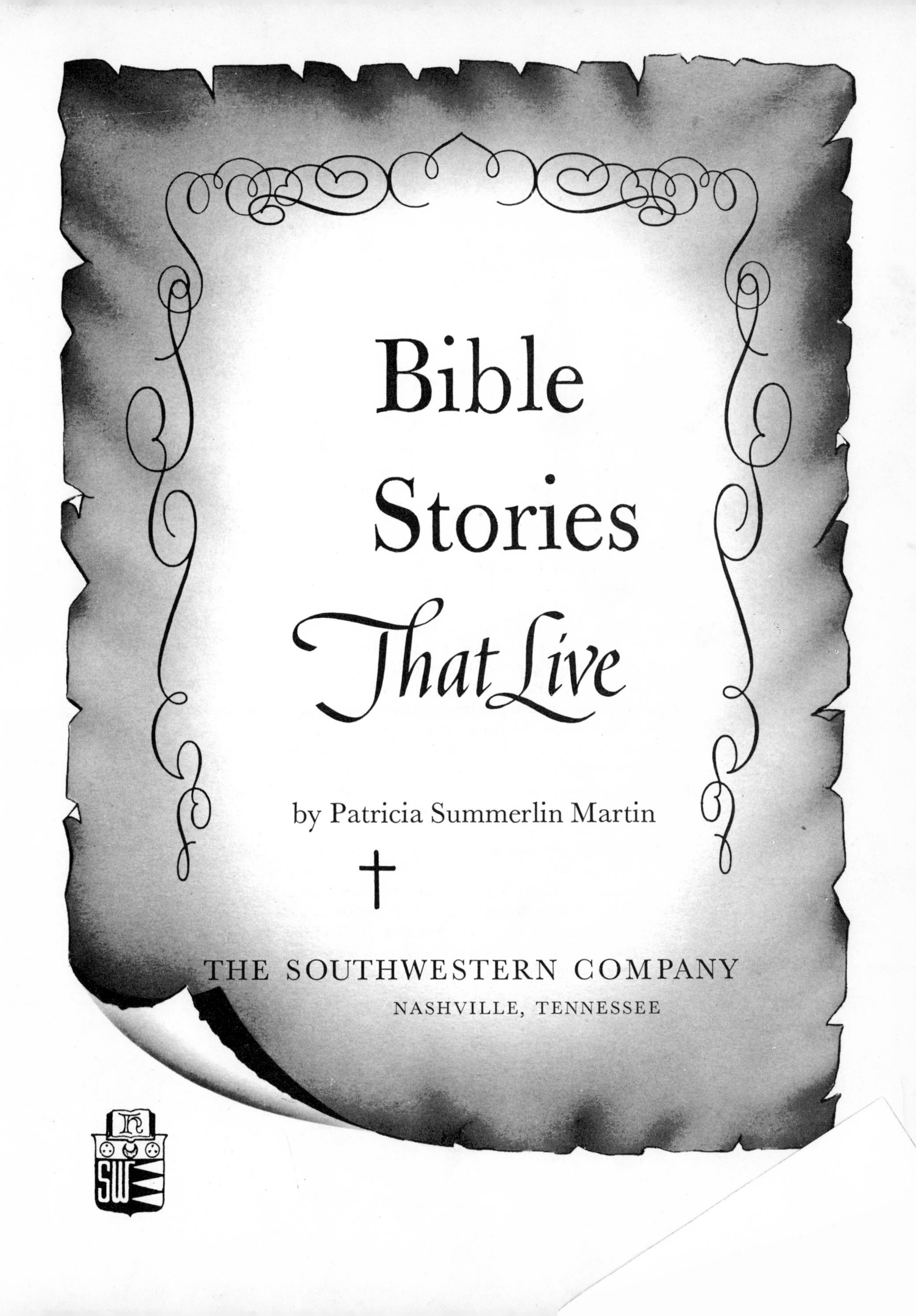
Bible
Stories
That Live
by Patricia Summerlin Martin
THE SOUTHWESTERN COMPANY
NASHVILLE, TENNESSEE

LORAN RAYMOND JONES, who painted the color illustrations in this book, was born in east central Indiana and spent most of his formative years in rural sections of that state. After high school, while employed by the Civil Service Commission in Washington, D.C., he studied evenings in the Corcoran Art School. Later, he attended the summer classes of Charles W. Hawthorne, Provincetown, Massachusetts. Coming to Chicago, he studied in a small professional class conducted by Audubon Tyler, and also evenings in the painting classes of the Art Institute of Chicago.

While employed in a commercial art studio he met, and later married, Miss Lena Gunderson of Wautoma, Wisconsin. She was earning her way doing drawings for advertising. Her background of art training and experience has been of great value in his work. They have a daughter and two grandchildren.

Mr. Jones has had many years' experience in general commercial and book illustration; also doing an occasional portrait. In this field some prizes were won. For several years he was an active and exhibiting member of several fine arts organizations in Chicago and the suburban area. He made many painting demonstrations for these organizations and served occasionally on juries of awards and admissions.

The painting of religious subjects for publishers has been his specialty for the past twenty years. He has also devoted part time to teaching in two of the country's prominent art schools for the past fourteen years. Many of his former students are quite successful. As a teacher, he feels that he is also a student, finding the two very controversial subjects of art and religion quite fascinating. He and Mrs. Jones are living at present in Sarasota, Florida.

Library of Congress Catalog Card No. 66-23204

Printed in the United States of America

R.R.D. 5-73

Foreword

Anyone who attempts to write a Bible story book is forced to examine his motives in face of the importance and weight the Biblical message carries. If the book is to be written for young children, one may easily justify his efforts—the Bible contains language and symbolism which must be "translated" into a child's language in order for him to understand them. In the case of older children or adults—the group for which this book is intended—the situation is somewhat different. One might suggest that the Bible itself is sufficient for them. On the other hand, I have found that even intelligent teenagers and adults find it difficult to grasp immediately the plot and message of certain scriptures. For them, a clearly-written story can lead effectively to a deeper study of the Bible itself.

Because it is aimed at an advanced age level, this book covers the most important Biblical stories rather completely. Naturally it is not possible nor advisable to reproduce everything, but I have tried with some detail to fill in the lesser understood periods of Biblical history, such as the era of prophets and kings. With each story, I have made an effort to use my imagination to make the story interesting and clear, but I have not deviated from the text to create characters or incidents. In fact, even the dialogue is often a paraphrase of the text, as in the stories of Joseph and David, both of which were written by the ancient historian with liberal amounts of interesting conversation. In these sections, as well as paraphrases of other sections of scripture, I have attempted to make the language plain without sacrificing the dignity of the message.

It was my desire to create a non-denominational book by following closely the Biblical text. The references are listed at the end of each story in the hope that the reader will be encouraged to use them with a new clarity. There are also questions given at the conclusion of each chapter that provide an easy review to the important characters, events, or lessons within the chapter.

My appreciation is extended to the publishers, who spared no expense in creating an attractive book. I feel they enhanced its value by supplying full-color illustrations which were the work of a single artist and are keyed to the stories. And I could go no further without commending the patience of my family, who have borne with me through months of pressure and deadlines.

Finally, it is my desire that *Bible Stories That Live,* like its reference work, will serve the spiritual needs of both children and adults; and that they, like its leading character, will "grow in favor with God and man."

Patricia Summerlin Martin

Table of Contents

CHILDREN OF ISRAEL

A FAMILY BECOMES A NATION

A NATION IN WAITING

THE CONQUEST OF CANAAN

THE JUDGE-WARRIORS

THE COMING OF THE SPIRIT

A LIGHT TO THE GENTILES

THE KINGDOM ESTABLISHED

List of Color Plates

OLD TESTAMENT *following page*

NEW TESTAMENT

Bible Stories That Live

Earliest Times

CREATION OF THE WORLD

God has always existed—even before the world and time, as we know it, were established. This is a concept that our minds simply cannot understand, for we must see a beginning and end. God's existence, however, extends beyond the limits of time into a realm we call "eternity." This means that he has always lived and will continue to live forever.

At some point in the endless span of God's existence, he began to create the earth and divide time into periods as we on earth measure it. Before this, the realms of our world were covered in darkness. Through this dark, shapeless space, God's voice said, "Let there be light," and piercing rays of light began to shine for the first time. God was pleased with the light, and he separated it from the darkness. The light he called Day and the darkness he called Night.

Next God separated waters that form the earth from the moisture that makes up the clouds and the sky. The great expanse of sky that filled the space around and above the earth was called the Heavens. God was again happy about his creative work.

Then God said, "Let the earthly waters be gathered together to form oceans and rivers and lakes and let the dry land appear." At his bidding it was so, and the world began to take on the shape that we know with masses of dry land separated by bodies of water. The dry land was called Earth and the waters were the Seas. When God saw how pleasing the new earth was, he caused plants, trees, and vegetation of every sort to bloom and grow upon it. Each had its own seeds so that its kind could grow again and again. The world was now a garden with shady trees bearing fruit of every sort and grassy meadows dotted with flowers.

God said, "Let there be lights in the heavens to mark the days and nights —the sun to rule by day and the moon and stars by night." When the earth was turned toward the sun, daylight reigned; then as it rotated away from the light, night began to fall and the light of the moon and stars became distinct. With the coming of the sun, time was not only divided into night and day, but into seasons as well.

The stage was set; the earth had taken on its form and the heavens were ordered by God's plan. Now God was ready to bring living creatures into being—the last stage of his work. He began by filling the waters with fish and the air with birds. They, like the plants, could grow and could give birth to those of their own kind so that they would continue to live. Their music and motion seemed to make God's creation even more complete. Next, he brought forth land animals of every sort—those that walk about on four feet and those that crawl. These, too, could produce offspring, for which God had so wonderfully provided.

God was pleased with his work at this point, and yet something was lacking—something important enough to make everything else appear to be preparation for this great event. *Genesis 1:1–25*

CREATION COMPLETED

God's marvelous scheme was almost complete—the fruitful earth was alive with growing, moving creatures in the waters, on dry land, and in the

Loran Raymond Jones

NOAH LEAVING THE ARK ON MOUNT ARARAT

Genesis 8:18; 9:1–17

Loran Raymond Jones

ABRAHAM AND LOT PART COMPANY

Genesis 13:7–9

Loran Raymond Jones

ABRAHAM RESTRAINED FROM SACRIFICING ISAAC

Genesis 22:2–14

Loran Raymond Jones

JACOB AND RACHEL AT THE WELL

Genesis 29:9–12

air. Overhead the sun, moon, and stars moved in their course, while God prepared for the final act of his creating work.

This time God used the materials from which he had fashioned the earth, and with these elements he made a man. Into this man God breathed the breath of life, and he stood alive, unlike any other creature yet made because he bore the image of God. He was capable of understanding more things than the other living beings. He could love with great depth and respond to God's love. He could communicate with God and be his friend.

This man—the final act of God's creation—was given the earth to rule over. The part of the world in which he lived was a lavish garden called Eden. Four rivers supplied the garden's vegetation with a plentiful water supply, and every sort of fruit and vegetable grew abundantly. Within the boundaries of Eden, various species of fish, birds, and animals could be found—these the man was to learn and to call by a name.

Man's life in this ideal outdoor home should have been perfect, but as he saw all the living creatures with others of their own kind, both he and God knew that something was yet lacking.

"It is not good for you to be alone," God told the man. "I will make a helper for you." So from the same elements that he had made the man, God fashioned a woman. This woman was a perfect helper for the man. The two could care for each other, work together, appreciate other things that God had made, and love the one who had created it all.

God looked upon this first man, Adam, and the first woman, Eve, and he was pleased with them, as he was with all his creative work.

Genesis 1:26–2:25

TROUBLE IN PARADISE

For a time, Adam and Eve lived a very happy, peaceful existence in Eden. God had supplied all of their needs and had given them enjoyable things to do in caring for the garden and observing the animals. Only one restriction did he place on them:

"Do not eat from the Tree of Knowledge of Good and Evil, which stands in the middle of the garden. On the day that you eat fruit from that tree, you must die."

Because Adam and Eve were adult, human beings, God gave them this chance to choose between right and wrong, just as he gives us the choice today. And it seemed that for a while, they were able to obey God's will and keep this single commandment.

The day came, however, when a serpent, more sly than the other creatures, approached Eve with this question: "Did God ask you to stay away from any of the trees in the garden?"

"He told us to eat from any of them," answered Eve, "that is, all but the Tree of Knowledge which stands in the middle of the garden. If we eat from it, we will die."

"Die?" remarked this strange serpent. "You will not die! God has told you that because he knows what will really happen. If you eat that fruit you will discover the difference between right and wrong and then you will know as much as God does."

When Eve heard this she looked at the fruit again. It did look ripe and delicious—could it be that it would truly make her as wise as God? Once the thought had entered her mind, she reached for the fruit and ate some of it. She even convinced Adam that he should try some also.

But eating the fruit did not make Adam and Eve like God at all. Instead, they both knew that they had done something terribly wrong. For the first time they felt scared and ashamed and dreaded meeting God. We still feel the same way today when we disobey God's commands. Adam and Eve felt so guilty that they tried to do an impossible thing—they tried to hide from God.

"Where are you?" called the voice of God. Adam knew that he could hide no longer. "We're afraid," he said. "When we heard you coming, we ran and hid."

"Afraid of me? Who have you been talking to? Have you disobeyed me and eaten of the forbidden fruit?"

Faced with his sin, Adam could not stand it. He turned to Eve and said accusingly: "She made me do it! She gave it to me."

So God looked at Eve. "What have you done?" he asked.

Eve tried to give an excuse also: "The serpent tricked me. That's the only reason I ate it."

At this, God faced the serpent. "You will always be despised, more than all other creatures," he said. "Because of this, you will always crawl in the dust of the ground."

Then Adam and Eve had to listen to their punishment. Because they had disobeyed and chosen to do wrong, God sent them out of the garden. Outside, life was very difficult. They had to work hard to get food to grow. They learned to know what sickness and pain were. Eventually, they knew that they would die.

At the gates of the garden, God stationed cherubim to keep Adam and Eve from ever returning. They guarded the entrance with a flaming sword that turned in every direction. But even though man had turned from him, God did not desert his creation. He promised that someday he would save them from the punishment and guilt that sin placed upon them. As we go through the Bible, we will discover just what God's plan was. *Genesis 3*

TWO BROTHERS—TWO OFFERINGS

Outside the Garden of Eden, Adam and Eve found their life much more difficult than it had been before. No longer did they have every sort of fruit and vegetable growing within their reach; now Adam had to dig in the ground and struggle against the weeds in order to produce their food. He tended to a few goats and sheep that produced milk and the skins from which Adam and Eve were clothed.

Eve's duties as a woman began at the birth of her first child, Cain, and were increased when his brother, Abel, was born. As soon as the boys were old enough, they had to help their father with the work that he did. Cain chose to do the farming and spent his time working in the fields. Abel cared for his father's flocks and became a shepherd.

One day the brothers each brought a gift to God: Cain had gathered the best of the produce that he had grown and Abel had chosen a prize sheep from his flock. Something about Abel's offering and the way that it was given was pleasing to God; on the other hand, God was displeased with Cain's gift.

When Cain sensed that his offering was unacceptable, his face grew ugly to look upon. Seeing this, the Lord spoke gently to Cain's conscience: "Why does your face show such anger? If you will do the right thing, your gift will be accepted, just as your brother's was. Be strong and conquer the sin that is within you."

But Cain did not listen to God's urging. Instead, he invited Abel to walk toward the field with him. There he sprang at his brother and killed him.

"Cain!" God called to the murdering brother. "Cain, where is Abel?"

"How should I know," answered Cain sullenly. "Am I my brother's keeper?"

Then God continued, "The blood of your brother calls to me like a voice from the ground. Punishment must come upon you as it fell on your parents when they sinned. The ground upon which your brother's blood fell will no longer produce for you. You will be forced to wander from place to place for the rest of your life."

At last Cain was struck with the weight of his wrong. "My punishment is too great. Those who see me wandering about will try to kill me."

"No one will harm you because I will put my special mark on you," answered the Lord once more.

As a branded man, Cain left the home of his father and wandered the face of the earth. *Genesis 4:1–16*

ADAM'S CHILDREN

After Cain was sent from God's presence, he went to live in the land of Nod. There he built a settlement and named it for his son, Enoch. His people continued to be avengeful and troublesome, as might be expected of the descendants of one such as Cain.

Fortunately, God sent Adam and Eve other children. Among them was a son named Seth, through whom the lineage to Israel and Christ was carried. As these early people began to grow in number, they also increased in their skills and ability to handle the materials they found on the earth. They made their first tent-homes of animal skins; they began to keep herds of cattle with them to supply milk and its products wherever they went. Some clever men learned the way to forge nature's metals into tools for cutting and gardening. They even discovered the entertaining value of music and fashioned the first crude musical instruments, forerunners of our wind and string instruments.

A few people remembered to call on the Lord, their maker and keeper, but most of them fell to the same temptations to which Adam and Eve and Cain had fallen prey. The book of *Genesis* mentions, as one of the exceptions, a man named Enoch, who "walked with God." Another of the famous names of this period was Methuselah, known because he was said to have lived longer than anyone else has ever lived—969 years.

The faithful men of these times were rare, however. People had not lived many generations upon the earth until God noted that their every thought and deed was evil continually. You can imagine how much sorrow it caused the creator to know that his creatures were so wicked. God became so grieved that he was sorry he had even made man. The only answer seemed to be to wash the earth clean of its wickedness. *Genesis 4:16–6:7*

SAVED IN A SHIP

As God looked upon the world which had become so wicked, he found one man who was pleasing to him. This man was Noah. Among all those of his generation, Noah was the only one who remembered the God of his ancestors and tried to live a righteous life. How strange his pattern of living must have seemed to his corrupt neighbors! But God had plans for Noah that were destined to make him look even more out of step with those of his time.

God revealed to Noah the desire he had to wash the earth clean of its wickedness with a flood, a flood so great that every living thing would be destroyed. "But you, Noah, will receive my special blessing and will be saved," the Lord revealed. "Here is the plan I have provided for the safety of you and your family."

God's plan was that Noah should build a ship, or an "ark," out of gopher wood. It was to be a great ship with cabins and three decks, all made water-tight. Windows were to be provided for air and a roof built over the top.

"When the flood rains come," God explained, "you and your family are to go inside the ark and to take with you pairs of all beasts and birds. Be sure to store enough food to supply all of you for a long period."

So Noah set about to follow God's instructions. Far from any great body of water, he and his three sons began constructing the huge ship exactly according to God's specifications. Can you imagine what comments this strange sight must have caused Noah's neighbors to make? But he kept right at his work until the ark was finished.

Then God spoke to Noah again: "The time has come for you to take your family and the animals into the ark. When the rain begins to fall, you alone will be kept alive."

For several days a strange procession made its way to the ark—creeping serpents, running beasts, flying birds of every kind came in pairs and found a place to rest on its decks. Then Noah brought his family, which included his wife, his three sons, whose names were Ham, Shem, and Japheth, and their wives. When they were all safely inside and the doors of the ark were closed, it began to rain.

From the first, this rain was not like any other; it seemed as though the very heavens had opened up. The rivers and streams filled and overflowed; the oceans ran over the land. Soon all the ground was covered. As the water grew deeper around the ark, it was lifted and began to float. It rose with the flood, higher and higher, until even the tallest mountains were covered and the ark drifted alone on an endless sea. Everything alive on the earth was drowned in the storm. Inside the ark, God kept Noah and those with him safe from harm. *Genesis 6:5–7:23*

CALM AND A COVENANT

For forty days and nights terrific rains fell on the ark, which floated alone on an endless sea. Even when the forty days were over and God caused the flood to stop, there was water everywhere for many more months. Winds blew and helped it dry up, but only very slowly did the tops of mountains begin to appear. At last the day came when the ark bumped against the dry land on Mount Ararat and rested there to stay.

Inside the ark, Noah, his family, and the animals waited for the earth to become livable again. How would they be able to tell when it was safe to leave the ship? Noah used some of the birds on board to discover when this time came. First, he sent a raven out. Now a raven has very strong wings, so it flew to and fro until the waters dried up.

Noah was still not quite satisfied when the raven failed to return to the ark. Once more, he selected a bird—this time a dove—and sent it forth. Doves are not as strong as ravens, and when the dove could find no trees in which to rest, she flew back to the ark. Noah waited a week and then let the dove fly out again. This time she came back with a leaf in her mouth, and Noah knew that trees were beginning to appear. When another week passed and Noah released the dove, she, like the raven, did not return.

At last Noah knew that the earth was dry. Still he waited for God to give the command: "Go forth from the ark." It was on the first day of a new year when God said those words—a wonderful day on which the door of the ark was opened and Noah, his family, and the animals stepped forth onto a clean, shining earth. How beautiful it must have looked after months closed up inside the ship! What gratitude they must have felt to the Lord who had chosen them to save for this day! With these thoughts on their minds, they gathered some stones together to form an altar and burned animal sacrifices in worship to God.

In return for their prayers and devotion, God made a promise, or covenant, with Noah and his sons. As part of this promise, he declared that he would never again send a flood to destroy the earth. "While earth remains," said the Lord, "seedtime and harvest, cold and heat, summer and winter, day and night, shall not cease." As a sign of the covenant, God set a beautiful rainbow in the sky. Its shimmering colors, spanning the heavens in the sunlight that follows rain, said to Noah and to all people after him that God would keep his promise.

Genesis 8:1–9:17

THE TALLEST BUILDING IN THE WORLD

When Noah's family stepped from the ark, they were the only people left on the earth. But like the first family, Noah's sons all had children and then grandchildren, and the earth was populated once more within a few generations. As much as possible, people tried to live close to each other and they spoke a common language, one that all understood.

From Mount Ararat, where the ark landed, people moved slowly, over the years, toward the south. Here, on a wide, flat plain in the land of Shinar, they found a location in which they wanted to settle. This land was supplied with materials for making bricks and mortar, so the people set about to make more permanent buildings than their tent homes had been. The sight of their strong new brick walls and homes gave these early people a sense of pride.

"Let us make a great city of bricks," they said. "In the center, we can build a tower so tall that it will touch the heavens. Why, we will even become famous for our tower. People everywhere will know that we are great because of it."

The foundations of the tower were laid and the building begun. As the bricks were stacked higher and higher, the people felt more and more important. They were pleased with their wonderful idea.

But God was watching the builders of that tower. As he heard them boast of their importance, he was displeased. He knew that their pride would soon cause them to think more of the things they had made than they did of him. So God confused the language of those people. He made them speak differently and they were unable to understand one another. When one man gave orders, no one understood how to follow them. With such a confused state of affairs, the building of the tower soon ceased.

Gradually, people found themselves grouped with others whose language they could understand. One after another, they moved away and left the tower unfinished. Later this city came to be called Babel, or "confusion," in memory of the confusion that resulted when everyone spoke a different language.

Genesis 11:1–9

QUESTIONS: 1. *Which existed first—God or the world? What do we know about God's existence that is different from ours?* 2. *Name the things in our natural world that* Genesis *relates as having been created by God.* 3. *What was the high point of God's creative activity?* 4. *In what way was man different from the rest of God's creation?* 5. *Describe Adam's and Eve's home.* 6. *What was the one rule God asked Adam and Eve to obey?* 7. *Who persuaded Adam and Eve to disobey? How did he do it?* 8. *What was the penalty for sin?* 9. *Who were the first children born into the world? What were they like?* 10. *What was God's reaction to Cain's and Abel's offerings?* 11. *Discuss Cain's sin and its consequences.* 12. *In what ways did the people on earth develop during these earliest times? In what ways did they fail?* 13. *Why did God decide to send the flood?* 14. *How did God plan to save Noah and his family? Why did he want to save them?* 15. *How did God preserve the earth's animal life?* 16. *How did Noah tell when it was safe to leave the ark?* 17. *What were Noah's first actions when he left the ark?* 18. *What was God's covenant and promise to Noah? What was the sign of that promise?* 19. *Why did men want to build a tower?* 20. *Why was the tower never finished?*

Father Abraham

JOURNEY BY FAITH

From the most ancient times and people, the book of *Genesis* now leaps forward in history to those first great heroes of the Israelite nation. Our question is: what have they to do with the incidents and men that have come before? Perhaps a review will help us understand. God created man and gave him every opportunity to do right, but Adam failed. Even though the Lord had to punish him for his sin and send him from the garden, he did not desert Adam. When Cain murdered his brother and was banished, God saved him by placing a mark on him which protected him in his wanderings. Finally, when the world became wholly evil and God was compelled to cleanse it with a flood, he saved a righteous man, Noah, and his family in the ark. Afterward he made a covenant with them, promising never to destroy the world in that way again.

But men failed to learn the lesson God tried to teach with the sending of the flood, and once more they defied his will in the building of the tower of Babel. Was God willing to forgive again? *Genesis* doesn't seem to answer that question; but rather, it moves forward many generations to the time when the first great heroes of the Israelite nation lived. At first, the story of Abraham may appear to have nothing to do with that which has come before it. But on a closer look, we see that Abraham's call *is* God's specific answer to man's sinfulness. With a chosen few, Abraham's children (the Israelite nation), God plans to save the world from its sin. We will continue to trace this theme of a sinful creation and a forgiving creator as it runs through the rest of the Bible.

Abram, like Noah, was a man who stood above the others of his time. Far to the east in the city of Ur, named for a moon-god worshipped there, he lived according to the will of the one true God. He heard when the voice of this God called him from Ur, and he moved with his family toward the west, finally settling in a place called Haran. But here God's voice came to him once more: "Leave this land and go to a country which I will show you. In time, I plan to make you the beginning of a great nation. Your name will be so great that all the people of the earth will be blessed because of you."

Now Abram did not understand all that God meant, but he trusted and had faith that God would keep his promises. Gathering together his wife Sarai, his nephew Lot, and his servants, flocks, and herds, he moved once more toward the west. This time he came almost to the sea, to a land called Canaan. As the company traveled across Canaan, they camped at several places whose names will appear later—Shechem and Bethel and Ai. Here Abram built altars and worshipped the Lord who was leading him.

"This is the land that will belong to you and your children," God revealed to him. Perhaps we can understand how much faith it took Abram to believe this when we realize that at this time he and Sarai had no children and the land was already inhabited by other people. But Abram continued to build his altars and follow God by faith. *Genesis 11:27–12:8*

A DIFFICULT CHOICE

In his journeyings in the countries bordering the Great Sea, Abram spent a time as far south as Egypt, but eventually he came back to the land

God had spoken of in his promise. During this time Lot, Abram's nephew, had grown to be a man, yet Abram and Sarai still had no children with which to share God's blessings. Abram's flocks and herds had multiplied, and by trading with the settlers in the lands through which he traveled, he had become a very rich man. Even Lot had gained many possessions and was wealthy in his own right.

For a time Lot and his flocks traveled along with Abram's, but the time came when there were too many animals to feed on the same land. Lot's shepherds and Abram's shepherds began quarreling over the pasture land and water that was available.

When Abram became aware of the situation, he called Lot to him. "We can't have trouble between us or our servants, for we're like brothers. There is no need for us to remain close together when there is plenty of land in this country for all our animals. You look around and choose the area you want for yourself, and I will take what remains."

Now Lot realized what a wonderful opportunity his generous uncle was giving him. As he looked over the regions before him, his eyes rested on the green valleys that lay to the east. This land was watered by the Jordan River that flowed through it, and several prosperous cities grew upon the plain.

"I choose the Jordan Valley," Lot decided, and he began moving his flocks and herds in that direction. It seems his selfish decision was all for his gain, but it eventually proved to be to his destruction.

After Lot left, God appeared once more to Abram with this encouraging message: "Look all around you, Abram, in every direction. One day all of this will belong to your children—and there will be so many of them that they will outnumber the specks of dust on the earth. Continue to travel the land that is yours."

So Abram moved his tents from Bethel to Mamre, where he built an altar to the Lord.

Genesis 13

ABRAM BATTLES KINGS

When Lot took his family and herds toward the Jordan Valley, they eventually came to live in one of those cities that he had seen upon the plain—Sodom. Abram continued to dwell in his tent in the mountains of Canaan.

Now in those times, the ruler of each city was called a king. There were other more powerful kings who ruled over several cities, or a whole area. Sodom and its four neighboring towns were under just such a king for twelve years. When they could bear it no longer, they made war upon this king, called Chedorlaomer. But the great king and his men proved too much for the five lesser kings; and after a fierce battle the five kings were either captured or fled to the mountains for safety. According to the customs of war at that time, the enemy went to the captured cities and took all the goods they could find for themselves. They also carried the people away with them to use as slaves. Among the prisoners taken in Sodom was Lot, Abram's nephew. One man who was able to escape the plundering soldiers ran into the hills to tell Abram of the bad news concerning Lot. When Abram heard of it, he gathered together 318 men from his own company to lead in pursuit of King Chedorlaomer. (This gives you some idea of what a wealthy man Abram was since he had over 300 hired men and servants.)

Down where the Jordan River begins, Abram and his men overtook the enemy king in the night and forced him and his men to flee far into the mountains, leaving behind the loot from their battle. This, along with Lot and the other prisoners, Abram gathered up to return to the king of Sodom.

News of Abram's victory traveled quickly and dignitaries came out to meet him on his way home. Among these was the king of Salem (probably Jerusalem). This king, called Melchizedek, was a priest of the true God whom Abram worshipped. He blessed Abram and fed him; in return, Abram gave him part of the goods he had captured.

Then the king of Sodom came out to meet him. Rightfully Abram could have kept all that he had taken from the enemy king, but he insisted that the king of Sodom take back the part that was his. He instructed the other small city kings to do the same.

"I did not fight to become rich," Abram said. "Just leave me my men and what belongs to them." Then he retired once more to his hillside home.

Here the Lord appeared to him and said, "Fear not, Abram; I will reward you greatly for serving me."

But Abram had a question that had probably been haunting him for some time: "Lord, God, what are you going to give me that I can keep? I have no children to whom I can give it. Will one of my servants be my heir?"

God reassured him: "Your own son will be your heir. Look up at the stars overhead—you will have as many descendants as that!"

So Abram believed God, and God loved him for it. *Genesis 14–15:6*

SPECIAL GUESTS

Abram's years in Canaan passed by, and again and again God renewed to him the promises concerning his children and the great nation they would become. But Abram grew to be an old man ninety-nine years old and still he trusted in the promises by faith because he and Sarai had not yet had a child. God even changed Abram's name to Abraham, which means "father of a multitude," and Sarai became Sarah, or "princess."

One day, as the heat of the sun beat down from overhead, Abraham rested in the shade at the door of his tent. Looking up, he saw three men walking toward him. As he was a kind, hospitable man, he ran to meet them and bowed before them.

"My lords," he said, "please be my guests. Refresh yourself here in the shade of the trees while I bring water to bathe your feet. While you are resting, I will find some food for you."

So the three strangers sat down under the oak tree at Mamre while Abraham and Sarah rushed to prepare a fine dinner for them. When it was done, Abraham proudly served it and stood to the side while his guests ate.

Then one of the strangers, who spoke as God himself, asked Abraham where Sarah was.

"She is in the tent."

"When I return in the spring," the Lord said, "Sarah will have a son."

Now Sarah, standing just inside the tent, heard these words and couldn't help laughing because she and Abraham were so old to become parents.

When the guest heard her laugh, he reminded her: "Is anything too hard for the Lord?"

Then the strangers got up to go, and Abraham insisted on walking part of the way with them. It seemed that they were on their way to investigate the city of Sodom, to see if its wickedness was as great as they had heard. When Abraham heard this, he grew fearful because he knew the city was indeed very sinful. He was worried for the sake of his nephew Lot, who still lived there.

"Do you intend to destroy the city?" Abraham asked God. "Will you destroy the good people who are there along with the bad? What if there are fifty righteous people there? Surely you will do the right thing concerning them since you are the perfect judge."

So the Lord replied, "If I find fifty good people there, I will save the city of Sodom."

But Abraham wasn't finished, and he spoke again, "I know it is not even my place to ask, but what if there are only forty-five righteous men to be found?"

"I will not destroy it if there are forty-five decent men."

"Suppose there are only forty."

"I will save the city for the sake of that forty."

"Do not be angry at my speaking, but what will you do it you find only thirty?"

"I will not do it for the sake of thirty."

"Maybe there are only twenty."

"That twenty will save their city."

Then for the last time Abraham begged, "Lord, don't be angry, but suppose there are only ten good people in the whole city."

"For the sake of ten, I will not destroy it," the Lord replied.

With the matter settled, the strangers went on toward Sodom, and Abraham returned home.

Genesis 18

A RUINED CITY

Two of Abraham's three guests journeyed on to Sodom to see if indeed ten righteous people could be found there. Whom should they meet, waiting at the gate of the city, but Abraham's nephew, Lot. You will recall that he was the one who had chosen the green plains for his flocks, had later been taken prisoner in Sodom, and had been rescued by Abraham.

When Lot met the two strangers at the gate he insisted they come home with him, but they refused. They preferred to wander around the streets of the city, to get a better picture of the people there. However, Lot, knowing how wicked his neighbors were, warned them that they were not safe on the streets. At last they accepted his invitation and went home with him.

No sooner had the two strangers eaten than there came loud knocks at the door of Lot's home. It was the men of Sodom, demanding to see Lot's guests.

Lot quickly went to the door, stepped out and tried to appeal to his neighbors. "These are my guests. Please go away and leave them alone."

But this only caused the men to make fun of Lot. "You think you can set yourself up as a judge over us," they taunted. Then they pushed Lot aside and began beating on the door.

At this point the two strangers pulled Lot into the safety of the house and struck the attackers with blindness so that they could not find the door.

What further proof did God's messengers need concerning the wickedness of the city of Sodom? "If you have any relatives in the city, you need to get them away from here. The city is about to be destroyed," they warned Lot.

But when Lot approached the two men who were engaged to his daughters, they only laughed at him. They had no desire to leave Sodom.

About the time for morning to break, the strangers gave Lot their final urging: "Your sons-in-law refuse to leave, but at least take your wife and two daughters and flee for your life."

The strangers grabbed Lot and his family by their hands and began to run. "Flee toward the hills," the men shouted. "Do not even take time to look back."

By the time the sun rose Lot and his two daughters had reached a point of safety in a nearby city. As they gazed across the plain, they could see Sodom and another city, Gomorrah, turned into swirling furnaces of flame. Near the edge of the city, where she had hesitated and looked back, stood Lot's wife, just a pillar of salt.

Genesis 19:1–29

A CASTAWAY BOY

Just as the strangers had predicted, Sarah had a baby within the year following their unusual visit. She and Abraham called their child Isaac, which means "laughter." Sarah said, "God has made me laugh—having this baby in my old age! Everyone who hears about it will laugh with me. Who would ever have said to Abraham that I would nurse a baby?"

Indeed, laughter did fill Abraham's home with the birth of Isaac, the promised son. Abraham dedicated him to God when he was only a few days old; and when Isaac was still only a toddler, his parents gave a great feast so that all their friends could come and see him.

Living in the house of Abraham was another boy whose mother was Sarah's maid. During the years when Abraham wondered if Sarah would ever have a child, he had thought that the servant's son might be the child to receive God's blessing, especially since Abraham was the boy's father.

It seems strange to us in these times to understand how Old Testament heroes often treated more than one woman as their wife, but this was the common custom of that day. Abraham was a man of his own time in this respect, but in many other areas he rose so far above his contemporaries that his was indeed a true greatness.

Nonetheless, God had planned for Sarah to be the mother of the child through which he had promised to bless all nations; and now that Sarah had that child, perhaps it was natural that she felt jealous when she saw the older boy around. She wanted no dispute as to which son would be Abraham's heir.

One day when Sarah saw the slave's child, Ishmael, playing with little Isaac, she grew very upset.

"Send the slave and her son out of this house," Sarah demanded of her husband.

Abraham was very distressed over this situation, but God spoke to him: "Go ahead and do as Sarah says. Isaac will be your true descendant, but I will bless Ishmael also. He too will be the father of a nation because he is your child."

So Abraham got up early the next morning and saw that Hagar, the slave woman, and Ishmael, her boy, had food and water for their trip. Then they began their journey, setting out toward the wilderness.

Days passed, and Hagar and Ishmael wandered about alone in deserted country. At last their food and water gave out and they were forced to stop. Ishmael was so weak that Hagar laid him under the shade of a small bush and went away a short distance because she couldn't bear to see him suffer.

Left alone, Ishmael began to cry.

Then, blended with his cry, the sound as of an angel's voice came to Hagar.

"Do not be afraid, Hagar," the angel said. "God will take care of your son. He will live to become the father of a nation."

As the weary woman lifted her eyes at the sound of the voice, she spied a well of cool water. She rushed to fill her vessels and give Ishmael a drink.

Just as he had promised, God took care of Ishmael. He and his mother continued to live in the wild country, where he grew up to be an expert archer. His people, like him, were tribesmen of the desert and were called Ishmaelites.

Genesis 16, 21:1–20

ABRAHAM PASSES A TEST

At last Abraham and Sarah had the child through whom God had promised to make their name great. One can imagine how much they loved Isaac, having waited so long for him.

Then one day God's voice called, "Abraham!"

And Abraham answered as he always did, "Here I am, Lord."

"Abraham, I want you to take Isaac, your son, to Mount Moriah and offer him there as a sacrifice on an altar."

What an incredible thing to ask! Yet God knew what he was doing. He was testing Abraham to see just how faithful and obedient he was.

Early the next morning Abraham got up and, with a heavy heart, prepared for the journey to Mount Moriah. He saddled his donkey, cut wood for the burnt offering, and called to Isaac and the two servants who were to accompany them. Slowly, the little group set off toward the lonely hills.

On the third day they reached the mountain which God had named. "You stay here with the donkey," Abraham told the two young men who were with them. "The boy and I are going on further to worship, then we will come back to you."

With that, he handed Isaac the wood he had cut for the offering, and he took the torch to start the fire and a knife. Together they climbed the deserted hill.

But Isaac began to be puzzled. "Father," he said, "we have the fire and the wood for our offering. Where is the lamb we are going to sacrifice?"

Abraham looked to the ground. "God will provide a lamb for the offering, my son," was the only reply he could make.

When at last they reached the place God had chosen, Abraham built an altar of stones, piled on top of each other. Then he put the wood neatly in place, bound Isaac hand and foot, and laid him upon the wood. He took his knife in his hand and raised it to kill his son, as God had asked.

Then in an instant he heard the voice of God's messenger, saying, "Abraham! Abraham! Do not touch the boy! Now God knows how much you love him; he sees that you are willing to give even your son for him."

When Abraham was able to lift his tearful eyes, he caught sight of a ram, entangled in a bush by his horns—a ram which could be sacrificed in place of Isaac. Joyfully, Abraham lifted Isaac down to the ground, untied him, and worshipped God with the ram he had provided.

Afterward Abraham called that mountain "The Lord Will Provide." And because Abraham had passed God's test, God renewed his blessing to him once more:

> I will indeed bless you, and I will multiply your descendants as the stars of heaven and as the sand which is on the seashore.
> And your descendants shall possess the gate of their enemies,
> And by your descendants shall all nations of the earth bless themselves.
>
> *Genesis 22:1–19*

QUESTIONS: 1. *How is the story of Abraham related to the previous events in the* Genesis *narrative?* 2. *Why was Abraham greater than others of his time?* 3. *Why did God lead Abraham to the west?* 4. *Why is faith mentioned in regard to Abraham?* 5. *What relation were Abraham and Lot? Why did it become necessary for them to separate?* 6. *What choice did Lot make? Was it a good one?* 7. *Why was Lot taken a prisoner? Who rescued him?* 8. *What message did three visitors bring to Abraham? Why did it make Sarah laugh?* 9. *Discuss the bargain concerning Sodom that Abraham made with God.* 10. *What incident proved Sodom's wickedness to the heavenly visitors?* 11. *Who were saved when Sodom was destroyed? Who was lost?* 12. *Who was the child that would be the heir of Abraham's promise? Who was Abraham's other son?* 13. *Why did Abraham have to send Hagar and Ishmael away?* 14. *How did Ishmael and his mother survive in the wilderness?* 15. *How did God plan to test Abraham's love and faithfulness?* 16. *What was the outcome of Abraham's test?*

Abraham's Family

A BRIDE FROM THE OLD COUNTRY

Following Abraham's great test on Mount Moriah, he and Isaac were happily reunited with Sarah, and God's chosen family continued to dwell in tents throughout the land of Canaan. After she had lived long enough to see her son grow to manhood, Sarah died and Abraham bought a cave in Machpelah in which to bury her.

Now Abraham thought that the time had come to select a wife for Isaac, a woman whose presence would help dispel some of the sorrow and loneliness that had pervaded their home since Sarah's death. (In those times, parents had more of a part in choosing their children's mates than the children themselves did.) Although Abraham had adopted Canaan as his home and wanted Isaac to remain there also, he did not want Isaac to marry one of the Canaanite women. He preferred a daughter-in-law of his own blood, one who understood their ways and worship. In order to find this kind of woman, he would have to send back to the old country.

So Abraham called for his oldest, most trusted servant, Eliezer, and gave him instructions to go back to Haran, where Abraham's brothers had remained, and there to find a suitable wife for Isaac.

Eliezer loaded ten camels with provisions and gifts and began the long journey east, over the same road Abraham had taken when God had first led him to Canaan many years before. After days and days of traveling, he finally saw that he was approaching the city that was the home of Nahor, Abraham's brother.

"Now, how am I going to tell when I have found the proper bride for Isaac?" Eliezer wondered. And as he halted his camels by the well on the edge of the village, he prayed, "Lord, show your love for my master Abraham by granting me success today. The women of the city are coming to the well now. I will ask one of them for a drink from her jar; and if she replies, 'Drink, and I will water your camels also,' let this be the sign that she is the one you have appointed."

Before he was even through praying, a lovely young girl named Rebekah walked down the steps to the well and filled the jar she was carrying with water. As she lifted it to her shoulder and started up the steps, Eliezer stepped toward her.

"Please give me a little water to drink," he asked.

"Here," she replied, as she graciously handed him her jar. "I will draw water for your camels also."

Back and forth to the well she went, drawing water until the camels were filled and content, while Eliezer stood wondering if God had indeed prospered his mission so quickly.

Then Eliezer unpacked a gold ring and two gold bracelets, which he gave to Rebekah.

"Tell me who you are," he asked of her. "Would there be room for me tonight at your father's house?"

"I am the daughter of Bethuel, the granddaughter of Nahor," Rebekah replied. Then she added, "You are certainly welcome at our home. We have sufficient room for you and provisions for your camels as well."

Then Eliezer bowed his head in thankful prayer. God had shown his love for Abraham and had answered his servant's request.

Rebekah ran back into the village to report the news of their unexpected guest, which brought her brother Laban out to meet Eliezer.

"Come in, come in!" invited Laban. "We have straw for your camels and food prepared for you."

But before Eliezer would eat, he asked permission to tell of his errand in the distant city. He revealed that he had been sent by their long-lost uncle, Abraham, who had now grown rich in the land of Canaan. He told of Isaac, Abraham's son, and of his mission to find Isaac a wife. He went on to tell of his prayer and the answer that he felt Rebekah must be.

Bethuel, the girl's father, and Laban looked at each other in amazement. "This must surely be of the Lord," they agreed. "He must mean for Rebekah to be the wife of your master's son."

Then to seal the agreement, Eliezer brought out lovely gifts of silver and gold and costly robes, which he gave to Rebekah and to her mother and brother. That night he and the men of the family celebrated the match with a great feast.

On the next morning, Eliezer was anxious to begin his return trip to Canaan. Although her family was reluctant to have her leave so quickly, Rebekah chose to leave immediately. She and her old nurse prepared the things she would take to her new home.

Many days later Isaac was out in the fields in the evening, just thinking. As he lifted his eyes toward the road, he saw ten camels approaching. At the same moment, Rebekah caught sight of him.

"Who is the man walking in the fields to meet us?" she asked Eliezer.

When he told her that it was Isaac, she alighted from her camel and drew her veil across her face in the way of maidens of that day.

And this was the way in which Isaac met his bride, a lovely girl who had traveled many miles to marry a man she had never seen. For the first time since his mother's death, Isaac felt comforted. *Genesis 24*

A FOOLISH EXCHANGE

After Isaac and Rebekah were married, Abraham took another wife named Keturah and had other sons, but there was none he loved as well as Isaac. This promised son was the one to whom Abraham gave all his possessions; and it was through him and his descendants that God planned to maintain his own people, those who would bless the earth. Finally Abraham died, and Ishmael, the son of Hagar, who had been sent into the wilderness many years before, came home and helped Isaac bury their father in the cave of Machpelah, near the body of Sarah.

Now Isaac was a rich man. He owned the flocks and gold Abraham had collected, and the one God guided in a special way as the leader of his chosen family. Isaac prayed to God for children through whom God's promises could be carried on, and at length Rebekah gave birth to twin boys.

From the time that the twins were born, they were as different as boys could be. Esau, the one born first, had red hair and ruddy skin. He spent every possible moment out of doors and developed into a strong hunting man with rough, hairy arms and legs. On his hunting trips he would kill deer, skin them, and cook them in a way that his father Isaac particularly loved.

Jacob, the younger twin, was a quiet, reflective person. He preferred to stay at home; and because he spent so much time in the tent with her, he grew very close to his mother.

One day, as Esau returned from a hunting trip, a wonderful smell wafted to him from the family tent. It was the delicious odor of a thick, lentil soup that Jacob was preparing.

"Let me have some of that soup," Esau demanded. "I am starved!"

Jacob's nimble mind tripped ahead of Esau's, who thought only of the things that immediately concerned him.

"First, give me your birthright," Jacob replied.

Now what was this birthright in which Jacob was so interested and why was it valuable? The birthright was the oldest son's inheritance from his father. It entitled him to twice the possessions of any other child and, more important, it made him the head of the family. This was the right that had made Isaac the family leader when Abraham died.

But Esau could not have cared less for his birthright at that moment. "Of what use is a birthright to me? If I don't get something to eat, I shall die anyway!"

"Swear to me the birthright is mine," Jacob insisted.

"I swear," answered Esau, as he looked longingly at the bubbling pot of rich soup.

And thus a very foolish exchange was made, one that would forever shape the destiny of God's people. *Genesis 25:1–11, 19–34*

A STOLEN BLESSING

Isaac and Rebekah, with their sons and their many servants and possessions, continued living in the land which God had promised to their family. Isaac was a peaceable man, yet he succeeded in increasing his father's fortune many times. To him, as he had to Abraham, God repeated the promise of his children becoming a great nation; and Isaac showed his devotion to God by worshipping him with sacrifices burnt on altars.

As Isaac grew to be a very old man, he became blind. One day he called his favorite son, Esau, to his side.

"My son," he began, "I may die now at any time. Once more I would like for you to kill a deer and prepare from it the savory dish you know that I love. When I have eaten it, I will give you the blessing that is yours as my eldest son."

Now Rebekah was listening to this conversation, and as soon as Esau left with his bows and arrows, she ran breathlessly to Jacob.

"I just heard your father and brother talking," she reported. "Esau has gone to kill some game. When he returns with it, he is going to receive the family blessing."

"Now, listen, my son, I have a plan in mind. Go and kill two goats from our flock and I will make the savory dish your father loves. Then you can take it to him and receive the blessing before Esau gets back."

"But, Mother," Jacob protested. "Father will never mistake me for Esau. Esau has hairy skin, and I am smooth. When Father realizes I have deceived him, he will give me a curse, not a blessing."

But his mother answered, "I'll take the blame. Do as I've told you."

So Jacob brought his mother the kids and she prepared them for Isaac, seasoning them the special way that he loved. Then she insisted that Jacob put on one of Esau's robes, and she tied the skin of the goats on the backs of his hand and his neck to make him feel rough and hairy.

Thus disguised, he brought the meat to his father.

"My father," he timidly began.

"Here I am. Which son are you?"

"I am Esau," lied Jacob. "I've brought you the meat you requested. Now eat of it, then you may bless me."

But Isaac was not so easily fooled. "How is it that you killed the game and prepared the dish so quickly?" he asked.

"The Lord your God gave me success," Jacob answered, entangling himself with another lie.

"Come near, my son, and let me feel to see if you are really Esau. You sound like Jacob."

But when Jacob held out his hands and his father felt the goats' hair fastened there, he seemed satisfied at last.

"You *are* Esau. Bring the food here to me."

Then Isaac ate the dish Rebekah had prepared and drank some wine. When he had finished, he drew Jacob near to him and he smelled the robe of Esau that Jacob had worn.

"Ah," Isaac smiled. "This is my son who smells of the fields which God has blessed."

And he proceeded to pronounce the blessing upon Jacob:

> May God give you rain from heaven and food from the earth.
> Let peoples serve you and nations bow down to you.
> Be the leader of your brothers and let my other sons obey you.
> May the Lord curse those who curse you
> and bless those who bless you.

Scarcely had Isaac concluded his blessing and Jacob slipped from the room, when Esau came striding in from his hunt.

"Come, Father. Eat of my venison and bless me."

A startled Isaac leaned forward. "What? Who are you?"

"I am your first-born, Esau."

Then Isaac began to tremble with anger.

"Who was it that just brought me meat? He is the one whom I have blessed."

Esau fell to the ground with a bitter cry. "Bless me, too, my father," he begged.

"I have already made Jacob head of the family," came the sorrowful reply. Then he gave Esau a lesser blessing, which was all that he could do.

"That Jacob!" Esau thought with tears in his eyes. "Twice now he has tricked me—he has taken both my birthright and my blessing."

And he determined to kill Jacob as soon as their old father was dead.

Genesis 27

JACOB'S LADDER

News of Esau's intent to kill Jacob soon reached Rebekah's ears. She suggested to Jacob: "You are not safe here while your brother feels that he has been tricked. Why don't you visit my brother Laban and his family? You could stay with them until Esau's anger cools down, and then I will send for you."

But Rebekah gave Isaac a different explanation for Jacob's sudden trip back to the old city of Haran. "These heathen wives of Esau's make my life unbearable," she complained to her husband. "It would break my heart if Jacob married one of their kind. Perhaps we could send him to visit my brother, and he could search for a wife among our own people."

So Isaac charged Jacob to do just that, and he sent him away with God's blessing.

Jacob set out on his journey, walking alone over the rocky country to the home of his kinsmen. One evening, as the sun set, he found himself in a particularly barren spot, but there was nothing to do but lie down on the rough ground and use a stone for his pillow. After his long day's journey, Jacob quickly fell asleep.

As he slept, he had a wonderful dream. He saw a ladder, set upon the earth, but stretching all the way up to heaven. Moving up and down on the ladder were angels of God; and at the top, the Lord God himself looked down on Jacob!

Then the Lord began to speak: "I am the God of your grandfather Abraham and your father Isaac. To you, as to them, I will give this land, and through your family will I bless the earth.

"I will be with you wherever you go and will bring you back to this land. I will not leave you until I have kept my promise to you."

Then Jacob awoke and said, "Surely the Lord was in this place and I did not realize it! This is really the house of God, the gate of heaven!"

To commemorate the place where his wonderful dream occurred and the awareness of God's presence was felt, Jacob took the stone that had been under his head and poured oil on it, showing in the way of that time that it was sacred. He called the place Bethel, or "House of God," a location that will appear again and again in the history of God's people.

Then, as his part of the agreement, Jacob made a promise to the Lord: "If the Lord will keep me on my journey, give me food and clothing, and bring me back one day to my father's house, then he shall be my God, this stone will be his house, and I will give to him a tenth of all I have."

To us, Jacob seems a strange combination of the religious and the sinful. Although he was willing to deceive his old father, he here acknowledges God's presence in his life in the bargaining sort of way that was typical of him. At least, unlike his brother Esau, he looked to the future with planning and insight, a quality that will greatly influence the course of history for God's family.

Genesis 27:42–28:22

LABOR OF LOVE

Days and days of traveling passed after Jacob's wonderful dream, but at last he approached the country of his mother's kinsmen. There at the edge of a city, as Abraham's servant had found on a similar journey, was a well where the villagers watered their livestock. On this occasion some shepherds were at the well, watering their flocks.

Jacob went over to the shepherds and inquired of them where he was. (Remember, he had no maps nor road signs to guide him.)

They replied that this was Haran. Indeed, it was the very place for which Jacob had been searching.

"Do you know a man in Haran named Laban? Is he well?" Jacob inquired.

Yes, the men knew Laban. "Look, there comes his daughter Rachel now with his sheep," they pointed out.

Surely enough, when Jacob looked up, he saw his cousin, the daughter of his mother's brother. He quickly stepped over to the well and helped her with the task of removing the stone cover. But then his emotions overcame him and he began to weep as he told Rachel who he was.

The news was so exciting that Rachel could not linger and talk. She ran to her father and brought him back to the well. What a happy family reunion! For Laban, here was the son of his sister Rebekah, who had left home so many years ago for a strange country and an unknown husband. For Jacob, these were some relatives who reminded him of his far-away home.

Naturally Jacob stayed with Laban and his lovely daughter. Before many days had passed he found himself much as one of the family, working with Laban's flocks.

But Laban did not want to take advantage of his nephew. After a month, he approached Jacob: "You should be receiving proper wages," he said. "What shall I pay you?"

Jacob's eyes began to shine. He knew exactly what he wanted from Laban. "If you will let me marry your daughter Rachel," he replied, "I will work for you free for seven years."

So the agreement was made, and Jacob served Laban seven years for Rachel. In the lovely words of *Genesis*, "they seemed to him but a few days because of the love he had for her."

At last the wedding day arrived. Laban gave a great feast and he brought the bride to Jacob covered with a heavy wedding veil. Imagine Jacob's surprise, when the wedding was all over, to discover that he had just been wed to Leah, Rachel's older sister who was not nearly so attractive as she!

Loran Raymond Jones

JACOB WELCOMED BACK TO CANAAN BY ESAU

Genesis 33:1–15

Loran Raymond Jones

JOSEPH SOLD INTO SLAVERY

Genesis 37:25–28

JOSEPH REVEALS HIMSELF TO HIS BRETHREN

Genesis 45:1–15

Loran Raymond Jones

FINDING OF MOSES BY THE DAUGHTER OF PHA

Exodus 2:2–10

"What have you done to me?" Jacob demanded of Laban. "Didn't I work seven years for Rachel?"

Laban tried rather weakly to justify himself. "Well, you see," he explained, "it is not the custom in our country for a younger sister to marry before the older one does.

"But," he went on, "I will give you Rachel, too, if you will work another seven years."

Realizing the way that he felt about her, Jacob had no choice but to consent to this plan. Thus, for fourteen years' work, Jacob obtained for himself not one, but two wives from among his mother's people. *Genesis 29:1–30*

A FAMILY FEUD

Years passed by and still Jacob remained in his ancestral land of Haran, working for Laban, his father-in-law and uncle. During this time he became the father of a large family himself—eleven sons and one daughter. The names of the sons were: Reuben, Simeon, Levi, and Judah, Dan and Naphtali, Gad and Asher, Issachar, Zebulun, and Joseph, the youngest. Their sister was called Dinah. Of all of these Jacob loved Joseph best, because he was Rachel's child.

The time finally came when Jacob felt that he must return to his own country; but because he was a dependent of Laban's, he had to have Laban's permission to take away the wives and children he had acquired while working for him.

As we observed in their wedding incident, Laban was a man as full of tricks as Jacob had proved to be. Realizing that his son-in-law was extremely valuable to him and that his fortunes had greatly increased during Jacob's period of service, he insisted that Jacob stay with him and invited him to name his own wages.

Jacob named his condition: that he be allowed to cut the speckled and spotted calves and goats and lambs from Laban's flocks to have for his own, as he desired to build up a herd. Laban readily agreed, but in truth he separated these mottled animals from the rest and hid them a three days' journey away.

Not to be outdone, Jacob was able to accumulate a number of spotted animals from the young born to the flocks that remained. Despite Laban's efforts against him, he grew quite rich and acquired servants and camels besides his flocks.

By the time this happened, Laban's own sons had grown quite jealous of their brother-in-law. "Look," they said; "Jacob is taking what is our father's and ours. He is getting rich at our expense!" Even Laban himself no longer looked on Jacob as the one who brought him prosperity.

If Jacob had any doubts about his next step, the Lord soon dispelled them. "Return to the land of your fathers," he commanded; "and I will be with you."

This time Jacob was not going to risk asking Laban if he could leave. Secretly, he made arrangements with his wives; and while Laban was off shearing sheep, Jacob gathered together his family and flocks and slipped away. They had traveled three days before news of what had happened reached Laban. By then, it took him seven days to overtake them.

"What have you done?" Laban demanded of Jacob. "You've cheated me and taken away my daughters like prisoners."

"I would have sent you away with great festivities if you had only asked," he insisted. "Why, you didn't even permit me to kiss my grandchildren goodbye. And to make it worse, you have stolen my household gods."

All this made Jacob quite angry. "You know you would never have let me take your daughters if I had asked," he replied. "And as for your gods—I know nothing about them. You may search us all."

In truth Rachel had stolen these household gods, or teraphim, but Jacob did not know it. She successfully concealed them by hiding them in her saddle and sitting upon it. Laban was rightly incensed about their loss because the possessor of them had claim to the family inheritance. There is no indication, however, that Jacob ever laid claim to Laban's fortune.

When Laban had completed his search and found nothing, Jacob confronted him again. "What have I done wrong? For twenty years I took excellent care of your flocks. I served the required time for your daughters. If God had not been with me, you know you would have sent me away empty."

Laban looked at his daughters and their children. "These are my family," he said, "and I could never do anything to hurt them. Come, let us make a settlement."

So Jacob and Laban set up a large stone on a heap of small stones and named this pillar Mizpah. "The Lord watch between me and thee while we are absent one from another," they pledged.

The final picture we see of Laban is no longer that of a plotting chieftain, but of an old grandfather, departing for home after kissing his daughters and their children goodbye for the last time. *Genesis 29:31–31:55*

A WRESTLING MATCH

Even though twenty years had passed since Jacob left home in the heat of a family disagreement, he was still uncertain whether or not his brother Esau had forgiven him. As he drew near to Esau's country, he sent messengers ahead to say: "Your brother Jacob reports that he has been with Laban these twenty years; that he possesses oxen, flocks, and servants; and that he desires now to find favor in your eyes."

The messengers returned with these words: "Esau is coming to meet you with four hundred men."

Jacob must have had a guilty conscience about the incident involving the stolen blessing because this message filled him with fear. He felt certain that Esau and his men were coming to repay him for his trickery. In order for at least some of his own to be saved from Esau's wrath, Jacob divided the company into two groups, reasoning that if one group were destroyed, the other would escape. Then he prepared a series of gifts to be presented to Esau before Esau actually met him. Included in this peace offering were sheep, goats, cattle, and camels, driven by several servants.

"Put a space between each one of you as you drive your herd," Jacob instructed the men. "When you meet Esau and he asks whose animals these are, you are to reply that they are a present from me to him, and that I am close behind."

In this way, Jacob hoped to soften Esau's anger by the time they met face to face.

Having taken these precautions, Jacob settled his family down for the night and crossed a little brook to be alone. There, in the darkness, he found himself in the strong grips of some stranger. All night the two of them struggled with neither ever gaining an advantage. Toward morning, this mysterious opponent, who was sent from God, threw Jacob's leg out of joint. Still Jacob would not release him

"Let me go; morning is near," the visitor insisted.

But Jacob was a strong man and was not one to let another get the better of him in a struggle. He insisted that this heavenly foe bless him before he left.

Instead of blessing him, however, this "man" asked a strange question: "What is your name?"

"Jacob."

"Your name shall not be Jacob, but Israel, for you have fought with God and men and have won."

Then the stranger blessed Jacob, but left before revealing his identity.

The significance of this event can be understood better when we realize that in these times names had a meaning that told something about their wearer's personality. Whereas the name Jacob means Cheater, and this certainly had fit in many respects, Israel means One Who Strives. Thus God's people gained the name they were to wear throughout history, one that refers to a strange wrestling match between Jacob and a visitor sent from God.

Genesis 32

HOMECOMING

The struggle with the angel was over, and as the sun rose, Jacob, or Israel, looked up and saw his brother Esau and the company of four hundred men approaching. Had the long train of gifts been useful in cooling Esau's anger? Jacob limped forward to meet him with the hope that they had served their purpose. Upon reaching his brother, he bowed before him seven times as a prince would before a great king.

But Esau walked over to Jacob and embraced him warmly. Tears of joy came to the eyes of the reunited twins. Jacob had had no need to fear at all!

Then Esau saw the impressive group of women and children standing behind Jacob.

"Who are all of these with you?" he asked.

"The wonderful family God has given me."

"And what was the meaning of the company of animals I met?"

"They are my gift to you."

"Oh, I have enough, my brother," Esau replied. "Keep what you have for yourself."

But Jacob insisted that Esau accept this portion of God's bounty, and Esau at last consented.

Naturally Esau wanted Jacob and his family to return with him to his home in Edom; but because the children and animals were so tired and traveled so slowly, Jacob went instead to Shechem in Canaan and rested there. Later he went on to Bethel, much as one might make a religious pilgrimage, and revisited the site of God's appearance to him on the heavenly ladder. He built an altar and worshipped as he had done there before.

So Jacob came home at last, but the joy of it was sharply broken when Rachel died giving birth to a son named Benjamin. When she, his true love, was gone, Jacob found himself strongly tied to this little one whom she had left and to her other son, Joseph.

Not long after Rachel's death, Jacob was reunited with his old father Isaac, who had lived much longer than he had evidently expected. The meeting took place at Mamre, where Abraham had entertained the heaven-sent strangers under the oak trees. Then Isaac, too, died after a long, full life and was buried by Esau and Jacob in the family burial place at Machpelah.

Genesis 33, 35

QUESTIONS: 1. *Why did Abraham decide that the time had come to find Isaac a wife? Why did he send away for her?* 2. *How did Abraham's servant tell which woman God had selected?* 3. *How did Isaac and Rebekah meet for the first time?* 4. *Describe the twin sons born to Isaac and Rebekah.* 5. *What did Esau exchange for the bowl of soup? Why was it valuable?* 6. *How did Rebekah and Jacob deceive Isaac?* 7. *What was Esau's reaction to Jacob's deception of their father?* 8. *Why did Jacob hurriedly leave home?* 9. *Describe Jacob's dream at Bethel. What was its significance?* 10. *How did Jacob obtain two wives instead of one? Which did he love best?* 11. *Why did Laban want to keep Jacob in his service?* 12. *How did Jacob succeed in obtaining a fortune of his own?* 13. *Tell of Jacob's exit from the home of Laban.* 14. *Why did Jacob fear to meet Esau? How did he plan to make peace?* 15. *With whom did Jacob wrestle?* 16. *What was Jacob's new name?* 17. *Did Jacob have reason to fear the meeting with Esau? Describe the encounter.*

Children of Israel

DOWN WITH THE DREAMER

As a wealthy old chieftain, Jacob settled as his father had done in the land of Canaan. Of all his sons, Joseph was his favorite. Because the boy was Rachel's child and because he was born when Jacob was older and more indulgent, Jacob allowed his partiality to become very obvious. Not only did this make Joseph an arrogant boy, but it caused his older brothers to be jealous of him and grow to hate him.

To begin with, Jacob singled Joseph out and gave him an especially lovely robe which he wore all of the time. Then with this show of favoritism already offending the older sons, Joseph made matters worse by carrying tales about them back to their father. Next, he began to have dreams with very obvious meanings.

"I dreamed last night that it was harvest time and we were all in the field binding grain into sheaves," he related to his brothers. "My sheaf stood upright, and your sheaves all bowed down to it."

"Is that so?" they asked in scorn. "I suppose that means that you will one day be the ruler of us all!"

Then, on another morning: "Listen to my latest dream! In this one, the sun, moon, and eleven stars were bowing down to me."

The significance of this dream was difficult even for Jacob to accept.

"Does this mean that your mother and I, as well as your brothers, will bow down to you?" he asked in a mildly rebuking way; but he wondered to himself if it might really come to pass. In his eyes, Joseph's future had no limits.

On his brothers, however, the dream had a much stronger effect. Their hate for Joseph grew to the point that they did not care what became of him.

Now it was true that these older sons of Israel were not of Joseph's caliber. They were matter-of-fact men, concerned with the tasks of the day. Much of their time was spent in distant pasture-lands, caring for their father's vast flocks, while Joseph stayed at home. Once, when they had been away like this for many days and Jacob had received no news from them, he sent Joseph to see how they fared. The boy, then seventeen, was to bring word of them back as soon as possible.

Rather than finding them where they were expected to be, Joseph had to look for several days before he located his missing brothers in Dothan. While he was still a long distance away, they recognized him by his well-known coat.

"Here comes the dreamer," one of them remarked.

"Listen, this is our perfect chance to be rid of him," the thought occurred to another. "We could kill him and throw his body down in a pit. Then we could see what becomes of his marvelous dreams!"

Reuben, the oldest and kindest of the brothers, was alarmed at this talk. "Let's not have any blood shed," he begged. "We could go ahead and put him in a pit, but I see no reason to kill him." (What Reuben intended to do was to return alone and rescue Joseph.)

Reuben's ideas seemed to appeal to the other men; so when Joseph finally arrived, they stripped the hated coat from him and threw him down in an empty pit, where he was not actually hurt. Then, with a feeling of accomplishment, they sat down beside the pit to eat. Reuben hurried off on some other task.

While they were having their meal, a merchant caravan, bound south for Egypt, passed the place where Jacob's sons were sitting. The sight gave Judah an idea: "What do we really gain by killing our brother?" he asked. "We could sell him to these traders, receive some money, but bear no guilt."

"A perfect solution!" the rest agreed.

So they lifted Joseph out of the pit and gave him to the Ishmaelite merchants for twenty pieces of silver. Exchanging satisfied grins, they watched their despised brother depart with the camel caravan for what they hoped was a distant land and a difficult future. *Genesis 37:1–28*

A DISGRACED SERVANT

As Joseph, now a slave, moved toward Egypt with his merchant owners, his oldest brother, Reuben, returned to the pit to rescue him. Upon finding it empty, he ran in despair to the other brothers.

"The boy is gone!" he cried. "Where shall I go to look for him?"

But the others gave no answer. They merely showed him the coat they had stripped from Joseph before they sold him, its beauty now stained with the blood of a goat they had killed. Later, when they arrived at home, they showed the same cruel evidence to their anxious old father.

"We found this," they said as they thrust the garment into his hands. "You can tell whether or not it is Joseph's."

Jacob reacted exactly as they had planned. "It is my son's robe," he moaned. "Some wild beast attacked and killed him." And Jacob could not be comforted over the loss of his favorite son. "There is nothing you can do for me," he told his other children. "I shall mourn for him until I die."

Meanwhile Joseph had reached Egypt and been sold as a household slave to an officer of the Pharaoh, a captain of the guard named Potiphar. Although it seemed that his dreams of greatness were now a mockery, Joseph did not let his humble position defeat him. His father's belief in him and his own self-confidence served him well and made him determine to do his job as well as possible.

Soon Joseph's careful and faithful work was noticed by Potiphar. He promoted his new slave boy again and again until Joseph actually had control of all Potiphar's affairs. Potiphar confidently left home each morning knowing that Joseph could handle his household better than he.

But someone else in the house besides Potiphar thought well of Joseph. This was the captain's wife. She found her husband's new assistant charming and handsome. Time and time again when Potiphar was away, she invited Joseph to make love to her. Each time he refused, saying: "My master has great confidence in me and has entrusted me with everything in his house, including you. How then could I do this great evil and sin against God?"

But the woman would not accept Joseph's "No" as his answer, and she followed him day after day. Once, when all the servants were gone and she was alone with Joseph, she grabbed at his robe in desperation. Joseph tore himself away, leaving the coat in her hands.

Potiphar's wife, angry at this rebuff, began shrieking for the servants. When they came, she showed them Joseph's robe, insisting he had tried to attack her. Then when her husband came home she told him the same story. "Your servant came in today and tried to insult me," she complained. "When I screamed, he ran out of the house, leaving his garment here."

Naturally this story enraged Potiphar. He promptly had Joseph arrested and put in prison.

Genesis 37:29–36, 39:1–20

MORE DREAMS

Once more Joseph found his dreams of success dashed when his master sent him to prison unjustly. But the great spirit that the Lord had given him kept him from giving up. He was not in the Egyptian jail long before he was noticed by the keeper of the prison, who made Joseph his chief assistant. As was always the case, he, under God's guidance, performed his tasks so well that the jail keeper was more than satisfied.

Among the prisoners in Joseph's care were two of the Egyptian king's servants—his head butler and head baker. One morning Joseph found these men troubled about the dreams they had had the night before.

"What can these dreams mean?" they complained to Joseph.

"Tell them to me," Joseph replied, "and perhaps God will reveal their meaning."

So the men related their dreams. The butler had dreamed of a grape vine with three branches. From this vine he plucked grapes and squeezed them into a cup, which he handed to the Pharaoh, or king. The butler, on the other hand, told of carrying three baskets on his head, filled with baked food for the Pharaoh. Some birds were eating the food from the top basket.

When the men had finished, Joseph explained: "The three branches the butler saw represent three days. In three days Pharaoh will restore him to his regular place and he will hand the king his cup once again.

"The three baskets the baker saw also stand for three days. In three days Pharaoh will have him put to death and the birds will eat his flesh."

Unfortunately for the baker, the dreams came true just as Joseph had predicted. Within three days Pharaoh had the baker hanged. He also had a birthday feast, for which he called the butler to serve him again.

"Mention me to Pharaoh," Joseph asked the man before he returned to the palace. "Tell his majesty that I was stolen and brought to this land and that I am not guilty of any crime."

But once the butler was gone, he promptly forgot about his prison friend. Years passed and Joseph grew to be a full-grown man, thirty years old, yet still he remained in prison.

Then one morning the Pharaoh woke up with dreams he could not understand. He called in magicians and wise men, but no one could explain to him what they meant.

News of the king's troubled dreams traveled all over the palace. When the butler heard of them, Joseph came to his mind. He hurried to the king and said, "I just remembered something that I should have recalled long ago.

"When the head baker and I were in prison, we both had dreams. There was a young man there, a servant of the captain of the guard, who was able to tell us exactly what they meant."

"Send for this man!" Pharaoh commanded, and his guards went running to the prison. As soon as Joseph could clean himself up a bit, they rushed him into the throne room.

Pharaoh frowned at the prisoner standing before him. "I hear you can interpret dreams," he said.

"It's not I who understands them," Joseph explained simply. "God gives me their meaning."

So Pharaoh related his dreams: "In one dream, I was standing on the banks of the Nile when seven fat, healthy cows came up from the water to feed on the grass. Behind them came seven poor, thin cows. Unbelievably, these thin cows ate the fat ones, but were still as lean as ever.

"In my other dream, I saw seven good ears of corn growing on a stalk. Then seven withered ears sprouted and swallowed up the good ones.

"These are the strange dreams which no one can understand," he finished.

"Both of these dreams have the same meaning," Joseph explained. "In them, God is telling you what he is about to do.

"The seven healthy cows and the seven good ears of corn are seven plentiful years. On the other hand, the seven lean cows and withered ears are seven years of famine. First, God will send the years of plenty, but they will be followed by years of severe famine. God sent this dream twice to impress it on you very strongly.

"Your honor should a select a wise, honest man to see that plenty of food is stored during the plentiful years to supply the people of Egypt during the time when nothing will grow," Joseph concluded.

Pharaoh shook his head in agreement with all Joseph had said. He turned to his court and asked, "Have you ever seen a man like this—one so filled with wisdom? Why, who could better fill the position that he has just described?

"Young man," he said to Joseph, "I am going to set you over all the land of Egypt to prepare for the famine—in all my kingdom, only I shall be greater than you."

Then the king reached forth his hand and placed on Joseph's finger a signet ring bearing the royal seal. Around his neck he hung a golden necklace. Joseph, the prisoner, had become a governor of Egypt! *Genesis 39:21–41:46*

BARGAINING FOR GRAIN

After years in prison, Joseph finally was released—as governor of Egypt! Clothed in gold and fine robes, he rode in a chariot right behind that of the Pharaoh's. When the Egyptians saw this procession coming, they would bow in respect for Joseph, just as they did for the king.

The seven years of plenty followed Joseph's appointment, just as he had predicted. For Joseph, these were happy, busy years. He supervised the storing of great amounts of food and grain in warehouses in every Egyptian city. He also married, and his Egyptian wife bore him two sons, Ephraim and Manasseh. This precious family helped him to forget his years of hardship in prison and symbolized to him the success he had found in his adopted country.

Then the good years ended, and the hot winds blew dust over the fields where grain had grown. When the people saw that there would be no food to harvest, they began to cry out to Pharaoh.

"What are we going to eat? Give us bread."

"Go to Joseph," Pharaoh replied. "Do what he tells you to do."

So Joseph opened up his storehouses and carefully parcelled out the food that had been set aside. Still the famine grew worse and worse, and barren fields spread to surrounding countries as well.

Canaan, where Joseph's father, Jacob, and his brothers still lived, was one of the lands hit by this disaster. There, the hungry people heard rumors that grain could be bought in Egypt.

"Why do you sit here looking at one another?" Jacob asked his sons when he heard the news. "Go down to Egypt and buy grain for us before we die!"

So Joseph's ten older half-brothers set out toward the south over the trail they had seen Joseph travel many years before. Jacob's other son, Benjamin, who was Joseph's real brother, remained at home because his father would not part with him. Probably more than twelve years had passed since Joseph's disappearance, but his father still felt the sorrow too vividly to let Rachel's other son leave his side.

Joseph's headquarters were a very busy place with hungry people from many lands bargaining for grain in their foreign tongues. In his chief place, Joseph sat, tanned and dressed as an Egyptian, while interpreters spoke to him on behalf of the poor people.

One day Joseph turned to hear an interpreter translating for him from his own native tongue. There before him stood ten ragged shepherds—his own brothers! Immediately Joseph recognized them, although they never dreamed that this mature, Egyptian official could be the brother they had sold as a slave.

To hide his feelings at the sight of them, Joseph spoke in a rough voice: "Where do you come from?"

"From the land of Canaan," they replied. "We have come to buy food because of the famine."

"No, you are spies. You've come to see how weak our land is."

"Oh, no, my lord! We're only here to buy food. We're all sons of one honest old man who lives in the land of Canaan. At home, there is a younger brother and another is dead."

"I still think you are spies," Joseph insisted," but you can prove yourself this way: I'll keep all of you in prison except one, who must go and bring back your younger brother."

So he had them arrested and held in prison for three days. At the end of this time he called them in and said: "Because I fear God, I am going to keep only one of you. The rest may take grain back to your father, but you must then return with your younger brother if you want to prove that you are not spies." And he took Simeon for a hostage to remain in Egypt.

All of this greatly upset Jacob's sons. "I know all of this trouble has come to us because of the way we treated Joseph," they said to each other, never dreaming he could understand their language.

"I told you it would happen," Reuben reminded them, "but you wouldn't listen."

During all of this Joseph, the stern official, could hardly bear to listen. He had to turn so that no one would notice the tears in his eyes. Secretly, he ordered his servants to put the money the men paid for the grain back into their sacks. Then he sent them on their way.

Back in Canaan, the ten related to their father how they had been accused of being spies. "The Egyptian lord insisted on keeping Simeon until we bring Benjamin," they sadly explained. Then they opened their sacks to show him the grain, and lo and behold, there was all their money!

Poor old Jacob! He was completely dismayed. "Joseph is gone. Simeon is gone. Now you want to take Benjamin," he grieved.

"Take my own two sons if I don't bring him back to you," Reuben offered. "I will take responsibility for him." But Jacob would not hear of it.

Genesis 41:47–42:38

IDENTITY REVEALED

The grain that the sons of Jacob had brought from Egypt was carefully parcelled out, but still the time came when it was gone. Since there was no food growing in Canaan to replace it, Jacob had to insist that his sons go to Egypt again to buy more.

"That man in Egypt said that we were not to return without our youngest brother," Judah, one of the older sons, reminded him. "I'm afraid to meet him unless we have Benjamin with us."

"Why did you even tell him you had a younger brother at home?" Jacob fumed.

And the sons tried to explain: "He kept asking us questions about our father and the rest of our family. How were we to know he would want us to bring our brother down?"

"Send Benjamin in my care," Judah begged his father. "Already we have delayed too long—we could have gone there and come back twice."

There was nothing for old Jacob to do but agree. "If it must be so," he said, "at least we can try to please that suspicious man. Take him some presents and twice as much money as before. Also, return that money that was found in your sacks.

"May God grant you mercy and the Egyptian governor permit you all to return."

Joseph was working at the storage headquarters when he recognized his half-brothers and Benjamin in the crowd waiting for grain. He pointed them out to his steward and said, "I want these men brought to my house to dine today."

The poor sons of Israel were completely confused and frightened when they were ordered to come to Joseph's home. "It is because of that money we found in our sacks on our other trip, "they worried. "He probably means to seize us and make slaves of us."

So they cornered Joseph's steward at the door of the house and began explaining: "You see, my lord, when we were here before we paid for the grain we took; but upon arriving at home, we found our money in our sacks. We have no idea how it got there. Look, we have it here to return to you."

"That's strange," the guard replied. "Your God must have put it there because I remember receiving payment."

Then he brought their brother Simeon, who had remained as hostage in Egypt, out to them. Water was supplied for them to wash themselves, and all prepared for dinner.

At length Joseph came in to eat. The brothers came up to him with their gift, bowing low before him. "How is your father, the old man of whom you spoke?" Joseph inquired. Then his eyes fell upon young Benjamin. "And this is your brother," he continued. "God be gracious to you, my son!"

But Joseph found that the sight of Benjamin nearly broke his composure. He turned quickly and walked from the room. Then, away from the rest, he leaned against the wall and sobbed. When he felt that he was able, he washed his face and returned to ask that dinner be served.

Once the meal was over, Joseph went out with his steward. "Fill these men's sacks with grain and replace the money in each one again," he whispered to his officer. "Also, put my own silver cup in with the grain in the sack of the youngest." The steward hurried away to obey the orders.

Early the next morning, the brothers loaded their donkeys and departed for Canaan with the grain they had bought. As soon as they had gone, Joseph sent his steward after them. "Follow those men!" he commanded. "Ask them why they stole my silver cup."

When the steward caught up with the eleven, he confused and terrified them all the more. They knew nothing of a silver cup!

"Why are you accusing us?" they asked the officer. "We brought you back the money we had found in our bags. Why would we turn around and steal gold and silver?

"Go ahead. Search us all. If you find it with one of us, he should be put to death and the rest of us made slaves."

"As you say," Joseph's servant agreed. "However, only he with whom it is found will remain as a slave."

Then one by one he went through each brother's bag, beginning with the oldest and going in order to the youngest. Sure enough, there in Benjamin's sack his hand touched the silver cup.

What groans and cries the men made! But there was nothing to do but follow the steward back to the city.

At the sight of Joseph, the men fell upon the ground.

"What is it you have done?" Joseph asked. "Don't you realize that you could not get by with it?"

Judah spoke for his brothers: "What can we say? How could we even begin to clear ourselves? We are all your slaves."

"That will not be necessary," Joseph replied. "Only the one in whose bag the cup was found will remain as my servant. The rest of you may return in peace to your father."

Judah tried once more to explain: "My lord, let me speak a word, and please do not be angry. Do you remember when you first inquired of our father and our younger brother? At that time we told you that our father would not let the young man leave his sight. Still, you demanded that he come with us when we returned.

"All of this we told to our father, but still he did not want to part with his son. You see, the boy's brother was taken from our father and he declares that he will die if something happens to this one.

"Surely you see that I cannot return to my father without him. Let me remain as a slave in his place."

At this touching story, Joseph could not restrain himself. Ordering everyone from the room except his brothers, he turned and let them see his tears. "I am Joseph," he stated simply. "Is my father still alive?"

No one could answer him. They were too stunned to think.

"Come near," Joseph said. And when they had, he explained: "I am your brother, Joseph, whom you sold into Egypt. Don't be angry at yourselves for sending me here. Actually it was God who guided me to this land so that I could save your lives in this famine. Yes, God made me Pharaoh's helper so that I could help our family.

"Now, hurry home to our father and tell him that I am alive. Bring him and all the rest of our people down to this land so they can be near me and I can take care of them in the five years of famine that are yet ahead.

"Please, make haste! Bring my father to me."

Then he threw his arms around Benjamin's neck and kissed him. He also embraced the rest of his brothers and they all wept for joy.

Even Pharaoh's household was excited about the discovery of Joseph's brothers. Pharaoh extended his own invitation to them to return with their father and families. "There is no need to bring all your goods with you," he told them. "The best of the things in our land will be yours."

So, dressed in fine robes and traveling in wagons that were gifts of Joseph, the eleven men set out once more for Canaan, this time with wonderful news for their old father, Israel.

Genesis 43:1–45:25

MOVING TO GOSHEN

"Joseph is alive. He is ruler over all of Egypt," Jacob's sons repeated. But the old man could simply not believe it. Why, his heart felt as though it would stop beating! Over and over they repeated the words and showed him the wagons and gifts Joseph had provided, until at last he began to shake his head, as though to clear a dream away.

"It is true," he reassured himself. "Joseph, my son, is still alive. I will get to see him before I die." And a smile began to break across his face.

So the old man Israel took a long, cautious journey to see his lost son. With him traveled his other eleven sons with their wives and children. They went past Beersheba, where God assured them that he was abiding with them on their travels to Egypt and would remain with them until they returned once more to their own land, the one he had promised them.

On the wagons rolled toward the borders of Egypt. When Joseph heard that they were approaching, he rode out in his chariot to meet them.

The reunion of Joseph and his old father was a touching one. So many years had passed since the day Jacob sent his favorite son to Dothan in search of his brothers, yet the devotion they felt for each other was unchanged.

"I am ready to die, now that I have seen your face," Jacob declared to his son.

As soon as possible, Joseph introduced his father and five of his brothers to the Pharaoh. As he had promised, Pharaoh gave them abundant land in Goshen which was particularly good for raising sheep, their main occupation. Joseph settled the whole family there comfortably and provided for them during the remaining years of the famine. Of course, he still held his position as Egyptian governor, which he carried out with great skill.

Jacob lived seventeen years after he came to live in Egypt and he lived to see his family survive the famine and increase greatly in size and possessions.

When Joseph realized that Jacob was at last near death, he brought his two sons out to Goshen to see their grandfather. As old men will do, Jacob talked to the boys of the past—of God's appearing to him in a dream, of a heavenly ladder, and of their lovely grandmother Rachel who died when Uncle Benjamin was born.

Then, at his bidding, the boys came and kneeled before him while he placed his hands on their heads and pronounced the old family blessing that had been passed down to him from Abraham and Isaac.

Joseph noticed that his father had placed his right hand on the younger boy, Ephraim, and had given him the blessing of the first son. When Joseph tried to correct him, the old man insisted that he had done it on purpose. "Both of these boys will become fathers of great peoples, but the youngest shall be the greatest.

"Now, one last request I make of you," Israel said when he had blessed not only Joseph's sons, but all of his children. "Take my body back to our land, to the cave where our fathers are buried." The sons promised.

Then Israel died, and true to their word, his family formed a great procession and brought his body back to Canaan. Here they placed it to rest with the other great father-leaders, or patriarchs, of their family—Abraham and Isaac.

Once their father was dead, Joseph's brothers began to wonder if he would try to repay them for their wrong. Joseph, however, was hurt that his brothers suspected such a thing of him.

"Do not fear me," he assured them; "God has used all that has happened for our good. I will take care of you and your little ones."

And Joseph was true to his promise. *Genesis 45:25–50:26*

QUESTIONS: 1. *Why was Joseph unpopular with his brothers?* 2. *How did the brothers get rid of Joseph?* 3. *What was Jacob told about Joseph's disappearance?* 4. *What did the Ishmaelites do with Joseph in Egypt?* 5. *Why was Joseph sent away from Potiphar's house?* 6. *Tell about Joseph's experience in prison with the baker and butler.* 7. *Why did Pharaoh call for Joseph?* 8. *What was Joseph's position in Pharaoh's government after interpreting the king's dream?* 9. *Why did Jacob's sons go to Egypt?* 10. *Why did Joseph keep one brother in Egypt as a hostage?* 11. *Why did Jacob not want Benjamin to go to Egypt? Why did the other sons insist that he go?* 12. *Describe the incident involving Joseph's silver cup.* 13. *How did Joseph reveal himself to his brothers?* 14. *Why did Jacob's whole family move to Egypt?* 15. *What was Jacob's last request of his sons? Did they carry it out?*

A Family Becomes a Nation

SLAVES IN A STRANGE LAND

Jacob's family, who moved to Egypt and temporarily settled in the land of Goshen, remained long after the famine was over. Actually, they found the new land that the Egyptian Pharaoh had deeded them was excellent for sheep-raising, their main occupation. Also, each of Israel's sons fathered large families which increased to the size of tribes, so the possibility of moving the whole group back to Canaan grew more difficult and improbable.

Meanwhile, the government of Egypt was going through periods when men from one family and then another ruled as Pharaoh. When the narrative of the book of *Exodus* begins, four hundred years had passed since Joseph had served as one Pharaoh's prime minister. No longer did the present king or any of his court remember a young Israelite who had interpreted dreams and wisely saved the Egyptians from starving to death. No longer were the Israelite people merely this man's large family, but a foreign group that needed to be kept in control and used to Egypt's advantage. Certainly they were no longer treated as privileged visitors. Rather, they were reduced to slavery and made to give up their sheep-raising in order to build government projects.

The ruler of Egypt reasoned this way: "There are so many of these Israelites living among us. Suppose we should become involved in a war—

these foreigners just might join our enemy and fight against us. We cannot let that happen. We will keep them from getting strong by giving them more hard work."

So he assigned to the Israelites the building of two huge store-cities. They had to make their own bricks and then construct strong walls with them. All the while, guards with whips watched to see that they never stopped.

Still, the families of the Israelites kept growing in number, and the king was afraid that hard work alone was not enough to keep them subdued. He added another command regarding them: all the baby boys born to Israelite women were to be drowned.

What about God's proud family, chosen by him to be a great nation? These miserable slaves do not seem to be the answer to the promises made by God to Abraham, Isaac, and Jacob. One explanation might be that God used the time in Egypt to prepare them for their responsibilities as a nation. During these years they kept to themselves, apart from the Egyptians, and developed the feeling of being a close-knit group. Even the Pharaoh's burdens contributed to this spirit.

But God was not to remain silent forever. He was about to speak to his people again in a dramatic way, through a mighty leader. *Exodus 1*

AN ADOPTED PRINCE

To one Israelite father, Amram, and to his wife, Jochebed, a baby boy was born during these difficult times. Already the couple had a son, Aaron, and a daughter, Miriam, but this new child was just as precious as the older ones. It was unthinkable that he be drowned by the Pharaoh's guards. So very carefully, everyone in the family hid the news that there was a new baby in their house. For three months no one suspected a thing.

But babies grow and make noise and need sunshine, and Jochebed found that she could not hide her son forever. However, she had a plan that she thought might keep him alive. To carry it out, she wove a little cradle-boat of reeds, which she coated inside and out with pitch to make it waterproof. Then she carefully laid her baby in it and took it down to a certain spot by the water's edge. Here, she set the little basket to float and left Miriam to watch it from the tall grass growing along the river bank.

As Miriam hid, she heard women's voices approaching. Here came the Pharaoh's daughter and her serving maidens to wash themselves in the cool River Nile.

"Oh, look—right there among those reeds!" the princess exclaimed to one of the servants. "It's some sort of a basket. Please get it for me."

Miriam held her breath.

"Why, it's a baby! He's about to cry—and what a sweet thing he is.

"He must be an Israelite child. Oh, we can't let anything happen to him!"

As the princess reached down to lift the child into her arms, Miriam stepped out from her hiding place and ran over to her. "Would you like for me to find one of the Israelite woman to nurse him for you?" she timidly asked.

Then, with permission granted, she ran home and came back with her own mother.

"Take care of this child for me," Pharaoh's daughter instructed the happy Jochebed. "I will see that he is spared by the guards and that you are paid for your work."

So the little boy was cared for by his own mother and allowed to live. When he was old enough, the princess adopted him and brought him to stay with her in the palace. She called him Moses, a name worn by Egyptian kings, yet its meaning recalled to her that she had drawn him out of the water.

Moses had a strange childhood in the palace. He lived a wonderful life of an Egyptian prince and had many friends among the court and royal family, yet he knew enough about his own people and their suffering to keep him from being completely happy. In many ways, he felt torn between the two, and the feeling grew as he became older. To which did he really belong?

As a grown man, Moses stood one day watching the Israelites hard at work on a great building. With the hot sun beating down upon them, they labored without rest hour by hour for fear the whip of the nearby taskmaster would fall across their shoulders if they dared to stop.

Off to the side Moses caught sight of one of the guards beating a poor workman. Without thinking, he ran over and struck the guard—so hard, in fact, that he killed the man. Looking in both directions, Moses decided that no one had seen it happen, so he hid the body in the sand.

But when Moses went out the next day, he found that his deed was the talk of the whole Israelite camp. Their reaction to it was strange: rather than looking upon him as being their defender, they were suspicious of him, thinking he was not really one of their own.

"What right have you to get involved with us?" they demanded.

"What right indeed?" Moses asked himself.

And he was afraid. "If all the Israelites know of the dead man, the news will soon spread to the Egyptians and to Pharaoh," he reasoned. "I must get away as quickly as possible."

So by the time Pharaoh did hear of it and sent guards to arrest Moses, he was far away in the land of Midian. *Exodus 2:1–15*

AN UNWILLING LEADER

In Midian, where he had fled from Pharaoh, Moses met the daughters of a priest, watering their father's flocks at a well. No sooner had they drawn their water than some shepherds came up and tried to make trouble for them. Moses jumped up and helped the girls.

Later, when they arrived at home, their father asked how they had finished their job so quickly, for he knew they were often disturbed by the bothersome shepherds.

"An Egyptian was at the well today, and he helped us water our sheep," the sisters explained.

"Where is the man now? Why didn't you invite him to eat with us? Run and see if he is still at the well."

So Moses came to eat with Jethro, the priest, and stayed to live. One of the daughters, Zipporah, became his wife; and he was content to work for his father-in-law, caring for his flocks.

Years passed, and Moses grew accustomed to the rough, lonely life of a shepherd—a very different existence than that of his early life as a prince. Over the hills he traveled day by day, always searching for fresh grazing land for his animals.

On one occasion, Moses had made his way to a mountain called Horeb, or sometimes, Sinai. Here, as he strolled along with his flocks, he noticed a strange light near the ground. When he stepped closer to look, he saw that it was a bush that appeared to be on fire and yet was not burned up.

Then he heard his name called by a voice that seemed to come from the flames: "Moses! Moses!"

"Here I am," he answered.

"Come no closer. Take off your sandals, for you are standing on holy ground," the voice continued.

"I am the God of your fathers—Abraham, Isaac, and Jacob. I have seen the sufferings of my people in Egypt and have heard their cries and moans. I am now ready to bring them out of Egypt and give them a new land of their own.

"Come, Moses: I have chosen you to be my messenger to Pharaoh."

"Who am I, that I should go to Pharaoh?" Moses protested.

"I will be with you," the Lord said. "As a sign, I promise that after you have led the people out, you will meet me again on this same mountain."

"How can I ever convince your people that I have spoken with you?"

"Tell them I AM GOD has sent you. Say that the God of Abraham, Isaac, and Jacob has appeared to you and told you that he was about to guide his people to their own land. First, meet with the leaders of Israel; and when you have convinced them, go and demand of the Pharaoh that he let you leave for three days to worship in the wilderness.

"Now Pharaoh will not want you to go at first, but I will perform mighty deeds through you that will make him release my people."

Moses seemed frightened by the importance of this difficult task. "The Israelites will not accept me as their leader," he said. "They won't believe that you have appeared to me."

So the Lord showed Moses signs to prove that he was with him—he turned a rod into a snake and then back into a rod again when Moses grabbed its tail. He made Moses' hand withered and white and changed it back to normal again.

"Show these signs to the people," the Lord told Moses. "Then they will believe you."

But Moses had another excuse: "I could not speak before such a group— I have never been good with words."

"Who made your mouth? Why, it was I, the Lord. I'll teach you what to say."

"But . . ." Moses began again.

"All right," the Lord said. "Your brother Aaron is a good speaker. He can go with you and do the talking for you.

"Now, go. Already Aaron is coming to meet you."

So Moses reluctantly accepted the leadership of God's people. After explaining the strange calling to his father-in-law, he took Zipporah and the sons that had been born to them, and departed for Egypt.

On the way, Aaron met them, and they traveled together. Once in Egypt, they summoned an assembly of the Israelite leaders, at which they explained the vision and demonstrated the signs God had shown them. It seemed that Moses' fear had been in vain—the Israelites were thankful he had come and were overjoyed at the news that the Lord was aware of their suffering. They bowed their heads and worshipped the one who promised to deliver them. *Exodus 2:15–4:31*

AN EXHIBITION OF POWER

The children of Israel had accepted Moses and Aaron as the leaders through whom God would bring them out of Egypt; the next step was to gain the consent of Pharaoh so they could leave. What a difficult task this proved to be!

First Moses and Aaron arranged for a meeting with the king and said very simply: "The Lord God of Israel wants you to let his people go into the wilderness to worship."

This merely amused Pharaoh. "Who is the Lord God of the Israelites?" he asked. "I don't even know him; and moreover, I won't let his people go. Those slaves must not have enough to do if they have time to plan trips into the wilderness. I'll see to it that they have plenty to keep them busy in the future!"

Until this time, the Egyptian overseers had supplied the Israelites with straw to strengthen the mud bricks they were making. Pharaoh ordered them to stop this practice. Now they would have to search for their own straw each day, while continuing to make as many bricks as ever.

Naturally this was an impossible task. When the Israelites failed to make enough bricks and were beaten by the guards, some of them tried to appeal to Pharaoh themselves.

"Make bricks!" Pharaoh ordered. "You shall not be given straw, but you must make just as many as you did before. This should take care of any talk about worshipping your God."

As they came away from the palace, the unhappy men met Moses and Aaron. "You've made things worse than ever for us now," they accused their would-be leaders.

Moses turned to God with their cry: "Why did you send me to make things worse for your people? Since I have come, Pharaoh hates them more than ever and you haven't saved them yet."

But God replied to Moses' plea by giving him confidence and sending him right back to Pharaoh.

"This time, when you see the king," the Lord instructed, "he will want to see a sign. Have Aaron cast down his rod and it will become a snake."

It all came to pass just as the Lord had said, but Pharaoh's magicians came in and changed their rods into snakes, also. Even when Aaron's snake swallowed all the others, the king's heart remained as stubborn as ever.

The next morning Moses was not so discouraged. He met Pharaoh as he walked down to the River Nile. "You are going to find out just who this God of the Israelites is and how powerful he is," Moses warned. "Watch now; by his power the water of this river is going to be turned to blood."

At that, the Nile ran crimson; dead fish rose to the surface. The smell and taste were so terrible that no one could drink from it. Before long, the Egyptians were digging around it to try to find some water they could use. But Pharaoh was not impressed.

A week passed and Moses and Aaron appealed to him again. When they saw that his heart was hardened, Aaron stretched out his rod over the Nile and frogs began to swarm from its waters. Into the houses, the bedrooms, the ovens, the dishes—everywhere the Egyptians looked, there were frogs.

Finally the little pests began to annoy the king. "All right," he said to Moses and Aaron; "take away the frogs and I will let you make sacrifices." But once he saw that the frogs were dead, he failed to keep his promise.

Another show of God's power was needed, and this time it came in the form of lice, crawling and flying until the air seemed thick with them. Pharaoh's magicians began to recognize the hand of a God more powerful than they, but Pharaoh failed to be moved.

Next, into the fields and houses God sent millions of flies. Their buzzing and their presence everywhere began to annoy Pharaoh. He summoned Moses: "Why don't you and the people worship here in this land?"

"The Egyptians wouldn't approve of our worship if we stayed here. We must go at least a three-days' journey into the wilderness," Moses explained.

"I will grant your request," Pharaoh replied. "You may go away, but only a short distance."

So Moses prayed to God for flies to be removed. Once they disappeared, Pharaoh changed his mind.

The next sign of the Lord's power was a sickness which affected the cattle of the Egyptians, but not those of the Israelites. Even when the Egyptians animals all died of the ailment, Pharaoh failed to see he would never win.

Again the Lord brought illness—this time in the form of boils which afflicted the people themselves. As sick and sore as he and his people were, Pharaoh remained hardhearted.

Damaging hail was sent which completely leveled the crops and fields of Pharaoh's people; and even though Pharaoh seemed to give in, he changed his mind as soon as the storm was gone.

Lest Moses be discouraged again, the Lord explained to him: "Continue to approach Pharaoh with your plea. I've purposely made him stubborn, so that I could show to all how powerful I am. For years the people will remember these signs and tell their children about me."

So after due warning to the king, Moses and Aaron called forth God to send another plague. It was locusts, which filled the land and destroyed all that was left unharmed by the hailstorm. By this time, Pharaoh's people began to beg him to end their suffering and let the Israelites have their way. In reply, he made a half-hearted attempt to please them by offering to let just the men leave.

"We must all go," Moses firmly announced. But Pharaoh would not agree to this.

Another sign was sent—a darkness so intense that it could be felt. For three days it covered the land of the Egyptians so that the people had to remain in their homes; but in the land of Goshen, a bright sun shone on the Israelites.

With the darkness, Pharaoh began to play the same game with Moses: he agreed to let the Israelites go under certain conditions of his own. When Moses refused to agree, he became very angry. "Get out of here!" he shouted at Moses. "If I ever see your face again you will die."

"You will never see my face again," Moses replied. "The God of the Israelites is going to show one more sign of his power; after that, you will be glad for us to leave!" And with that, he and God turned their backs on Pharaoh forever.

Exodus 5–11

A MEMORIAL MEAL

The struggle for power between God and Pharaoh was nearly over. God was about to deliver the crushing blow that would show Pharaoh and the idols he worshipped to be completely powerless. By this act, a group of slaves would be freed and become a new nation, one that God had truly

Loran Raymond Jones

THE FIRST FEAST OF THE PASSOVER

Exodus 12:3–17

Loran Raymond Jones

MOSES AT SINAI

Exodus 32:15–24

Loran Raymond Jones

CONSTRUCTING THE ARK OF THE COVENANT

Exodus 37:1–9

Loran Raymond Jones

MOSES STRIKING THE ROCK

Exodus 17:1–7

created. In a dramatic way, Moses made sure that the people would never forget it.

"At last the time has come when the Lord is going to lead us away from here to a new life," he warned the Israelites. "You must get ready."

"Get ready! Get ready!" The news and excitement swept through the land of Goshen, where God's people had settled in the time of Joseph.

Then Moses told them exactly how they should prepare: "At midnight the Lord is going to pass through the land and smite the Egyptians with the last plague: he will cause the first-born in every house to die. If you will follow my instructions, however, your children will be spared. Each family must kill a lamb and sprinkle its blood on the sides and crossbeam of the door of the house where you live. This blood will be the sign that shows the Lord which houses belong to his own people, and he will pass them by in his destruction.

"On the same evening, you will roast the lamb that you have killed and eat it. You may also eat bread, but make it hurriedly, without yeast, for there is little time. Be dressed and ready for traveling when you eat this meal," he went on. "Have your coat tied and your sandals and hat on. Eat standing up so you will be ready to leave at any minute, for when the Lord strikes, Pharaoh will let you go."

By this time, Moses did not have to show the Israelites any signs to make them trust his word. The mighty acts of God, or plagues, had shown both to them and to many of the Egyptians, as well, that he had been divinely appointed by the one true God.

Quickly the lambs were killed and the doorposts marked with blood. A darkness fell, the people dressed for a journey, while their lambs roasted. When the meat was cooked, they ate their unusual meal, one that is still eaten every year by their descendants, even though over 3000 years have passed since its first observance.

Today, it may seem strange to Jewish children to watch their parents eat this memorial meal, the Passover, while wearing a hat and standing up as though they were about to go somewhere. They may even wonder at the bread which has no yeast in it. Moses was able to sense this when he told the Israelite elders: "You and your children after you should observe this feast every year. When the children notice strange things about it, they will ask what these things mean. You will be able to say: 'This is the feast of the Lord's passover, for he passed over the houses of our people on the night when the Egyptians were slain.' "

At midnight the Lord came, as he had warned. Pharaoh, who had gone to bed with the notion that he was at last rid of Israelite trouble, was awakened with the news that his oldest son was dead. From the house of every Egyptian came cries that the same thing had happened. No family was spared. In the middle of the night, the defeated king summoned Moses and Aaron to the palace.

"Take your people and flocks," he begged them. "Go worship your God as you asked." Then, in a pathetic voice that recognized a power far above his, he added, "Bless me."

So the waiting Israelites gathered up what they could and began to move out of Egypt. A long-awaited day was dawning as God led his people toward home.

Exodus 12, 13

PATH THROUGH THE SEA

From Egypt, the shortest road to the land of Canaan lay up toward the Mediterranean Sea and along its coast. At various points on this road, the Egyptians kept outposts of soldiers stationed, awaiting any emergency or enemy; so God led his people away from this route. He knew that they were not yet prepared to fight a regular battle with trained soldiers. Instead, he led them down toward the southeast, guiding them overhead with a cloud, like a pillar, by day and a pillar of fire by night. The land in this direction was rather deserted and wild and seldom traveled.

Now during their four hundred years in Egypt, the families of Israel's twelve sons had grown to include more than 600,000 men. This gives you some idea of the size of the group that began this exodus across the wilderness. It also gives an explanation for Pharaoh's reluctance to have them leave Egypt: they caused a mighty loss in slave labor to his kingdom. They had not been gone long, in fact, when these very thoughts made Pharaoh regret what had taken place.

"It is not too late to capture them," he reasoned, and he called for his chariots and army. Away they galloped toward the Israelite encampment on the banks of a sea, once thought to be the Red Sea, now called Sea of Reeds.

From a distance, God's people heard the din of the chariots and horses approaching. All their courage melted at the sound. The infant nation still had so much to learn; freedom was a new thing. In that moment, life in Egypt did not seem so bad. It was hard, but it was certain; whereas, this new life was unknown.

"Did you bring us out in this wilderness to die?" they asked Moses. "It was better serving in Egypt than it is dying here."

Moses tried to calm them down. "Don't be afraid; remember that the Lord is on your side," he reminded them.

Then night came on, and the pillar of cloud by which the Lord showed the way moved between the camps of the Israelites and Egyptians. In the dark Moses held out his rod over the sea, and the wind began to blow. All night it blew at the sea until it pushed the water aside and left the ground underneath showing.

Across this sea-road the Israelites lined up to pass. As quickly as they could, they filed to the other side. After them, in a chase, rolled the Egyptian chariots, but the swampy lake bottom that had supported people on foot gave way under their heavy wheels. As the wheels dug in and the horses floundered, the last of the Israelites reached the opposite shore.

Once more Moses held his rod over the water. This time the wind began to die down. When it did, the walls of water came rushing together, drowning the soldiers who had ridden out into the river bed.

Safe on shore, Moses and people could not hold back the joy and thanksgiving they felt. They sang a song to the mighty God who had delivered them. Quite naturally, Moses' sister Miriam picked up a tambourine and, dancing, led the women in a beautiful hymn:

> Sing to the Lord, for he has triumphed gloriously;
> The horse and the rider he has thrown into the sea.

Exodus 13:17–15:21

QUESTIONS: 1. *Why did Jacob's family remain in Egypt so long?* 2. *What was their status in Egypt?* 3. *Why did Moses' mother have to hide him?* 4. *How did Moses come to live in Pharaoh's palace?* 5. *Why did Moses flee to Midian?* 6. *What was Moses' occupation in Midian?* 7. *What was the message of the burning bush?* 8. *How was Moses to convince Israel that God had sent him?* 9. *What did Moses ask of Pharaoh? Why was his request not granted?* 10. *How did Pharaoh make the Israelites' work more difficult?* 11. *In what ways did God demonstrate his power to Pharaoh and the Egyptians? What was Pharaoh's reaction?* 12. *What was the last plague?* 13. *How did the Israelites escape being harmed by the plague?* 14. *Describe the Passover meal.* 15. *Why did God lead the Israelites toward the wilderness?* 16. *What was Pharaoh's reaction when he saw the Israelites had gone?* 17. *How did the Israelites escape from the Egyptian army?*

A Nation in Waiting

DIFFICULT DAYS

God's people, the Israelites, had escaped from Egypt. With the crossing of the sea on dry land, they were free of their life of slavery to Pharaoh. But Canaan, their promised homeland, was still a long distance away. Between them and their destination were miles and miles of rocky desert with grim mountains rising all around.

At the sight of the wasteland ahead, the happy mood of the singers by the banks of the sea began to change. God had led them out of Egypt—but surely not for this. There had been slave labor in Egypt, but there had also been homes and food and plentiful water. In the civilized cities along the Nile, no one feared attacks of plundering desert tribes. Life had a certain security in Egypt; now survival alone seemed difficult.

But Moses was not daunted by the trip ahead. He had wandered this very country as a shepherd and knew that the people could survive. He also trusted in God to lead the marchers safely to Canaan. So despite the complainings, he set out into the wilderness and the people followed. For three days they moved out into the desert, walking slowly in the blistering heat of the day and huddling in their tents during the cold nights. On the third day, they spied their first sight of water ahead. A few hurried to be in the first to sample it, but they quickly spat it out. It was too bitter to drink!

"What shall we do?" they cried to Moses.

The Lord told Moses to throw branches from a certain bush into the water. Once this was done, it became pleasant to taste, although the people still remembered the place as Marah, or "bitterness."

From Marah, Moses led his followers to one of the few green spots that relieved the terrible desert. Here, at Elim, twelve springs of water were surrounded by a grove of palm trees; and the people briefly enjoyed a pleasant, shady campsite. However, there were many miles yet to go, and the company had to leave Elim and set out once more across the wilderness. By this time only a few weeks had passed since the journey had begun, but the road ahead already looked endless to the weary travelers. When they thought back on their life in Egypt, it seemed better and better.

"We had food and water back in Egypt," they reminded Moses. "Did you bring us out in this terrible country to die of hunger?"

"When will you learn that the Lord is taking care of you?" Moses asked. "Even now he had told me that he will send food from heaven each day."

That evening a cloud of quails flew into the camp. When they landed on the ground, the people caught as many as they wanted for food. In the morning, they awoke to find little white flakes covering the ground as dew would.

"What is it?" they asked each other, or "Manna?" as one would say it in Hebrew.

"This is the bread God has sent," Moses explained. And when the people touched some of it to their tongues, they saw that it tasted like sweet wafers. At Moses' command, each family gathered up its daily supply early in the morning before the "Manna," as they called it, disappeared. If anyone was greedy and took more than he needed, that part spoiled.

On the sixth day of the week, however, it was all right to pick up a double supply, because God desired that his people rest and worship him the seventh day. This extra measure for the Sabbath, or seventh day, remained fresh until it was eaten. Day by day, the people continued to eat this "heavenly bread" until they reached Canaan.

The need for food was now taken care of, but several weary days on the desert brought more complaints about the lack of water. In answer to the cries for help, Moses struck a rock with his rod, and water sprang forth at a place he named Massah and Meribah.

Another oasis lay ahead at Rephidim, but the Israelites found that these green spots were much sought after by the wandering tribes that roam the desert. While they were camped at Rephidim, one such tribe called the Amalekites swept down out of the mountains and attacked them. Moses appointed a young man named Joshua to choose men from among the Israelites to make a stand against the raiding tribe.

Now, by this time, the rod of Aaron and Moses that had been used to bring plagues upon Pharaoh, part the Sea of Reeds, and bring water from rocks was thought to have some special power. In order to give Joshua and his men confidence in their battle, Moses stood on a hill above the fight and held up this rod where the men could see it. Whenever it was in sight, the Israelites fought bravely; but when Moses's arm grew tired and dropped, they were beaten back.

When Aaron and a man named Hur saw what was happening, they moved a stone for Moses to sit on; and they stood on either side of him, holding up his arms until the sun went down. Thus Joshua "mowed down Amalek and his people with the edge of the sword." *Exodus 15:22–17:16*

MOSES ON THE MOUNTAIN

Still ahead of the Israelites lay the towering mountains that rose out of the rocky wilderness. It was in these very mountains that Moses had spied the burning bush and had heard the voice of God. As the Lord had promised on that occasion, Moses led the people right to the base of one of the peaks called Mount Sinai. Here, at God's command, they set up camp and prepared to stay for a while.

Although Abraham's descendants were far from perfect, under Moses' leadership they had gradually come to know something about God. The wondrous signs and deliverance from Egypt, the crossing of the sea, the provision of food and water, and victory over the Amalekites had made them aware that he looked on them with special favor and planned to make them his own in a particular way. Now the time had come for him to seal his choice of Israel with a covenant.

A covenant has always been a common thing; it is merely an agreement made between two parties. Most covenants are made between people or groups that are equal, but this agreement the Lord made with his people was not a covenant between equals. The Lord of all creation, the ruler of the universe, was being gracious enough to enter into a pack with this homeless, overgrown family of Abraham.

The scene at Sinai was set to impress upon the people the might and power of this king of heaven. With their tents spread out around the base of mountains, the Israelites spent two days preparing for God's scheduled appearance by cleaning themselves and the camp thoroughly. On the third morning, they awoke to the sound of thunder from high upon the mountain. Lightning flashed and a very dark cloud hovered around the mountaintop. The noise of a trumpet sounded, louder and louder.

"Don't come any closer to the mountain," Moses warned the people. "It is a holy place, for our God is calling from it." Then in answer to the voice that had spoken to him before, Moses began to climb up the rugged mountainside. Watching below, the people saw him disappear into the hovering smoke.

The words God spoke to Moses on this occasion were the wise commands that were to guide the lives of the chosen people in a manner pleasing to the Lord who chose them. We know them as the Ten Commandments:

> I am the Lord your God, who brought you out of your life of slavery in Egypt.
> Worship me as your only God.
> Do not make images to worship or serve.
> Speak of me with honor and respect.
> Always keep the Sabbath day as a time of rest and worship.
> Love and respect your parents.
> Do not murder another person.
> Be faithful to your husband or wife.
> Do not steal.
> Do not tell something untrue about anyone.
> Do not desire to have something that belongs to another.

Moses heard these words of the Lord, but he found that the people below had been frightened by the thunder and lightning and majesty of the Lord's appearance.

"We're afraid," they said to Moses. "You listen to God and then tell us what he says."

So Moses returned to the mountaintop and listened for all the people while God completed his divine covenant. *Exodus 19:1–20:21*

THE GOLDEN CALF

God had many wise rules worked out for the good of his people, and he spent a long time discussing them with Moses on the peaks of Mount Sinai. The first important rules, the Ten Commandments, were written by the Lord himself on slabs of stone for Moses to deliver to the people. Other commands regarding the Israelites' worship and life in their new home were also entrusted to Moses to remember. We might compare this meeting to a "summit conference" of today, where stipulations of a treaty—or covenant—are agreed upon.

Because the people were afraid of God's power that showed itself like a storm on the mountain, they waited in their tent-camp at the base of the mountain for Moses to return to them with God's word. Day after day passed and still they saw no sign of their leader. Had he disappeared forever? If so, who was protecting them now in this forsaken wilderness?

"Aaron!" they called to Moses' brother. "Where is Moses? We think something bad has happened to him, and we're afraid with no leader. Make us a god that will lead us and take care of us."

So Aaron said, "Take off all your gold rings and give them to me."

When the Israelites had done as he suggested, Aaron took this gold, melted it into one mass, and shaped it into the crude form of a calf.

"Here is your god, O Israel!" he said as he presented it to the impatient people. "This is the one who brought you out of Egypt. Tomorrow we shall have a great feast in honor of this god!"

"Hurray!" the people shouted, and they forgot all about their worry. There, right in the shadow of God's presence above their heads on the mountain, they offered animal sacrifices to the calf and sang and danced around it as they had seen the Egyptians do.

When God saw this, he told Moses, "Go down! The people have already broken our covenant. They are worshipping an idol that they have made. It makes me want to destroy them now!"

So Moses turned and hurried as fast as he could down the rocky ledges of the mountainside. His traveling was careful and cautious for in his hands he guarded a wonderful treasure—the tables of stone on which the law was written in God's own handwriting.

As he neared the base of the mountain, Moses was met by Joshua, the young warrior, who had been faithfully waiting during the forty days

Moses spoke with God. From this point they could already hear sounds of the celebration that was being carried on around the golden calf.

"It sounds like war in the camp," Joshua said.

"Those are not sounds of war," Moses replied. "That is the noise of people singing."

Then they turned a corner and came within view of the camp. The whole awful scene was spread out before them—God's own people, singing and dancing around a golden calf while their sacrifices burned before it.

Within Moses welled a very great anger. He hurled the precious tables of stone down and shattered them into pieces. Then he grabbed up the golden idol, burned it, ground it into powder, and mixed it with water for the people to drink.

"Why did you let the people do this?" Moses demanded of Aaron.

"Now, Moses," Aaron tried to explain; "don't be angry with me. You know how the people are—always set on doing evil. They wanted a leader when you failed to return. I merely took the gold they gave me, threw it into the fire, and this was what came out."

Moses had had enough excuses. He strode to the entrance of the camp and shouted: "Who is on the Lord's side? Come to me!"

The loyal men gathered in a company before him.

"See that you serve the Lord this day by punishing those who worshipped the idol."

So they went out and slew about three thousand on that day, the first of many purges for a lesson that Israel seemed never to learn.

The next day, Moses' anger had disappeared. On behalf of the people, he bowed and prayed: "Lord, the people committed a terrible sin. Please remember it no more."

So the Lord forgave the people and consented once more to bind himself to them with a covenant.

"Cut two more slabs of stone like those that broke," he told Moses, "and I will write my law upon them."

So Moses went up on the mountain again and talked with God. When he finally returned with the new tablets, his face was bright and shining with the radiance of God's presence. This time the people had waited patiently; they were ready to hear the terms and demands of God's covenant.

Exodus 31:18–32:35, 34

A PORTABLE PLACE OF WORSHIP

With the exodus and the covenant on Sinai, the religion of Israel was born. God had played a real part in the life of the Israelites before this time, but it had not taken a definite form. He had spoken directly with the first fathers of the people—Abraham, Isaac, and Jacob—but his voice had been nearly silent during the long period of slavery in Egypt. From the time of Abraham until Moses, there was no strict code that told the people how to worship and act.

Now, in his covenant, the Lord had made specific demands on the Israelites, and in turn, he gave them definite promises. They would receive the promises if they obeyed the commands. These commands were generally wise rules dealing with worship and moral behavior.

In the rules for worship, God had made it very plain that the Israelites were not to make some form that represented him and then bow down to it. He was larger and greater than any idol or even a building. But the people still needed a building that they could use for the religious ceremonies he had commanded them to observe. The structure could not be a temple on Mount Sinai because they were going to leave and move on toward Canaan. It would have to be a portable place of worship—one they could move around until they arrived in the land of promise. The tabernacle that the Lord asked them to build was just that.

This house of worship described in the law given to Moses was really an elaborate tent. It was built of a wooden framework covered with curtains of linen, mohair cloth, and animal skins. Inside it were two rooms. In the larger, there was a golden candlestick with six branches, an altar for burning incense, and twelve loaves of bread, changed each week. The loaves represented the twelve tribes of Israel. A curtain divided this room from a smaller room called the Holy of Holies or Most Holy Place. Here lay a chest made of wood overlayed with gold, within which three precious treasures lay: the tablets on which God wrote the Law, the rod of Moses and Aaron that called forth so many signs of God's power, and a pot of manna, the bread from heaven. To the Israelites, these three things seemed to symbolize God's promise and his presence. This ark, as the chest was called, was so sacred that it was never even touched. Instead, it was always carried by poles slipped through the rings on its four corners.

The people did not meet inside the tabernacle itself. Instead, it was built at one end of a courtyard, which was large enough to hold a crowd. This courtyard had wooden frame walls, covered with linen curtains, but no roof. Besides the tabernacle, the courtyard also contained an altar where sacrifices were offered to God and a great brass bowl for washing.

In order to build this place of worship as God had commanded, the people had to show their trust and love for him by giving materials and time.

Moses made his plea: "Whoever has a generous heart, let him bring an offering now to God. Bring your gold jewelry, your fine material, and animal skins. Bring good wood and sweet incense.

"Bezalel and Oholiab will oversee the work because they are expert craftsmen with gold and with wood. Bring your gifts and offer your time to them."

Everyone wanted to have a part in building the place of worship. They brought all the things Moses had mentioned. They carved wood and wove cloth and processed animal skins. Finally Bezalel and Oholiab sent word to

Moses: "Every morning the people come with new gifts. Tell them we already have more than we need; they have done more than the Lord demanded."

So because they were generous and industrious, the Israelites finished their new place of worship. When it was done, they gathered for a meeting. Moses set everything in place as God had commanded him. Aaron and his sons, in special priests' robes, conducted services and offered sacrifices according to the new laws. And the cloud which had covered the top of Mount Sinai came down and rested on the tabernacle. *Exodus 35–40*

CONFLICTING REPORTS

One day the cloud of God's presence that hovered over the tabernacle moved away. The people knew that it was time to leave Sinai and follow as God led toward the promised land. Now they had a prized possession to move along with them—the tent of meeting with its special furnishings. The men of Levi's family were given the task of dismantling and moving this holy equipment. Aaron and his sons were named to serve as priests, leading the worship services that were held in the tabernacle.

Days of weary travel passed by and the people began to wonder: Would they ever reach their new home? One after another complained to Moses. They liked the food they had eaten in Egypt better than manna. They were tired of walking about in barren wilderness. Some were jealous of Moses' power and leadership, including Aaron and Miriam, his own brother and sister. Through all of this, Moses remained patient and spoke with God again and again on behalf of the people and their weaknesses. In answer, the Lord molded him into the mighty leader he had feared he would never become.

Despite their slow progress, the Israelites finally reached a camping place in the wilderness of Paran that was near enough to Canaan for an exploring party to go forth and bring back a report on the new land. Moses chose a group of twelve men to make this trip—an outstanding leader from each of the twelve tribes of Israel.

"See what the land is like," he commissioned them. "Find out whether there are many people or few, and whether they are strong or weak. Explore the cities that you see, as well as the farming land and woodland. Bring back some of the fruit that you find."

So the scouts went over the hills and into the Jordan Valley. All over the land of Canaan they wandered, making notes on all they saw. They also gathered fruit that they found growing—figs and pomegranates and a cluster of grapes so big that two men had to carry it on a pole between them.

The people crowded around the twelve when they returned, anxious to hear what the new land was really like and how difficult it would be to take it from the people already living there. There was no dispute among the spies as to whether the land was good. "The land is rich indeed, flowing with milk and honey. Just look at this fruit we have brought and you can see for yourselves."

But at this point the report began to differ. "Let us take the land and occupy it right away," urged Joshua and Caleb, two of the men. "With the Lord to help us, we can do it."

The other ten scouts disagreed. "The people who live in the land are very strong and live in walled cities. Some of the men are so big they make us look like grasshoppers. We do not have a chance against them."

Then the people—the very ones God had led from Egypt, fed in the wilderness, and made a covenant with at Sinai—began to cry with fear. "We would rather have died in Egypt!" they said. "The Lord has brought us out here only to be killed. Let's choose a captain and start back now."

"Oh, no!" Joshua and Caleb tried to tell them. "This is a wonderful land the Lord is going to give us. Do not fear the people there; the Lord will deliver us from them."

But by this time the people had worked themselves into a fever of disappointment and mistrust. They began to hurl stones at Joshua and Caleb.

Suddenly the voice of God came from the tabernacle: "How long will it take for you to believe in me? What more must I do to prove myself? Perhaps I should send some disaster upon you and disown you now."

"Pardon them, Lord," Moses begged as he had before. "You are patient and loving. Forgive them as you have from the time we left Egypt."

So the Lord agreed to pardon once more, but he pronounced a punishment on those who had not trusted him to lead them into Canaan—they would not enter the promised land at all. Instead, they would wander in the wilderness for forty years until they died. Then their children would be grown and they, along with Joshua and Caleb, would inherit the land.

When they heard this, the people regretted their decision. "Joshua and Caleb were right. We'll go on now and take the land," they said.

But their decision came too late. "The Lord has turned away from you now," Moses warned. "You'll be killed if you go." And this was precisely what happened to those who went ahead. The Canaanite people rushed down on them from the hills, killing some and driving the others back.

So the Israelites who remained sadly turned away from the promised land and started their journey back into the wilderness, following Moses and the cloud.

Numbers 13–14

YEARS OF WAITING

Back into the wilderness the Israelites marched, and for many years they camped in and around Paran. During this period there were rebellions against Moses which arose and were put down. Finally, to prove Moses' right to the leadership of the people, God caused buds to sprout on his rod, a dry stick. As a constant reminder to the rebels, it was placed inside the ark.

There were also more complaints about the lack of water. Once when this happened, Moses and Aaron took the problem to the Lord in their usual way. An answer came from God: "Take your rod, and in front of the whole company, call forth water from a certain rock. Before their eyes, water will pour out, enough for them and their cattle."

So the brothers led the people to a dry rock. This time Moses' patience had worn thin. "Look here, you rebels!" he shouted. "Watch while *we* bring forth water from this rock." Then he hit the rock twice with his rod.

Water came pouring out, but God was not pleased. "Why did you claim to produce that water instead of giving the honor to me?" he demanded of Moses. "As a punishment, you will not live to lead the people into the promised land, although you will bring them to its borders."

Thus the wandering in the wilderness passed, a sad and discontented time. Nevertheless, as God in his wisdom knew, these were valuable years. The older generation who had served as slaves in Egypt died away. It was their preference for the security of Egypt to the challenge of a new land that had kept Israel out of Canaan for forty years. Meanwhile, their children grew up. These young people remembered nothing of the life of slavery; they were more adventuresome and bold than their fathers had been. When they heard stories of a good land awaiting them, they grew anxious to go and take it. Altogether, they made a more impressive group to move behind the Lord into promised country.

Yes, the time of waiting ended; finally the Lord was ready to move into Canaan. Of those adults who had fled from Egypt only Moses and Joshua and Caleb remained alive to lead the Israelites. First, the leaders sought to travel from the wilderness northward to Canaan through Edom, the home of Esau's descendants. Since these people had close family ties with the people of Israel, they wanted to pass through the land in a peaceful way. Moses sent a message to the King of Edom: "Let us come through your land. We will walk straight down the highway, taking nothing from your fields."

But the king of Edom did not welcome Moses' request. He was afraid to have such a large group of strangers in his country. To make sure they did not come, he sent armed guards to stand watch at the borders of the land.

For this reason, Moses led the Israelites on another difficult journey, circling the land of the Edomites to avoid having a conflict with them. This route led to the edge of the land of the Amorites. As before, Moses asked the king permission to pass through his country. When this king refused and sent men to battle with the Israelites, they did not make a peaceful retreat. Instead, they fought with the Amorites and won. Sihon, the king, was killed and one after another of the Amorite towns were captured. From this victory, they moved on and took possession of the land of another king, Og of Bashan. God's people were on their way to the promised land.

Numbers 16; 17; 20; 21

BALAAM AND HIS DONKEY

For years, the kingdoms bordering Canaan were aware of the band of ex-slaves camping throughout the wilderness to the south, but none of them was troubled by the fact. The one time the Israelites had made an assault (following the report of the scouts), they had easily been put down; and they had remained peaceful afterward. Then suddenly, almost without warning, they started marching northward, defeating Sihon and Og on their way. Balak, king of the Moabites was distressed. The Israelites were camped near his borders; he was bound to be their next victim. And judging from the size of the encampment, he knew that his army would not stand a chance against them. He was going to need something more than soldiers on his side—only supernatural assistance would give him a victory.

With this thought in mind, Balak sent far away to another country for a man named Balaam who was supposed to have special powers to work charms. "A great horde of people have come out of Egypt and are encamped near me," went Balak's message. "Come now and put a curse on them, for they are too strong for me. I have heard that those whom you curse are cursed, and those whom you bless are blessed."

But Balaam refused to return with Balak's messengers. "I am not able to go with you and curse these people."

Balak was not content with Balaam's refusal; he felt that his only hope lay in the magician's curse. So he sent a more impressive delegation to Balaam, giving them permission to offer him a generous reward for aiding their king. This time Balaam was still reluctant; but at last he saddled up his donkey and set out with the princes of Moab.

On the journey, an angel of the Lord appeared in the road. Of all those in the company, only Balaam's donkey saw the vision. The poor beast was so frightened that she headed off the road and into a field. At this, Balaam whipped her and finally managed to get her back on the road.

They had not traveled far, however, until the donkey saw the angel standing before her again. Caught in a pathway between the walls of two vineyards, the animal pushed up against the wall, crushing Balaam's foot. Again, Balaam got out his stick and beat the donkey until she moved.

Ahead, in a narrow place, the angel confronted the party again. This time Balaam's frightened beast sat right down with her master on her back. Irritated, Balaam began to beat her in earnest.

But the donkey opened her mouth and spoke: "What have I done to make you strike me three times?"

"You're fortunate that you've only been beaten," Balaam replied. "If I'd had a sword instead of a stick, I'd have killed you."

Then he looked up and saw the cause of all the furor. At the sight of the angel with a drawn sword, he fell on his face. "I know I should never have come," Balaam admitted. "I'll return home now."

But the angel permitted him to continue on to Moab, charging him to speak only the words the Lord directed him to say.

King Balak was waiting impatiently for Balaam. "What has taken you so long?" he wanted to know.

The very next morning he took Balaam out to a mountain which permitted a view of the Israelite camp. "Now, these are the people I want you to curse," Balak said. "Work your magic."

So Balaam opened his mouth to curse the Israelites, and this was what he said: "How can I curse whom God has not cursed? From this mountain I see them—I cannot count them, these sons of Jacob, they are so many."

"What are you saying?" Balak demanded. "I brought you here to curse my enemies, not bless them. Let us try again, in another place."

So he and Balaam moved to another mountain with a closer view of the Israelites. This time they went through the same procedure they had before—building altars and preparing for the curse on Israel. And when Balaam opened his mouth, his message went this way: "Behold, I have received a command to bless, and I can do nothing else. The Lord is with these people; he has brought them out of Egypt. There can be no enchantment against Israel."

These words infuriated Balak. "Either curse these people or say nothing at all," he commanded Balaam. And he agreed to give the magician one more chance.

But another mountain and more altars did not change the message. "How beautiful are your tents, you sons of Jacob," said Balaam. "Your enemies shall fall before you, and a great king shall rise from your people."

Balak hit his hands together. "I called you here to curse these people, promising you a great reward," he reminded Balaam. "You can be sure there will be no reward now. In fact, you had better get away from here while you can."

Balaam shrugged his shoulders, reminding the king that he had known all along he could only speak the words the Lord gave him to say. "A house full of gold or silver couldn't change that," he said. Then, to the king's dismay, he added something more about Israel:

A star shall come forth out of Jacob,
A king will rise in Israel.
He will crush his enemies,
no matter how strong they be.

And with this Balaam hurried home. *Numbers 22; 23; 24*

VIEW FROM THE MOUNTAIN

The Israelites were on their way; little stood now between them and the land of promise. To most of them, it seemed life was just beginning; but to their great leader, the end had come. As the Lord had decided, Moses would not enter Canaan with his people. He had finished his work.

First, he ordered a count made of all the people, according to tribes, so they would know the size of their fighting force and have some idea as to how to divide the land when it was theirs. Next, he appointed Joshua—warrior, scout, and companion—to be his successor.

Then Moses made his farewell speech to the people, most of which makes up the book of *Deuteronomy*. He reminded them of all the things God had done for them. He spoke again the words of God's law that they should keep and should teach to their children. With his hands on Joshua, he charged them:

"Be strong and of good courage, for you will go into the land God has promised. You will take possession of it because it is the Lord who goes before you. He will be with you; do not be afraid."

The people wept at the final words of their leader. In his life they had caused him misery; now, in his death, they realized that he had stood apart from them because he stood with God. As he finished his message and walked away from the tabernacle for the last time, they stood silently trying to realize how life would be without him.

Through the camp Moses passed, and alone he climbed up the side of one of the mountains of Moab. Here he met with the Lord, who showed him in the distance the land that the Israelites would soon possess. Moses looked across the Jordan River to the walled cities and the green fields of Canaan. "Here is the land of my fathers, Abraham, Isaac, and Jacob," he thought, and he was happy.

Then Moses died, alone with God on the Mount Nebo, and was buried in an unknown tomb.

Deuteronomy 31:7–8; 34:1–8

QUESTIONS: 1. *Into what kind of land did the children of Israel escape when they left Egypt?* 2. *How were they fed by God in the wilderness?* 3. *What did Moses do to help Joshua win his first battle?* 4. *Explain what a covenant is. How does the Law of Moses fit your description?* 5. *How were the people made aware that God was on Mount Sinai?* 6. *Name the Ten Commandments.* 7. *Why did the people appeal to Aaron for a god?* 8. *What was Moses' reaction to the calf worship?* 9. *Why did Israel need a portable place of worship?* 10. *How was the tabernacle built? How were the materials supplied?* 11. *What did the Ark of the Covenant contain?* 12. *Who served as priests in the tabernacle services?* 13. *What was the report of the twelve scouts who went into Canaan?* 14. *What was the Israelites' penalty for not trusting in the Lord to help them take the land?* 15. *In what ways were the years of wandering valuable?* 16. *Why was Moses told he could not enter the promised land?* 17. *Why did Moses by-pass Edom?* 18. *Why did Balak of Moab consult a magician? What was the outcome?* 19. *Describe Moses' farewell to Israel and his death.*

The Conquest of Canaan

SPIES IN RAHAB'S HOUSE

With the death of Moses, Joshua became the new leader of Israel. Now Joshua was a man of action, and he knew that the time to act had come. The promised land, a home for the wandering Israelites, was before him and was his for the taking, with God's help.

So Joshua led the people down from the mountains of Moab to the eastern side of the Jordan River, which runs through the land of Canaan. At this point, three of Israel's twelve tribes had a request: could they settle here on the eastern side of the Jordan instead of crossing into central Canaan? The land had been taken from the Amorites and Moabites, and they were quite satisfied with it. Joshua gave permission for the three tribes—Reuben, Gad and Manasseh—to take possession of the land that had just been conquered. "But," he reminded them, "the fighting men among you will have to come with us across the river to help the rest of the tribes take land for themselves. It would only be fair since they gave you the strength to obtain this part for yourselves. Your wives and children can remain here and begin building your homes."

"If that is your command, we will obey," the men agreed.

Not far on the other side of the Jordan River, within sight of the Israelite camp, stood the walled city of Jericho. If the land of Canaan was to be taken, it was clear that Jericho would have to be conquered first. Like any general preparing for battle in an unknown territory, Joshua sent spies over to Jericho to discover what the city was like.

Secretly, the two spies crossed the river and got through the city gates and into Jericho. Posing as ordinary travelers, they stopped at an inn owned by a woman named Rahab. They felt they would be safe in such an unsuspicious place.

But the king of Jericho had his spies, also; and they had seen the two strange men enter the city and go to Rahab's house. As soon as this information was related to the king, he sent soldiers over to Rahab's house to arrest the men.

In the middle of the night the soldiers banged on Rahab's door. "Bring out the two strangers. We know they are spies."

"Strangers come in and out of here all day," Rahab replied calmly. "How could I have known those two were spies? They left right before the city gates were closed at dark. I don't know where they were going, but I think you could overtake them if you rode out quickly."

So the soldiers followed Rahab's advice, riding out into the land surrounding the city. All night they searched for the spies, but found no one.

The reason they found no one was because Rahab had really hidden the men on her roof. She had made them lie down there and then covered them with flax that she was preparing to spin into cloth. This way, they could not be seen. Once the soldiers were gone, she hurried back to the roof to uncover them.

"I know all about you," she whispered to the two Israelites. "I know that your God has given you this land—everyone in Jericho had heard of it and we're terrified. We heard how your God brought you out of Egypt and helped you defeat the people on the other side of the Jordan. He must be the true ruler of the universe. No one here has the heart to fight him.

"Now, I have done this favor for you tonight. Would you do one for me in return? When you come back to take the city, spare me and my family."

"Our lives for yours," the men agreed. "Don't breathe a word of this to anyone, and we will remember you with kindness when the Lord gives us the land.

"Gather all your family into this house and mark your window with a red cord," they instructed her. "When we see it, we'll know where you are and keep you safe."

Then Rahab helped the men escape by lowering them from her window with a rope. You see, her house was part of the city wall.

"Run to the hills and hide for three days," she called to the men as they touched the ground. "By then the soldiers will have returned and you will be safe." And as the two figures disappeared into the shadows of the night, Rahab tied a red cord strongly to her window.

Three days later the spies stood before Joshua, ready to give their report. What a good report it was! "God is ready to lay the country in our hands. The people are already so afraid of us they won't even put up a fight!"

Joshua 1; 2

CANAAN AT LAST

The priests slipped the poles through the rings on the side of the sacred ark and lifted it to their shoulders. The day for marching had come! Joshua had called out the order, "Forward!" and the people stood waiting to follow.

With their precious burden, the priests passed through the crowd and made their way to the head of the procession. At a respectful distance behind, the rest formed lines and began to move. But their journey could not be a very long one. The Jordan River was just ahead and there was no way to cross it—no way unless God provided one.

The priests reached the water's edge, but they did not stop. They stepped right out into the water! And when their feet touched the swollen stream, the Jordan stopped flowing upstream and piled up like a dam, leaving dry land where the priests stood. On the rocks of the river bed, the holy men walked out into the middle of the Jordan and stood, guarding the ark. Then it was time for the people to cross. Hurrying, anxious to set foot on their new homeland, they made their way to the other side of the river.

When everyone had crossed except the priests, who still stood with the ark in the middle of the dry river bed, Joshua called for a representative from every tribe. "Each of you twelve men go back out where the priests are standing and pick up a large rock," he said. "We will pile them here for a stone memorial."

So the men did as Joshua commanded. "Now," Joshua said, as the twelfth stone was set in place, "when your children ask why these stones are here, you can tell them about God's bringing us safely over the Jordan River."

Next, Joshua signalled to the priests to join the rest of the company on the shore. As soon as they did, the river began rolling along in its usual way.

The Israelites' campsite on the western side of the Jordan was called Gilgal. Here they set up the tabernacle, with the ark inside, and celebrated the Passover feast, as their fathers had done just before leaving Egypt. They found grain growing ripe in the fields of the land, and they used this to make real bread. No longer did they need for God to supply manna. They had reached the land "flowing with milk and honey." *Joshua 3–5:12*

THE WALLS TUMBLED DOWN

Across from the Israelite camp at Gilgal stood the city of Jericho. Its walls were shut tight; no one came out or went in. The people of the city knew that a siege was about to fall upon them. They had been frightened when they heard of the Israelites' defeating the kings across the Jordan; but the story of God's stopping the flow of the river had completely terrified them. No one had the heart to fight such a powerful Lord.

Joshua stood outside the walls of Jericho, looking over the scene of the coming battle. Suddenly, a man appeared before him, his sword glinting in the sun. Joshua gave a start, but he walked bravely over to the stranger. "Whose side are you on?" he asked.

"I am the Commander of the Army of the Lord," came the reply.

Joshua fell to his knees. "What plans do you have to give me?"

"Jericho is yours—even its king and mighty men. But you must keep none of the treasure you find there for yourselves. It belongs to God; it must be put in his treasury." Then the armed man told Joshua of the plot to conquer the city, a plot that could not fail because it came from God.

The next morning Joshua summoned the priests to come forward with the ark. It was time for the strange attack to begin. Ahead of the priests marched the armed soldiers; then came seven priests with trumpets made of rams' horns; next the men bearing the ark; and in the rear, the rest of the Israelites. This strange procession began winding its way around the city walls of Jericho. No one made a sound; the only noise came from the seven trumpets. Within the city, the people huddled in fear, waiting for the battle to begin. But all they heard were trumpets and marching feet—once all the way around the city wall. Then the Israelites returned to their camp.

The second day the same thing happened—Joshua and his people marched silently around the walls of Jericho, but that was all. For six days they followed the same routine. What kind of attack was this?

On the seventh day Joshua called for the Israelites to form ranks just as dawn was breaking. "Forward, march!" came the order, and they began circling the city as they had before. But on this day, they did not stop marching after one time around; they kept going until they had encircled the city seven times. Then they stopped.

The priests blew their trumpets and Joshua said to the people, "Shout! The Lord has given you the city!"

The trumpets began to blare again and the people began to shout. The silence was broken so violently that the city walls began to tremble. Great cracks broke through the stones and one by one, they began to fall. Crashing, tumbling, the walls fell flat before the attack of the Israelites. The city lay wide open for them to capture.

One house in the city wall, however, still stood among the rubble. From its window bravely fluttered a dusty red cord. "Go into that house," Joshua commanded, "and bring the people you find to the safety of our camp." So the promise of the spies to Rahab was kept. She and her family were saved and came to live with the people of Israel.

From that day on, the fame of Joshua and the Lord's army began to spread throughout the land of Canaan. *Joshua 5:13–6:27*

SIN IN THE CAMP

The conquest of Canaan was more than just another war; it was a Holy War of God, and as such, it was fought according to certain principles. For one thing, the Lord was Commander-in-Chief of the Israelite army. He gave the orders to attack and planned how each battle was to be fought. Usually his presence was signified by the ark, which was carried in the midst of the battle lines. When God fought alongside his people in this way, it really did not matter how few or many troops they brought into combat. With him on their side, they could not lose. (You can see how all these characteristics fit the battle of Jericho. It will be interesting to see if they apply in the ones to follow.)

Another feature of Holy War concerned the disposal of the treasure and loot taken in an attack. Although the city itself was to be destroyed, the valuable things found there were to be put into the treasury of the Lord. Since he had won the battle for Israel, these things belonged to him.

After the successful attack on Jericho, Joshua made plans to invade the hill country that lay ahead. A small city, Ai, was chosen as the target, and spies reported that it was so weak that only part of the army was needed to conquer it. There was no need for the whole company to make the trip.

So Joshua confidently sent a detachment of three thousand men to take Ai. You can imagine his surprise when they returned to camp defeated. The men of Ai had chased them back, killing many of the group.

Joshua fell to the ground in anguish. What a blow! "Oh, Lord," he prayed, "did you bring us here to destroy us? When the rest of the Canaanites hear of this, they will come and kill us. Why didn't you help us win?"

The Lord explained to Joshua: a rule of Holy War had been broken. Someone had taken treasures from Jericho and kept them for himself instead of giving them to the Lord. "Until you find this person and punish him, I will not fight on your side," God warned.

So Joshua began a search to find the one whose sin had caused the defeat at Ai. From all the tribes, God pointed out the tribe of Judah, then the particular family, and finally the man himself. Achan was his name.

"Tell me what you've done," Joshua asked the man.

Achan confessed, "I have sinned against the Lord God of Israel. Among the ruins of Jericho I found a beautiful coat, some silver coins, and a bar of gold that I wanted to keep for myself. I buried them under my tent so no one would know I had them."

Joshua sent messengers to Achan's tent, and there in the ground they uncovered the treasure Achan had described. It was returned to the Lord, but Achan had to die as punishment.

Once the sin had been removed from the camp, Joshua was anxious to attack Ai again. "I will be with you in this battle," God assured him and planned together for the fight.

This time, Joshua led only a small group of soldiers against the city, but he commanded a large force to wait in ambush behind it. He and his band lured the men of Ai to chase them, pretending they were the same small group that had been so easily defeated. Then, when they had led them some distance, Joshua raised his spear. This was the signal for men who had been hiding to rise up and swarm the deserted village. The men of Ai looked back to see their homes going up in smoke. They were caught in a trap!

So Joshua, with the Lord on his side, captured Ai. *Joshua 7–8:29*

TRICKED INTO A TREATY

Following the battles of Jericho and Ai, the fame of Joshua and his army spread throughout Canaan. In every city, men prepared to defend their homes against these bold invaders.

Now Gibeon was a city not far from the Israelite camp at Gilgal. Its citizens felt that their town would probably be Joshua's next object of attack, yet they knew that a battle against the mighty Israelite God would be hopeless. The only way their city could be saved would be to make a peace treaty with Joshua. Since God had forbidden Joshua to make any agreements with the Canaanites, they would have to be very tricky to make their plan work.

One day some men from Gibeon came walking into the Israelite camp. They looked as though they had been traveling for many days. Their clothes were ragged and torn; their sandals were worn-out and patched. The food they carried was dried-up and molded.

"Far away, in our homeland, we heard of the powerful God who helps you win battles," they told Joshua. "We have come to make a treaty of peace with him and with you."

"How can we tell that you are not from some nearby city?" Joshua asked. "We cannot make peace with the people living around us."

"Oh, our home is in a very distant country," they assured him. "Look—see this old, molded bread? It was fresh from the oven when we left home. These torn, worn-out clothes were like new when we began our journey. It has taken that long for us to walk all the way to Canaan."

So without consulting God, Joshua and the Israelite leaders made a pact with the men from Gibeon. They promised never to make war on them.

Three days later Joshua discovered that these visitors from a "faraway land" were actually his close neighbors. How embarrassed he was to learn that he had been tricked! All of the Israelites felt very foolish. Some of them wanted to go and destroy Gibeon without any regard to the peace treaty.

"No," Joshua said, "we made a promise to them and we must keep it. We will not kill them, but they must become our servants. They will cut wood and draw water for us."

Being alive as servants was better than being destroyed, so the Gibeonites agreed.

Now, when the kings from the neighboring cities heard that the Gibeonites had banded together with the Israelites, they grew very upset. They had counted on the Gibeonites' helping them against the Israelites. Five of these kings set out to punish the people of Gibeon.

The frightened Gibeonites sent a hurried message to Joshua as soon as they heard what was about to happen. "Come!" they said. "You won't have us as servants long unless you help us."

This time Joshua consulted God about his plans. "Go ahead, Joshua," the Lord said. "None of these men are strong enough to stand up to you."

So Joshua led a rescue party from Gilgal to Gibeon, marching through the night. When he and his men suddenly appeared on the scene, the five kings were dismayed. Some tried to flee, but they were not fast enough to escape Joshua's able men. The Lord trapped others by sending a terrible hail storm. For hours and hours the chase went on, seemingly without end. Even so, the day was not going to be long enough. The words of an old song tell us that Joshua prayed:

> Sun, stand still at Gibeon,
> And moon, remain in the valley.
> And the sun stood still, and the moon stayed,
> Until the people had won the victory.

Because the Lord was fighting for Israel, he answered Joshua's prayer and gave him enough sunlight hours to win the battle—the battle of the longest day.

Joshua 9–10:15

THE LAND AT REST

The kings that Joshua battled at Gibeon were from the southern part of Canaan. After he had won a victory over them and killed them, it was fairly simple to take their cities, one by one. When this was done, Israel had claim to the central and southern parts of their new homeland.

Next, they turned to northern Palestine; and again, the team of Joshua, as general, and the Lord, as commander-in-chief, proved unbeatable. City after city fell before them, until the rule of the land was in their hands.

Now all of this fighting had taken several years to complete. In the camp at Gilgal, the people were getting restless to settle in the land they had taken. They wanted to build homes and plant crops. On the other side of the Jordan, the families of the fighting men from the tribes of Reuben, Gad, and Manasseh, were anxious to have their husbands and fathers rejoin them.

Loran Raymond Jones

THE FALL OF JERICHO

Joshua 6:1–21

Loran Raymond Jones

GIDEON'S VICTORY OVER THE MIDIANITES

Judges 7:15–23

Loran Raymond Jones

THE DEATH OF SAMSON

Judges 16:25–31

Loran Raymond Jones

ORPAH, RUTH AND NAOMI

Ruth 1:1–18

"You have done your work well," the Lord commended Joshua. "You may stop fighting and divide the land among the tribes. Each tribe can defend its own territory against the Canaanites who remain there."

So a peace settled over the land, and Joshua parcelled out the territory in a fair way. The tribes who had descended from Judah, Simeon, Benjamin, and Dan were given land in the south. The people of the family of Ephraim, Joseph's son, got a portion in the central section. Toward the north, the tribes of Issachar, Asher, Zebulun, and Naphtali moved with their families to live. Three other tribes—Reuben, Gad and Manasseh—had already claimed the land east of the Jordan River.

That left one tribe without a home—the descendants of Levi. If you remember, these people had been appointed to serve as priests when the Law was given on Mount Sinai. In the new homeland, they were to continue to do their special work. They would live scattered among all the tribes so they could minister to them. In turn, all of the tribes would help support them since they had no land of their own.

When the people broke camp at Gilgal and scattered to their new homes, Joshua had the tabernacle dismantled and brought to Shiloh, near the center of Canaan, now "the land of Israel." Here it was set into place, with the precious ark of the covenant inside the Holy of Holies room. All the Israelites were urged to come to Shiloh and worship at the tent of meeting on the important feast days during the year.

Then Joshua grew very old and the time came when he knew that he would not live much longer. He sent for the people to meet him at a central place called Shechem.

For several days the people arrived from various parts of the land. They knew that Joshua would have wise counsel to give them. When they had all gathered, he began his speech, words that God gave him to say. He retold the story of Abraham, the first one to whom God had promised the land,

and of Joseph, Abraham's great grandson, who brought the children of Israel down to Egypt. He spoke to them of the years of slavery, then of the exodus from Egypt. He reminded them of the wilderness wandering and of the battles they had won in the new land.

"By the hand of God, you are now living in cities you did not build and eating fruit from trees you did not plant," Joshua went on. "In return for God's fulfilling every promise, you must honor him faithfully. Do not forsake him to worship the idols of the Egyptians or the Canaanites. Choose this day whom you will serve—as for me and my family, we will serve only the Lord."

"We will serve the Lord, also," the Israelites replied in chorus, "for he is our God."

And as long as Joshua, or those who had known him, lived, God's people were true to their promise. *Joshua 10:16–24–31*

QUESTIONS: 1. *Who took Moses' place as leader of the Israelites?* 2. *Why did two men go to Jericho?* 3. *What part did Rahab play in saving the lives of the spies? What was to be her reward?* 4. *Describe the crossing of the Jordan River.* 5. *In what order did the children of Israel march around Jericho? What was the procedure each day?* 6. *Explain some of the principles involved in Holy War.* 7. *Why did Joshua lose the first battle at Ai?* 8. *How did the Gibeonites trick Joshua into making a treaty with them?* 9. *Why was a certain battle of Joshua's referred to as "the battle of the longest day"?* 10. *How was the land of Canaan divided?* 11. *Where was the tabernacle located in the promised land?*

The Judge-Warriors

SIN AND PUNISHMENT

"You shall worship me, and me alone," the Lord demanded of the Israelites in their covenant. But he did not intend for it to be an act of blind devotion, performed only because he asked for it. Rather, he gave them a reason to love and serve him—he led them in victory over all their enemies until they obtained a fruitful land for their own. Once they were settled in the new land, it seemed they would naturally be faithful to God because they owed him so much. Sadly, this did not prove to be true.

How could Israel possibly turn away from God so soon? For one thing, after Joshua died, there was no strong leader to remind the people of their duty. For another, they were scattered all over the land, with one tribe isolated from the rest, and they lost the sense of being one people—God's chosen people. With the adjustment to a new land and a new way of life, it grew easier and easier to neglect meeting for worship at the tabernacle. A third reason lay in the fact that the Israelites shared the land with the Canaanites. When the land was divided, not all of it had been conquered. Each tribe was to deal with the natives it found in its own territory. Not only did some of the tribes fail to conquer the remaining Canaanites, they began to accept them. Worst of all, they accepted their idol gods, whose temples and altars were so conveniently located in every village.

God watched all of this with disappointment; he could not let it go unpunished. Therefore, he turned away from his people; and when he did, they lost their strength. Their enemies came from the lands around, or from within, and overcame them. The plunderers robbed their fields and carried away those whom they wanted for slaves.

These misfortunes seemed to wake the people from their neglect. They remembered that the source of their strength lay in the one true God, and they turned away from the useless idols to call on him for help. The Lord could not resist the sincere plea of his people. He would answer them by raising up leaders among them, deliverers who could break the power held over the Israelites by their enemies. These warriors would lead the people to freedom. Often they would continue to lead in peacetime by settling disputes and upholding the law of God. For this reason, they are referred to as "judges." Unlike Joshua and Moses, these judges were not usually leaders of all Israel, but of one tribe, or of several tribes that lived close together.

The first judge came forward in a time when Israel had been under bondage to the king of Mesopotamia for eight years. He was Othniel, a relative of Caleb, one of the two faithful spies. Othniel not only freed the people from foreign rule, but he kept them faithful to the Lord for the forty years that followed.

The next enemy king to take advantage of Israel's sinfulness was Eglon of Moab, the nation just east of the Dead Sea. Ever since King Balak, the Moabite, had tried unsuccessfully to persuade Balaam to curse the Israelites, there had been hard feelings between the two nations. Now King Eglon enlisted the help of some neighbors and took possession of the territory belonging to the tribe of Benjamin at a time when God had deserted them for their idolatry. For eighteen years he demanded heavy tribute from the Israelites.

After this long period of time, the people finally realized that their trouble had come upon them because they had forgotten God. They called upon him to help them. The judge-leader who came to the rescue on this occasion was named Ehud.

When it came time that year for the Israelites to pay their tribute money, Ehud was chosen to deliver it. But this warrior was not content just to hand the gift over to the king; he wanted a private audience.

"I have a secret message from God to give you," he told King Eglon. So the king sent all the members of his court from the room, and he stepped close to Ehud so he could hear the message better. At the moment the king reached his side, Ehud whipped out a small dagger that had been hidden in his coat and thrust it into Eglon's body so quickly that he died without making a sound. Then Ehud locked the doors and slipped from the palace unnoticed.

By the time Eglon's servants found his body, Ehud was on his way to Israel to round up an army. Inspired by his daring leadership, the "minutemen" that he marshalled completely subdued the Moabites who came out against them.

After this, Israel was at rest for eighty years. *Judges 2:11–3:31*

TWO BRAVE WOMEN

As we mentioned before, Joshua was unable to take certain areas of the promised land away from Canaanite control. One of these was a valley through the central part of Canaan. The people of this area united under King Jabin and Sisera, the commander of his army, to oppress the Israelites after Ehud died and his good influence was forgotten. King Jabin had an exceptionally impressive military force of nine hundred iron chariots. Without God's help, the Israelites could not begin to match this strength, so for twenty years Jabin was able to steal from them and demand that they pay heavy taxes.

Finally these Israelites realized they were in trouble because they worshipped useless idols rather than the true God who could help them. Sorry and ashamed, they asked God to free them from King Jabin.

At this time, a wise woman named Deborah was serving as a judge over Israel. She was not a warrior-judge as Ehud and Othniel had been, but she was good at settling disputes and knowing the will of God concerning certain matters. People came to consult her as she sat under a particular palm tree, and she helped solve their problems.

When Deborah heard of the plight of her fellow-Israelites under Jabin and Sisera, she prayed to know God's will concerning the matter. Then, confident that he was guiding her, she sent for a man named Barak.

"God has commissioned you to gather an army of ten thousand together on Mount Tabor," she told him. "There, Sisera and his men will be given over to you."

But Barak did not want to fight Sisera unless Deborah would consent to go with him.

"All right, I will go," Deborah said, for she was not afraid. "But because you did not trust God without me, the honor of winning this battle will be given to a woman."

Then Deborah and Barak rounded up their fighting force and went out to meet Sisera. From their camp on Mount Tabor they watched the impressive Canaanite army approach. Again Deborah showed her courage, urging Barak: "On to battle! The Lord is going with you!"

This time Sisera's iron chariots were no match for an army with the Lord at its command. The Israelites advanced with such force that Sisera deserted his chariot and began running for safety. Left on their own, not a single one of his men escaped.

Sisera himself fled until he came to an isolated tent on the plain. Jael, the woman who lived there, knew Sisera, and she called him aside. "Have no fear. You can rest here."

The panting general fell beside her tent. "Please, just give me a little water," he asked.

Jael poured him some milk to drink instead. The combination of the soothing drink and his exhaustion from running overcame Sisera. "I will rest here just a little while," he told Jael. "You stand at the door of the tent, and if anyone comes, say that I'm not here." Then he fell fast asleep.

Once she was sure he was asleep, Jael crept quietly back into the tent. With a tent peg in one hand and a hammer in the other, she killed him with a blow through the head.

Eventually Barak came across the plain looking for Sisera. Jael went out to meet him. "Are you looking for Sisera? I'll show you where he is." Then she pulled aside the flap of her tent, exposing the sight of the Canaanite general with a tent peg through his head.

So Israel was freed of King Jabin's tyranny; but as Deborah had foretold, the honor of the victory went to a woman. *Judges 4–5*

MAKING SURE OF GOD

Following Deborah, the deliverer whose adventures are related in the book of *Judges* is Gideon. Gideon grew up in a time when Israel was in grave trouble. In his own village and throughout the nation, the Israelites prayed to Baal to send them good crops. But there was no time to enjoy the grain that grew. Before it could be harvested, the Midianites, a desert tribe, overran the country and trampled all the fields under the hooves of their awesome camels. Hungry and frightened, the Israelites deserted their homes and gardens and ran for safety to caves in the hillside. Here they huddled and prayed to God to forgive them and to save them from the Midianites.

Now Gideon had managed to salvage a bit of grain from his father's field, and he tried to thresh it in a wine press where the Midianites could not find him. While he worked, an angel of God appeared to him. The angel spoke: "The Lord is with you, Gideon. You are a brave man."

Gideon's life had been hard. He was skeptical of this heavenly message. "If the Lord is with us, why has all this trouble come our way?" he asked. "I've heard of mighty deeds the Lord performed in the past, but now he has turned us over to the Midianites."

"The Lord is going to save Israel from the Midianites through *you*," the angel answered.

This was difficult for Gideon to believe. "I am from a small tribe and I'm the least important person in my tribe," he insisted. "Show me a sign so that I can really believe that you speak the truth."

Then Gideon went in and prepared a meal for the angel. When he brought it out and set it on a rock, the messenger reached forth his staff and touched the meat and bread that lay there. Immediately, fire sprang out of the rock and consumed all the food. The angel disappeared in the same moment.

This was the sign Gideon had requested. Now he believed that the Lord's spirit was with him.

That night the Lord and Gideon began planning their attack. First, it would be necessary to get rid of the root of all the trouble—the altar to Baal where the Israelites offered their sacrifices. In the dark Gideon crept out and tore down the offensive altar. In the morning smoke was burning from sacrifices he had offered on an altar to the true God he had built in its place.

The men of Gideon's town had grown to believe that Baal, the Canaanite idol, was really the one who made their crops grow. When they saw his altar destroyed, they became very angry. "Who has done this terrible thing?" they asked.

"Gideon, the son of Joash," someone answered.

So the indignant men marched over to the house of Joash. "Bring out your son Gideon!" they demanded of the old man. "He dared to tear down Baal's sacred altar last night."

Joash stepped out and faced the crowd quite unafraid. "Is this Baal so weak that you have to fight his battles for him?" he asked them quietly. "If he is really a god, let him defend himself."

The men had no reply.

Then in answer to the Lord's command, Gideon sent forth a call throughout the tribes for men to come forward and join him in battle against the Midianites. While he waited for his army to assemble, he went out alone to look over the formidable invaders as they camped in a valley near the Jordan River. There were so many of them and their camels were so unlike anything Gideon had known before! He prayed to God: "Give me confidence before my men arrive. Tonight I will lay a lamb's fleece on the ground. If it is wet with dew in the morning and the ground around it is dry, I will know you are with me."

The next morning Gideon wrung a whole bowl full of water from the fleece, although the ground was as dry as could be. But, as we mentioned at the beginning of this story, he was not a man who believed things easily. He begged God for one more proof: "Tonight I'll put out the fleece again. This time, let it be dry and the ground around it wet with dew." And God did just as he asked.

Now Gideon was very, very sure of God's presence. He had been a reluctant man to convince; but now that he believed God would make him the victor over the Midianites, nothing could stop him. *Judges 6*

TORCHES, PITCHERS, AND TRUMPETS

Soon it was recognized throughout the tribes of Israel that the Lord's spirit had come upon Gideon. When he called for the fighting men to gather forces under his command, thirty-two thousand volunteers came forward and offered their services. Encouraged to have such a large army, he confidently led them to a brook just south of the great Midianite encampment and set about to pitch his own camp.

But this was not the way the Lord had planned for the battle to go. "Your army is too large," he told Gideon. "If you took this many out against the Midianites, they would think they had won by their own strength. Dismiss all those who would rather have stayed at home."

So Gideon made a surprising proclamation to his men: "All who are afraid to fight may return to their homes." He watched twenty-two thousand of his soldiers pack up and leave. This left him with an army of ten thousand.

But the Lord was not yet satisfied. "Your army is still too big," he insisted. "All you need are a few of the bravest, most choice fighting men. Bring the whole group down to the brook and I'll show you how to tell which ones you should keep."

So the men followed Gideon down to the brook, and he watched to see how they behaved. All were thirsty and most lay down their spears and knelt to drink. A few, however, held their spears and would not take their eyes away from the Midianite camp. They reached down and scooped up some water in one hand, then held it to their mouth and lapped it up with their tongue.

"See the men who lapped the water with their tongues? They are only three hundred out of ten thousand, but by their hands, I will deliver the Midianites," God instructed Gideon.

So Gideon weeded his army down to a group of only three hundred men. The small camp they made looked ridiculous next to the endless rows of Midianite tents that stretched out before them. But if this caused Gideon to have any fears, the Lord dispelled them that night. "Take your servant and creep down to the Midianite camp," he told Gideon. "You'll be glad to hear what they're saying."

Gideon slipped out in the darkness and came close enough to the enemy camp to hear voices. One man was telling his friend of a dream. "It was the strangest dream—a little piece of bread tumbled into camp and knocked a whole tent over."

"The bread must be Gideon, the son of Joash," replied the friend.

Gideon was overjoyed. He hurried back to his own camp. "Rise up, men!" he commanded. "The Lord is giving us the victory over Midian tonight!"

Then he divided his troops into three companies of one hundred each and told them to surround the Midianite camp. To each soldier he gave the strange weapons of this battle—a lighted torch, a pitcher, and a trumpet.

"Cover your torch with the pitcher so the light is hidden, and we'll advance upon the enemy," Gideon said. "When we reach the outskirts of the camp, watch me and do just as I do. I'll blow my trumpet; then you blow yours and shout, 'For the Lord and for Gideon!' "

Very quietly the men crept all around the place where the Midianites lay sleeping. When they had completely surrounded it, Gideon gave a blast on his trumpet that broke the silence of the night. Instantly, all his men responded by blowing their horns and shouting, "For the Lord! For Gideon!" Then "Crash!" went the pitchers, and the torches of Gideon's men lit the countryside in every direction.

Trumpets! Shouts! Lights! Men! The awakened Midianites could not tell what was happening or what they should do. In their confusion they picked up their swords and began lashing out at one another. Then Gideon's trumpet sounded again, and the Midianites broke and ran.

The chase was on! Across the hills and plains, all the way to the Jordan and beyond, the men of Israel pursued the Midianites. There the enemy leaders were caught and punished, and the power of Midian was broken.

Judges 7:1–23

A VOW OF IMPULSE

After Gideon's time, there was a period of unrest when Abimelech, one of his sons, sought to rule Israel; but the divine spirit was not with him and he led briefly as an outsider, not as one of the Lord's appointed. Then, as part of the cycle that is now becoming familiar, the people forsook God to worship native idols; and as punishment, he allowed their enemies to overcome them. This time, it was the Ammonites who swept down from the desert and molested the tribes that had settled east of the Jordan. For eighteen years the oppression continued until Israel decided to "put away the foreign gods from among them and serve the Lord." Only then were they ready to begin a fight for freedom.

The deliverer who rose to lead Israel against the Ammonites was a half-Israelite outlaw named Jephthah. He had become the leader of a band of guerilla fighters when his half-brothers disowned him for being his father's illegal son. Now, when a revolution was being planned, Jephthah came to people's minds as one with enough daring and bravery to win an assault.

"Come and lead us in a fight against the Ammonites," the Israelite elders asked Jephthah.

He reminded them of the way he had been treated by his own people. "Why do you come to me now—when you're in trouble?"

"That is exactly why we've come to you—we *are* in trouble," they answered frankly. "Will you be our commander in this battle?"

But Jephthah did not want to fight for Israel and then find himself rejected again once the war was done. "I'll come," he agreed, "if you will let me continue to be your leader when the battle is over."

"The Lord is our witness. We will do as you say."

So Jephthah accepted the leadership of Israel in a battle against the Ammonites—a battle he wanted desperately to win. His desire was so intense that he made a vow to the Lord just before the fighting began: "If you will make me victorious against the Ammonites, Lord, I will offer to you the first thing that comes from my door to greet me when I return." He hoped somehow that this sacrifice would prove his devotion to the Lord.

Jephthah did lead the Israelites to victory and freed them from the Ammonites. Afterward, he and his men made a triumphant march back to their homes.

But Jephthah still had a debt to pay: his vow of impulse that he had made before the battle. What was the first living thing that met him on his return? It was his only child, a daughter, who came out singing and dancing with joy at her father's success.

Jephthah grabbed at his clothes in despair when he saw her. "Oh, my daughter!" he cried. "What great anguish this causes me! And now it is too late to take back my vow."

So the victory of Jephthah was a hollow thing; and the price he paid for it, very dear.

Judges 10:6–11:40

A RIDDLE AND ITS ANSWER

The most formidable opponents of the Israelites during the time of the judges, and even the kings, were the Philistines, a people of the coastline near the Great Sea. In turn, one of the most impressive individuals with whom the Philistines ever had to deal was Israel's strong fighter, Samson.

His heroic adventures, well-known to people for thousands of years, show him to be more a champion of bravery than a religious leader. Nevertheless, he was a judge of God's people and he relieved them from the Philistine oppression of his day in a unique way.

Samson's parents were a childless couple of the tribe of Dan. One day an angel appeared in a field to the woman who was to be Samson's mother and told her that she would bear a son who would deliver the Israelites from the Philistines.

"Your child will be given to God in a special way from the time of his birth," the angel revealed. "He must never drink any wine or strong drink or eat any of the foods forbidden to Israel. As a sign of his lifelong vow, his hair is never to be cut."

The woman hurried to tell her husband Manoah this wonderful news, but he could hardly believe it. It was too good to be true! "Dear God," he prayed, "send your messenger again to teach us how to rear this child."

So, in answer to Manoah's request, the angel appeared in the field again within a few days. This time Manoah heard the message with his own ears. He was to be the father of a son whose entire life would be lived under a vow. Manoah was so grateful to hear the this news that he prepared a sacrifice to the Lord who works such wonders. When he lit the fire under the offering, the angel and the fire seemed to blend, ascending at once into heaven.

In time, the boy Samson was born, as the angel had foretold. His parents took good care of him, following the Lord's instructions. He never ate of forbidden food and scissors never touched his hair. Even as a long-haired boy, stories circulated about his unusual strength and daring.

Then Samson grew up and fell in love with a Philistine girl. He told his parents that he wanted to marry her. "Why can't you find a girl that you like here among our own people?" Manoah asked his son. "It will disappoint your mother and me if you choose to marry this foreigner." But Samson did choose to marry the Philistine girl, and he was not a person to give preference to the wishes of another. He tended to do precisely as he liked—and who was strong enough to stop him?

So Samson started for Philistia to ask for the girl of his choice to be his wife. Walking alone through a vineyard, he suddenly encountered a young lion. The lion roared and leapt in attack, but it had met its match. In a second, Samson reached and caught it, tearing it to pieces with his bare hands. Then, leaving the body there on the ground, he continued on his way to visit his sweetheart.

Plans for the wedding were made and at the proper time, Samson returned to claim his bride. As he walked once more through the vineyard, he wandered into the brush to see if he could find any of the remains of the lion he had killed. Sure enough, there on the ground lay its bones, now the adopted hive of a swarm of bees. Samson reached into the honeycomb and scraped some of the honey into his hands. It tasted good to him as he walked along on his long journey.

Now it was the custom in those days for the groom to hold a celebration after his wedding; and in grand style, Samson prepared a weeklong feast. During the party, he and other young men entertained themselves with riddles and games.

"I have a riddle," Samson bragged. "If you guess it within these seven days, I'll give you each a new set of clothes. If you don't, each of you must give me a new outfit.

"This is the riddle:

Out of the eater came something to eat.
Out of the strong came something sweet.

For three days Samson's companions puzzled over his riddle, but none of them could figure out the answer. Finally they came to Samson's bride.

"Get Samson to tell you the answer to his riddle, or we will burn your father's house."

Desperately the Philistine girl pled with Samson to tell her the secret. She cried and said, "If you really loved me, I know you would tell me."

So Samson gave in and told her about the lion he had killed and the honey he had found among its bones. Naturally, she relayed the answer to the young men. They waited until the evening of the last day of Samson's feast. Then they came to their host with a smile and said,

What is sweeter then honey?
What is stronger than a lion?

Oh, was Samson angry! He knew where his companions had gotten the answer. "If you had not plowed with my heifer, you wouldn't have found out my riddle," he told them. Then, to pay off his bargain, he killed thirty Philistines of another town and took their clothes. Afterward, he went angrily back to his father's house.

Judges 13–14

SHORN OF HIS STRENGTH

Samson was angry when his riddle was guessed at the wedding celebration, but it hardly compared with the irritation he felt later when he returned to Philistia and found that his wife had been given to his best man in his absence. As far as he was concerned, the battle was on. It seemed that nothing he could do to the Philistines was enough repayment for the trouble they had caused him. First, he went out and captured three hundred foxes. Then, of all things, he tied their tails together, two by two, secured torches in their tails, and let them loose in his enemies' grainfields. Dragging the firebrands around, the foxes burned up the surrounding vineyards, as well as the standing grain.

After this, the Philistines came to Israel, looking for Samson. On this occasion, Samson let the men of Judah bind him and lead him out, as if they were handing him over to the Philistines as a prisoner. Then, just as the Philistines were about to take him, the spirit of the Lord came on him and he broke the ropes that bound him, grabbing the jawbone of an ass that lay nearby. His song tells the rest of the story:

> With the jawbone of an ass I have slain them,
> Heaps upon heaps.
> With the jawbone of an ass I have slain them;
> I have slain a thousand men.

Another time the Philistines caught him in Gaza, one of their cities. They locked the city gates and thought they had him captured, but he escaped by merely lifting the gate from its posts and depositing it on a distant hill.

Then, for the second time, Samson fell in love with a Philistine woman; this one was named Delilah. "Samson has lost his heart to this woman," his Philistine enemies reasoned. "We'll use her as our tool to rid ourselves of him once and for all."

So the men went to Delilah and proposed a bargain. "If you will find out the secret of Samson's strength, we will each give you eleven hundred pieces of silver," they said. This was agreeable to the scheming young woman.

Now Samson was deeply in love with Delilah and he never suspected that she loved him any less, or would betray him. Still, when she coaxed him to tell her what made him so strong, he teased her. First, he told her that if he were ever bound with seven green switches, his strength would disappear.

Delilah passed this word on to the Philistines, and they brought her the green switches. When Samson was asleep, she tied him with them, then called out, "Wake up, Samson! The Philistines are coming!" At that, he jumped up, breaking the switches with ease.

"You were teasing me, Samson," Delilah pouted. "Now, tell me truly, how could you really be bound?"

Samson thought this was all a clever game. So he answered her, "If I were tied with brand-new ropes, why, I would be no stronger than any other man."

Once more Delilah bound him, this time with new ropes, but again he broke them as though they were thread.

Next he told her that his strength would leave him if his hair was woven in a loom; but, of course, this did not work either. He stood up with the loom still fastened to his locks.

By this time Delilah had begun to tire of Samson's games; she was anxious to have the silver she had been promised. So she asked him, "How can you say that you love me when you don't tell me the truth?" Every day she begged and plead in this way until he got tired of listening to her.

"All right," he snapped. "I will tell you my secret if you will promise never to mention this matter to me again. My hair has never been cut because I am under a special vow to the Lord. If my head were shaved, my strength would leave me."

Delilah knew that she had the truth at last. She called for the Philistine rulers to bring her the silver they had promised; then she hid the men in her house. Unknowing of all this, Samson came in and went to sleep. While he slept, one of the men came in with a razor and cut off the long locks of hair that had not been touched since his birth. As they fell from his head, his strength began to fail.

"Wake up, Samson! The Philistines are here!" Delilah called. But the Lord had deserted Samson. He was at the mercy of the men who stepped from their hiding places and took him their prisoner.

The next picture we have of Samson is a pitiful one. With his eyes gouged out, he stood chained to a millstone, grinding wheat as an animal would. The Philistines were very proud to have Samson in such a condition. To celebrate his downfall, they gave a great festival in the temple of Dagon, their idol god. During the celebration, some of them got the idea that it would be great sport to bring Samson out before the crowd. They dragged him from the prison and stood him between two great pillars in the center of the hall so all could see. What a sight he must have made!

In the midst of all the jesting, Samson whispered to the boy who was leading him around, "Would you guide me to the pillars which support the temple so I can lean on them and rest?"

Then, when he felt the pillars in his hands, he prayed silently to God: "Lord God, give me my strength just once more that I may repay the Philistines for the trouble they have caused me." The old strength began to surge through Samson's body. Grasping the two pillars tightly, he cried out, "Let me die with the Philistines!" And with one mighty push, he cracked the pillars, collapsing the temple. All the thousands who were gathered there, including Samson, were killed.

So, Samson, in his brave death, did more for the Israelites than he had done during his lifetime. *Judges 15–16*

A LOVE STORY

In many respects, the time of the judges was the most violent period in the history of Israel. The primitive quality of the heroes seem to contradict our concept of spiritual leadership. Yet not everything that happened in this time was characterized by savage brutality. Like a breath of fresh air, the story of Ruth appears next in the Biblical narrative to tell us of another phase of life in that same day.

Elimilech was an Israelite of Bethlehem. He lived there with his wife Naomi and his two sons until a famine arose and food became so scarce that he was worried whether or not they could survive. Then word came that there had been rain in the neighboring country of Moab and food was plentiful. Naturally, Elimilech decided to leave Bethlehem and take his family to Moab until the famine was over.

Alas, that was the last time Elimilech saw Israel, for he died while in Moab. Naomi continued to live there as a widow with her two boys.

When the sons grew to manhood, each of them chose a Moabite girl to be his bride. One was named Orpah; the name of the other was Ruth. Then misfortune struck again! both of the sons died. Naomi and her two daughters-in-law were left alone.

By this time, word came that food was plentiful back in Israel once more. Naomi grew homesick and decided to return to her homeland and her people. Both Orpah and Ruth made plans to go with her on her journey, but she would not hear of it. "My daughters," she said, "there is no reason for you to leave your families and your homeland. You are still young, and you have time to find other husbands and have families. Return to your homes."

Tearfully Orpah kissed her mother-in-law goodbye, but Ruth would not leave. "Follow your sister-in-law," Naomi begged. "You should return with her."

Ruth had a beautiful reply: "Do not ask me to leave you or to quit following you. I want to go where you go and live where you live. Your people will become my people and your God, my God."

When Naomi saw that Ruth would not change her mind, she said no more. The two made the long trip to Bethlehem together.

News traveled quickly that Naomi was back in town and many came out to greet her. They hardly recognized their old friend. "Can this be Naomi, the Pleasant?" they asked.

"My name no longer fits," Naomi answered. "A better one for me would be Mara, or Bitter."

Now Naomi and Ruth returned at the time of the barley harvest, and Ruth went out in the fields to gather grain with the other reapers. It was the law in Israel for the harvesters to leave some of the grain for the poor people to gather, and this was what Ruth picked up as she followed along.

It so happened that Ruth had chosen to gather grain in a field which belonged to a rich man of Bethlehem named Boaz. When Boaz came to look over his fields, he noticed Ruth among the reapers. He asked his foreman, "Who is the young woman there?"

"She is the Moabite woman who returned to Bethlehem with Naomi," the man replied. "She asked to glean here and has been working hard since yesterday."

Boaz went to Ruth and told her, "Stay here in my fields and work for the rest of the harvest. I will see that everyone is kind to you. When you get thirsty, feel free to take some of our water."

Ruth bowed and thanked Boaz for his kindness to her, especially since she was a stranger in Israel.

Boaz smiled. "You are really no stranger, for I have heard how good and kind you have been to your mother-in-law. I know that you left your home and family to come with her. May the Lord, in whom you have come to trust, reward you."

Boaz then watched Ruth return to her work. He gave quiet instructions to his harvesters: "Drop some extra grain for the young lady to gather and let her take some from the sheaves."

That evening Ruth was excited when she returned to Naomi. "Look how much I have gathered today," she said. "I met the owner of the field, and he is the kindest man! He told me to gather there until the end of the harvest."

"Who was the man?" asked Naomi.

"He is called Boaz," Ruth replied.

"Why, he is my husband's near kinsman," Naomi exclaimed. "Stay in his field as he has invited you to do."

By the end of the harvest, Boaz had fallen in love with Ruth; and when he got permission from the wise men of the city, he took her to be his wife. In time, Ruth had a baby boy, and Naomi came to be his nurse. "You may call me Naomi again," she told her friends. "Once more, my life is pleasant."

The son born to Ruth and Boaz was named Obed, who later became the grandfather of King David. Thus Ruth, the young Moabitess who followed her mother-in-law to Bethlehem, became the grandmother of Israel's greatest king.

Ruth 1–4

QUESTIONS: 1. *Why did Israel grow unfaithful after she had taken over the land of Canaan?* 2. *How did God punish this unfaithfulness?* 3. *What kind of ruler led Israel in these early days in Canaan?* 4. *Who was the only woman judge? Why did she go to battle?* 5. *How did a woman receive the honor of defeating Sisera?* 6. *For what tests and signs did Gideon ask?* 7. *How did Gideon reduce the size of his army?* 8. *How did the Israelites use torches, pitchers, and trumpets against Midian?* 9. *How did Jephthah live before he became leader of Israel?* 10. *What was Jephthah's impulsive vow?* 11. *Describe the stipulations of the vow under which Samson lived.* 12. *What was Samson's riddle? What did its answer mean?* 13. *How did the Philistines discover the source of Samson's strength?* 14. *How did Samson die?* 15. *Why did Naomi and her family go to Moab?* 16. *Who returned to Israel with Naomi? What happened to them after they returned?*

From Judges to Kings

A MOTHER'S PRAYER

For two hundred years the Israelites had lived in Canaan. Only with the aid of God and his appointed hero-leaders had they managed to survive the invasion of many neighboring people. Yet, even though they still existed as a league of tribes, they were loosely bound and governed.

What had become of the religion of the people by this time? Where was the tabernacle? Were worship services still observed there?

The tabernacle had been set up in Shiloh after Joshua captured the Promised Land, and the descendants of Aaron still served there as priests. When the people periodically turned from their wickedness to honor God, the worship was carried on more faithfully. In such a time, it was natural for them to look to the high priest for guidance—not only in religious matters, but in all affairs pertaining to the nation. This was especially true when no warrior, or judge, came forward to lead.

For just such reasons, the high priest Eli became a chief figure in Israel. Those who remembered the Lord and desired to have forgiveness came to Eli. They offered sacrifices and prayed near the holy place where the Ark of the Covenant was stored.

Among those who brought gifts to Shiloh was a man named Elkanah. He and his family came every year from their home in the hill country, worshipped God at the tabernacle, and then celebrated with a feast. But on one such visit, Elkanah's wife Hannah was in no mood to celebrate. Instead she quietly left the festive meal and slipped back into the place of worship. Here alone, she fell to her knees and let her pent-up tears begin to fall.

You see, Hannah had no children, and this caused her great sorrow. As she wept, she began to pray to God, saying: "Oh, Lord, please remember me. Let me have a baby, a son, and I will give him to you all the days of his life." Whispering these same words, she begged the Lord again and again to answer her request.

As it happened, Hannah was not alone in the temple as she thought. Nearby Eli, the priest, sat observing her strange behavior. Although he could see her tears falling and her lips moving, he could hear no sound, so he guessed that something was wrong.

"How long will you go on like this?" he asked her. "Put away your wine."

But Hannah answered: "I've not been drinking, sir. I am greatly troubled and have been pouring out my sorrow to the Lord."

"Then go your way in peace," Eli replied more gently. "And may the God of Israel answer your prayer."

So Hannah rejoined her husband at the feast in a happier mood.

A year later Elkanah had to go alone to worship at Shiloh, for Hannah stayed at home to tend her newborn son. She had named him Samuel, for it meant "asked of God." As soon as the child was old enough, the whole family journeyed together to the tabernacle. There Hannah sought out Eli and set Samuel before him.

"Sir," she said, "I am the woman you saw praying to God for a child. Now God has given me that child; and, as I promised, I am returning him to the Lord. As long as he lives, he belongs to the Lord."

So the boy Samuel came to live with Eli near the tent of worship at Shiloh.

I Samuel 1

VOICES IN THE NIGHT

After Samuel was brought to Shiloh, his parents came back each year to offer sacrifices and visit. Hannah always brought with her a little linen coat, just like those the priests wore, that she had made in Samuel's size. So the boy looked like a young priest as he worked alongside Eli.

Indeed, Samuel did much of the work in the temple, for Eli's own sons, Hophni and Phinehas, who should have assisted him as priests of the Lord, were worthless men. Oh, they were often present at the tabernacle, but only to take bribes of the people and to carry on indecently. Eli tried half heartedly to control the young men, but he had been permissive for so long that he had no power for good over them. He turned for comfort to Samuel, and the boy did small jobs around the tent of worship, as well as performing services for the old man, who was growing feeble and blind.

One night, as the lamp in the house of God burned lower and lower, Eli lay fast asleep in his bed. Nearby, Samuel, too, was lying down.

"Samuel!" a voice called.

The boy sat up, wide awake. Then he ran to Eli's side.

"Here I am," he replied, waiting to hear what the old priest wanted.

But Eli answered: "I didn't call you. Go back to bed."

In bed Samuel lay, falling asleep, when the voice came again: "Samuel!"

"Here I am," he called, as he rushed to Eli's bed.

"I have not called, my son. Lie down again."

Then a third time the same thing occurred, only Eli finally realized what was happening—the Lord was calling Samuel.

"Go and lie down," he instructed the boy, "and when the voice calls again, you must say: 'Speak, Lord. Your servant is listening.' "

Before long, the voice was heard once more: "Samuel! Samuel!"

This time Samuel was ready. "Speak, Lord. Your servant is listening."

Then God talked to Samuel: "Eli's sons are very wicked and must be punished. Because Eli knew of their sin and did not stop them, the office of the priesthood has been shamed and the whole family must suffer."

Samuel lay until morning, thinking of this sad prediction. As soon as the sun rose, he got up and went right to work, trying to avoid Eli. But the old man finally caught up with him and stopped him.

"Now, my son," he said, "tell me what the Lord said to you last night. Don't try to hide anything from me."

So Samuel told him everything God had revealed. Naturally it made Eli very sad, but he said quietly, "The Lord knows what is best. Let him do what seems right to him."

Word soon spread that God had spoken to Samuel. People began to look on him with respect; and as he grew, they could see that he had the favor and guidance of the Lord, as had Abraham and Moses. *I Samuel 2:12–3:21*

ADVENTURES OF THE ARK

While the judges ruled, many invaders attempted to take food and prisoners from Israel, but none of them was as formidable as the Philistines, who launched their strongest attacks during the time Eli served as priest and judge. These mighty people from the coastland near the Great Sea had grown in power since the time when Samson harassed them. Now they threatened to steal the land away from the Israelites, making them Philistines and ending their existence as God's separate people. With their well-trained army and iron weapons, it seemed as though the Philistines would succeed.

In one particular battle, the Philistines were so thoroughly victorious that they left four thousand Israelite soldiers strewn across the battlefield.

"Why were we beaten so badly?" the Israelite troops asked as they dragged themselves back to camp.

"Could it be that the Lord is not with us?" someone questioned.

"If that is the case—let's be sure he's with us next time. He has said he would always be present in the Ark of the Covenant—why not remove it from the tabernacle and take it into battle with us?"

So some of the soldiers went up to Shiloh and took the Ark from its place inside the Holy of Holies. They brought it, along with Eli's two wicked sons, back to army headquarters. When the other Israelite soldiers saw the Ark in the middle of the camp, they gave a great shout.

"What is that noise?" the Philistine soldiers wondered when they heard the shouting.

"Their gods have come into the camp."

At first this message filled the Philistines with fear; but on second thought, it made them want to fight harder than ever. "Take courage, and act like men," their leaders said; and the army took them to heart. In battle the next day they completely routed the Israelites, slaughtering thirty thousand foot soldiers. In the disaster, they killed Eli's sons and captured the unguarded Ark.

Back in Shiloh old Eli, now blind, sat waiting for news of the fighting. He feared for the lives of his sons, but most of all, his heart trembled for the holy Ark, unprotected on a battlefield. Finally a soldier, his clothes dirty and torn, reached the city with the unhappy word; and when the people heard it, they began to cry out.

"What is this uproar about?" Eli asked.

"A man has returned from the battle," someone told him.

"How did it go?"

"Many Israelites were killed, and the few who were left have retreated from the enemy. Your sons are dead, and the Ark has been taken."

Such bad news was too much for old Eli. At the mention of the Ark, he fell backwards off his seat and died.

"The glory has departed from Israel," the people mourned, "for the Ark has been captured."

To Ashdod, one of their chief cities, the Philistine soldiers proudly carried the Ark of God. They set it up for display in the temple of Dagon, their part-fish, part-human idol. But when the people came out early in the morning to see it, Dagon, a statue carved of heavy stone, had fallen before the Ark of the Lord. Quickly they set him upright, but the next day he had not only fallen—his head and hands were broken off as well. None of the visitors would dare to step inside the shrine.

Then, to make matters worse, a plague broke out in Ashdod. "It's that Ark," the people complained. "It has brought nothing but trouble to us." So they sent it over to Gath, another Philistine city.

No sooner had the Ark reached Gath than sores and sickness began infecting its citizens. They passed it on to Ekron, but by this time it had gained a reputation.

"We don't want that Israelite trophy among us," the people of Ekron cried.

So the wise men of Philistia met to decide what could be done with their unwanted prize of victory. The only course of action seemed to be to send it back to Israel, where it belonged.

"Send offerings along with the Ark," the advisers said. "In that way we can try to appease this angry God."

Thus the Ark and gifts of gold were loaded on a wagon pulled by two cows and headed for Israel's borders. The Philistines breathed a sigh of relief to see the cows pass out of sight, lowing as they went.

It was a surprised group of Israelite harvesters who looked up from their work to see the same cows coming toward them. When they recognized the precious cargo the cart held, they knelt there in the field to worship God.

"The Philistines have returned the Ark—come and get it," they sent word to the people of a nearby town. So the Ark was taken to the house of Abinadab and his son Eleazar became a priest and tended it for twenty years.

I Samuel 4:1–7:2

A KING TO LEAD

With Eli and his sons dead, the tabernacle at Shiloh fell into ruins. Times were difficult in the land of Israel, for the Philistines persisted in their raids, stealing crops and animals—even land. In their despair, the Israelites looked for guidance to Eli's boy-helper, Samuel. Now a grown man, Samuel lived at Ramah, his birthplace. As the last of the judges, Samuel more often led in a moral and religious struggle rather than physical warfare. His strength lay in his close communion with God and his ability to translate the message of God to the people. Because of this capacity, this speaking for God, he may be classed with the prophets, as well as with the judges.

Samuel performed his work much as a circuit minister or judge. He traveled a certain route each year, stopping at Bethel, Gilgal, and Mizpah. At each place he would hear cases, make judgments, and also lead in worship services. Then his duties took him back to his home in Ramah.

Like Eli, Samuel had sons who were unfit to follow in their father's footsteps. When the wise old men of Israel saw that the young men were incapable of making fair judgments, they approached Samuel with a new idea. They wanted a king for a leader.

At first, this may seem like a strange notion; but at another glance, it appears to be the natural desire of a nation that was loosely bound, weakly governed, and faced by an enemy as powerful as the Philistines. They thought that a king could bind the twelve tribes together as one. Thus unified, they could face their enemies with some strength and force.

In view of this, is it surprising to learn that Samuel was displeased with the request of Israel?

"Why do you need a king to rule over you?" he asked. "You do not need to be like the other nations—they do not have the Lord God as their leader.

"Life under a king's rule will be different from what you imagine," Samuel went on to warn. "He will take your sons to be his servants and warriors. He will take your daughters to be his cooks and bakers. He will take your land—the best land—for his own. He will make you pay taxes that will equal nearly everything you make and own.

"Then you will cry out because of this king you demanded, but it will be too late," he finished.

"None of this matters," the people assured the old judge. "We want a king anyway. Israel will be like other nations when we have a king to lead us to war."

"Do as they ask, Samuel. Choose for them a king," came the voice of the Lord.

I Samuel 7:15–8:22

THE FIRST KING

Near Ramah, Samuel's home, two young men were walking. Their eyes roamed over the countryside as though they were searching for something. The tall, handsome one was Saul, the son of a rich man named Kish, whose donkeys were missing. He and the servant with him had been hoping for many days to find the lost animals. Now their travels had carried them so far from home, Saul began to be worried.

"We had better start back," he said to his companion. "Father will be worrying now about us instead of his donkeys."

"Listen, we are near the place where the wise man lives," the servant said. "Let's not give up on our search until we ask him where to look."

"Well said," Saul agreed. So the two went the short distance into the city.

Samuel, the wise one whose reputation had spread to Saul's home, was just coming out of his house on his way to the place of worship when the men approached. Although he had never seen them before, Samuel was not entirely unprepared to meet the strangers. The day before the Lord had sent a special message: "Tomorrow about this time, I will send a man of the tribe of Benjamin to you. Anoint him prince over Israel, for he will save my people from the Philistines."

Samuel's eye caught the impressive sight young Saul made—the most handsome man in all Israel, head and shoulders taller than the rest.

"Here is the one I was speaking of! He is the one to rule over my people!" spoke the voice of God to Samuel's heart.

Now none of this was known to unsuspecting Saul. He was merely in a strange place trying to find a seer, one who could foretell, who would point him to the path his father's donkeys had taken.

"Can you show me which house belongs to the wise man?" Saul greeted Samuel.

"I am the one you are seeking," Samuel answered. "Come, be my guest today at worship and in my home. You must spend the night with me and we can discuss the things that are on your mind.

"As for your donkeys—give them no more thought. They have already been found. Nothing is more important at this moment than you and your family."

Saul was stunned. "What can you mean?" he asked. "I am from the most humble family in Israel's smallest tribe."

But Saul allowed Samuel to lead him to the feast of worship. When the sacred celebration was over, he went to the judge's home to spend the night. On the flat roof top, under the stars, they spoke of Israel and the future. Later, Saul slept in this choice spot.

Early the next morning Samuel walked with his guests to the edge of the city. "Tell your servant to go on ahead," he whispered to Saul. "I want to speak to you alone."

Then, when the servant was beyond hearing, Samuel took a small bottle of oil from his robe, broke it open, and reached up to pour its content on the young man's head.

"The Lord has anointed you prince over his people, Israel," were the prophet's solemn words.

Then Samuel told Saul what would happen to him on his way home so that he would know that all that had happened was of the Lord, not merely a dream.

"First, you will meet some men who will tell you that the donkeys have been found. At another place some men will give you two loaves of bread. Finally, near the Philistine fort, you will encounter some prophets with the spirit of God. For a while, the spirit will come upon you and you will join them in their praise to God."

As Samuel had predicted, each of these things eventually came to pass. When Saul met the band of prophets, he behaved as though he had become a new man. His praise was so joyful and so full of God's spirit, that it set people to talking.

"What has come over Saul?" they asked. "We would never have imagined him as a prophet."

But Saul gave no reason for the change that had occurred. When he reached home, his uncle asked where he had been. He answered simply: "I went to hunt the donkeys; and when they were not to be found, I went to Samuel."

"Pray, tell me what Samuel said," demanded Saul's uncle.

"That the asses had been found."

And that was the only answer Saul gave.

I Samuel 9:1–10:16

Loran Raymond Jones

SAMUEL PRESENTING SAUL—FIRST KING OF ISRAEL

I Samuel 10:17–25

Loran Raymond Jones

DAVID AND GOLIATH

I Samuel 17:1–54

Loran Raymond Jones

SAUL'S JEALOUSY OF DAVID

I Samuel 18:10–16

Loran Raymond Jones

DAVID AND HIRAM PLAN THE TEMPLE

I Chronicles 22:1–19

A KING INDEED

Saul had been anointed king of Israel, but only he and Samuel knew of it. Now the people had to be told the news; and for this purpose, Samuel called a meeting of Israel at Mizpah.

When they had gathered, he addressed the crowd: "The Lord God made you his people and brought you out of Egypt. He delivered you from your enemies and calamities, yet now you say you want a king to lead you. Come, present yourselves as families before the Lord."

So the people lined up and passed by Samuel according to tribes. He chose Benjamin's tribe to stand aside. Next, all the families within the tribe presented themselves, and from the number, Saul's family was selected. But Saul himself was not with his father and brothers! After a search he was discovered hiding behind the baggage. As he stood and came forward, Samuel pointed him out.

"Look whom the Lord has chosen. There is none like him among all Israel."

Indeed, tall, handsome Saul made a wonderful impression. At the sight of him, the people let up a great cheer: "Long live the king! God save the king!"

But Saul still had to prove himself as king, a difficult and uncertain task in a nation that had never before been ruled by such a leader. While he waited for an occasion to exert his leadership, his life followed the same pattern it had before his anointing; he lived at home and worked as a farmer. This shows us how far the kingship had to develop before it reached the level it attained two generations later, in Solomon's time.

Then word came that the Ammonites were attacking the town of Jabesh-Gilead and threatening to punish its citizens by putting out their right eyes.

This kind of cruelty was often practiced in those days by the victors in a struggle. Nevertheless, the men of Jabesh-Gilead took a chance on their only hope: the newly-appointed king. Would he prove to have any power?

When Saul received word of the Ammonite oppression, he became so angry that he cut apart the oxen with which he was plowing and sent pieces of their bodies throughout Israel. With them went the message: "This shall be done to the oxen of anyone who refuses to answer the call of Saul and Samuel."

In answer to this threat, three large companies of men came forth to fight under Saul's command. Their fierce attack against the Ammonites lasted only until noon of the day it began. It took only that long for the enemy to be thoroughly scattered and the people of Jabesh-Gilead to be freed.

With this victory, Saul's position as king was made secure. Even those who had questioned his authority agreed to support him. In a great service of rededication to God, the Israelites met at Gilgal and made Saul truly their king—in deed, as well as name. On the occasion, Samuel made a moving speech. He reviewed Israel's history from the time of Moses and the Exodus; he reminded them of the judge-heroes who had risen to lead them. Then he related their desire for a king and the choice of Saul, even in view of the dangers a king's leadership would bring.

"Nevertheless," he finished, "God will not turn away from you if you will serve him with all your heart." *I Samuel 10:17–12:25*

WARS OF KING AND PRINCE

The most formidable enemy Saul was forced to meet during his reign was the Philistines. Indeed, the aggression of these coastland people was one of the leading factors in Israel's demand for a king. As he had no course but to attempt to subdue them, Saul set out with an army of two thousand men and put his son, Prince Jonathan, over another thousand. Jonathan's men were successful in defeating one Philistine garrison at Geba, but this only produced full-scale trouble: it set the whole Philistine military strength into motion against the Israelites. This impressive force included iron chariots and weapons that the Israelites could not obtain or duplicate, so Saul had a difficult time mustering enough troops to withstand an attack. Many of the Israelites fled across the Jordan River or hid in caves and among rocks.

Finally King Saul brought his uneasy force together at Gilgal. Here they waited for Samuel to come and offer sacrifices to God on their behalf. Seven days passed and still there was no sign of Samuel. Was this proof that God had deserted them also? The army looked as though it might disintegrate at any moment, so Saul took it upon himself to offer the sacrifices. No sooner was this done than Samuel appeared as he had promised.

"What have you done?" the man of God demanded of Saul.

"Because the people were scattering and you were delayed, I was forced into offering the sacrifices myself," Saul explained.

"You have done foolishly," Samuel said. "You had no excuse. You knew what God's will was concerning the sacrifice and you disobeyed him. Now the kingdom will not be allowed to remain in your family. God will find a man closer to his heart to be the next ruler of his people."

Meanwhile the Philistines had to be met; and at this point, Prince Jonathan comes to the forefront as a hero of greater stature than his father. With only his armor-bearer, Jonathan slipped away to a pass where twenty Philistine men were posted.

"Listen," he told the armor-bearer, "with the Lord, it will not matter that there are only two of us. Let us take this outpost."

"I am with you," answered the servant.

So, never fearing the ten-to-one odds, Jonathan and the other man fell upon the Philistines and slaughtered all of them. You remember a point made earlier concerning Holy War and the fact that numbers made little difference to the Israelites when God fought with them.

The panic that this attack caused among the Philistines was enough to give heart to the Israelites. Some that had been in hiding rejoined Saul and added to the strength of his force. Even the Israelites who had been captured and were held in the Philistines camp rose up and helped King Saul send the enemy fleeing for their own country. Altogether, the impression they made was enough to maintain peace for several years. *I Samuel 13–14:23*

AN ACT OF REBELLION

Following the victory of the Philistines which he and Jonathan brought about, Saul led other battles against enemies on every side—the Moabites, the Ammonites, the Edomites, even the Philistines again—and succeeded in most of them. As the people had hoped, their king united them against these bothersome tribes that surrounded them and rid them of the constant threat of attack and oppression.

Still one group had to be subdued. This was the Amalekites, who had been Israel's enemies since the days of the Exodus.

Samuel gave Saul the Lord's orders: "Go now and utterly destroy the Amalekites. Do not spare a single person or animal, for they all belong to God." (Do you remember this provision of Holy War—dedicating the spoil of battle to God?)

By this time Saul had a large, well-armed fighting force, a far cry from the pathetic group which first met the Philistines; and when they marched against the Amalekites, they were completely victorious. However, Saul, in his confident mood, began to reason this way: "We've captured the king of the Amalekites alive. It would be a shame not to spare him. And all of these marvelous sheep and cattle—some of them should be saved."

Now Samuel had not gone south with Saul's army, so he knew none of this, but still he had an uncertain feeling about Saul. With this in mind, he went to Gilgal to confront Saul on his return from battle.

Saul came forward smiling to meet the old prophet. "Blessed be the Lord," he said. "I've done all that he commanded."

Samuel did not return the smile. "If you speak the truth, what are the animal sounds I hear?"

"Oh, those are just some of the best from the Amalekite flocks. We spared them so we could offer them to God. Otherwise, we did as you said and destroyed them."

"Stop!" Samuel interrupted. "I am going to tell you what the Lord has already told me.

"You were nothing until God chose to exalt you as the king of his people. Now you have taken it upon yourself to disobey his command and to spare part of the spoil from your battle."

"That is not true," Saul insisted. "I obeyed the Lord. I spared these animals only in order to sacrifice them."

"Would God rather have sacrifices or your obedience?" Samuel asked. "To obey is better than to sacrifice. And to listen is better than any gift you could bring.

"Because of your rebellion and stubbornness, you have rejected the Lord's command. Now he has rejected you from being king."

Saul began to lose some of his confidence under these accusations. "I have done wrong—I listened to the people instead of God.

"Now, forgive me," he begged. "Come and worship with me."

But it was too late. As Samuel turned his back on the rejected king and began to walk away, Saul grabbed at his robe and tore part of it.

"God has torn the kingdom away from you. He will give it to a better man," were Samuel's parting words.

So Saul lost his kingdom because he had disobeyed the Lord; and Samuel, faced with disappointment in both God's people and their king, mourned and wept. Saul had shown such promise as a shy young man, hiding among the baggage. Would his successor be able to prove more competent as king than he?

I Samuel 14:47–15:35

QUESTIONS: 1. *What was Eli's role in Israel?* 2. *Why did Elkanah bring his family to Shiloh?* 3. *For what did Hannah pray? Was her prayer answered?* 4. *Why did Samuel come to live with Eli?* 5. *Who spoke to Samuel in the night? What was his message?* 6. *Why was the Ark of the Covenant removed to the battlefield?* 7. *Describe the adventures relating to the Ark while it was in Philistia.* 8. *How was the Ark finally returned to Israel?* 9. *What was Samuel's role after Eli died?* 10. *Why did Israel want a king?* 11. *What warnings did Samuel give regarding a king?* 12. *What errand brought Saul to Samuel's home?* 13. *Tell of Saul's anointing.* 14. *How was Israel told of the new king?* 15. *With what incident did Saul prove himself a leader?* 16. *Describe Jonathan's brave adventures against the Philistines.* 17. *How did Saul disappoint God and Samuel?* 18. *What punishment did Saul suffer because of his rebellion?*

Israel's Greatest King

ANOINTED IN SECRET

For a time after God's rejection of Saul, Samuel grieved for Israel and her leader; but finally he had to admit that Saul would never again bear God's spirit. True, Saul remained king, but the knowledge that God was displeased with him and would not let his son reign after him set his mind off balance, and his life became more and more a failure as years went by.

Meanwhile, a new leader had to be found, and God sent Samuel down to Bethlehem to make the discovery. "Go to the house of a man named Jesse," the Lord directed. "I've chosen the new king from among his sons."

"How can I openly anoint a new king?" Samuel asked. "Saul would kill me if he heard of it."

"Go under the pretense of offering sacrifices. Invite Jesse and his sons to the worship service."

So Samuel went to Bethlehem and invited the people to assemble for worship. When Jesse walked in, Samuel was pleased to note that there were seven fine-looking sons with him.

The oldest, Eliab, passed in front of Samuel. "Surely this is God's choice," the prophet thought.

But the Lord's answer came: "Eliab is handsome and tall, but he shall not be king. I judge a man by his heart not his appearance."

Then the rest of the sons passed by—Abinadab, Shammah, and four others—but the Lord refused to designate one of them.

"Are these all of your children?" Samuel finally asked Jesse.

"There is one more, the youngest; but he is out keeping my sheep."

"Send for him. We will not begin our service until he arrives."

So Jesse sent for his youngest son. When the boy, David, walked in, cheeks flushed from the mountain air, Samuel knew that this was God's chosen one.

Later, in the presence of only the family, Samuel raised the sacred oil over David's head and pronounced him God's anointed. From that time on David felt God's presence with him in a special way, guiding him toward a divine work.

Saul, on the other hand, grew more and more lacking in the very spirit David now possessed. In its place, a very depressing mood overtook the older man and made him act strangely.

"What can we do to make King Saul feel better?" his distressed servants asked. "He has a terrible temper these days, and he no longer trusts anyone."

"Perhaps a musician could be of help," someone suggested. "His soothing songs might break the evil spell that binds the king and makes him ill."

Another member of the court knew just the young man who could perform this service. "Jesse of Bethlehem has a son who is skillful with the harp," the courtier suggested. "He performs beautiful songs which he has written. Besides that, he is a man of valor, honesty, and a fine appearance—the sort of man marked with favor by God."

So the son of Jesse was summoned to appear at court, and it was none other than David! Yes, David was the musician sought to cure Saul of his troubled thoughts. Whenever he played, as though by some magic spell, the bad spirit left the king and he grew calm. Thus Saul came to love David, the shepherd boy who had been chosen to be his successor. *I Samuel 16*

FELLED BY A STONE

All the time that David had spent as a shepherd had been combined beautifully with his development as a musician, and both had increased his devotion to God. While he wandered the hills he had time to sit quietly and meditate. During these periods of meditation he thought about God and about his relationship as a man to his heavenly creator. Then he translated these thoughts into lovely poetry and song. In the thousands of years that have passed since, David's music has been lost; but his moving verse still lives on. None is more memorable than that which compares the divine relationship of man and God to that tie which binds shepherd and sheep, one most familiar to David. It is preserved, as are many of his other songs, in the "songbook of the Bible"—the Psalms.

> The Lord is my shepherd, I shall not want;
> He makes me lie down in green pastures.
> He leads me beside still waters;
> He restores my soul.
> He leads me in paths of righteousness for his name's sake.
> Even though I walk through the valley of the shadow of death,
> I will fear no evil; for thou art with me;
> Thy rod and thy staff, they comfort me.
> Thou preparest a table before me in the presence of my enemies;
> Thou anointest my head with oil,
> My cup overflows.
> Surely goodness and mercy shall follow me all the days of my life;
> And I shall dwell in the house of the Lord forever.—*Psalm 23*

David's older brothers, however, did not live lives that provided such peace. They had been drafted to serve in King Saul's army against the Philistines. These warring people, stilled for awhile through Saul's efforts, launched fresh attacks. Their new confidence was placed in a huge warrior who marched to battle with them, the giant Goliath. The Philistines were placing all their trust in this man's ability to defeat any one Israelite.

The two nations camped across from each other in a valley, but no fight took place. Instead, Goliath would come out every morning and hurl his challenge to the Israelite army:

"Men of Israel, why are you here? Choose a man and send him out to fight me. If he kills me, the Philistines will be your servants; but if I kill him, Israel must serve us.

"I defy you on this ground. Send forth your man."

But these words only filled Saul and all his army with dismay. None was willing to face the giant. For forty days they listened silently to Goliath's roar without giving an answer.

While this was occurring, David was in Bethlehem caring for his father's sheep, for he was too young to join the army. But Jesse, his father, had begun to worry about his three sons who were on the battlefield.

"David," he said, "go visit your brothers at army headquarters and bring word of them back to me. Take this bread and cheese to leave with them."

So David happened to be in Saul's camp one morning when Goliath strutted out to issue his challenge.

"Do you see that man?" David's brothers and their friends pointed out. "The man who kills him will be honored in Israel. The king will give him great riches and let him marry the princess.

"What? This Philistine is defying the army of the living God?" David answered with contempt. And he went straight to King Saul.

"Tell your men not to be afraid any more. I will fight the Philistine."

"Why, you are just a boy," Saul replied in astonishment. "This fellow has been a man of war for years."

"I'm not as weak as you might think," David assured him. "I've killed lions and bears with my hands to protect my father's sheep. The same God who helped me do that will take care of me now."

"Go, and the Lord be with you," Saul agreed after a pause. But he insisted on dressing David in his personal armor—his helmet, his coat of mail, and his sword. David had to take only one step thus armed to know that it would not work.

"I'm not used to this," he admitted to Saul. "I cannot wear it."

Instead, he picked up his shepherd's staff and chose five smooth stones from the brook. The stones he placed in the leather bag that hung from his wait. In his other hand, he grasped a slingshot; and thus armed, he walked out to face Goliath.

The giant was angry when he saw David coming to meet him, for he thought the Israelites were making fun of him. "What do you mean, sending a boy?" he asked. Then he followed the question with several curses.

David answered: "You've come to meet me with a sword and a spear, but I come to you in the name of God. He will help me to win, and all the world will know that Israel worships the true God."

Then David began running toward the giant, slipping a stone in the sling. He drew back his arm and quickly let it fly.

His aim was deadly. The stone hit Goliath on the forehead and he pitched over on his face. David ran over, picked up the giant's own sword and cut off his head.

When the Philistines saw that their champion was dead, they began to run. Behind them followed the Israelite army, killing many and forcing the rest back into their own territory. *I Samuel 17*

IN AND OUT OF FAVOR

After the defeat of Goliath, Saul would not hear of David's returning to his father's house. Instead, he made him an officer in the army, and kept him so close to the royal family that David and Prince Jonathan became closest friends. The two loved each other so much that they pledged vows of friendship, and Jonathan gave David his own robe and sword and bow.

But the Philistine campaign ended and the army began its march back to Saul's capital. All along the way they found that David had become the hero of Israel. Women in every city came out singing the newest, most popular song:

> Saul has killed his thousands,
> And David his ten thousands.

The meaning of this song did not please the already unbalanced King Saul. "They are giving David credit for ten thousands and me only thousands," he pouted. "What more can he want now but my kingdom?"

And in his jealousy, another of his black moods came upon him.

"Send for David. Let him play and ease the king's mind," the servants suggested.

But David's music was the last thing Saul desired to hear. The mere sight of his "rival" threw him into a rage and he hurled his spear at David. The young man jumped aside twice and narrowly missed being hit before he was able to escape from the room.

From that time on it was clear that God was with David and had departed from Saul. No one was more aware of this than Saul himself; and it made him afraid. He would have liked nothing better than to have gotten rid of David, but the people would not have permitted it. Already they loved David far too much.

So Saul sent David into dangerous battles, pretending to honor him as an officer while secretly hoping he would be killed. Still David met with success on every hand, and each adventure only increased his popularity.

As pointed out before, there was none with whom David was more well-liked than Saul's own son, Jonathan. When the young prince became aware that his father was trying to kill David, he tried to appeal to the spark of goodness that he hoped still dwelt in Saul.

"Father," he begged, "why do you want to kill David? He's done nothing but good for you. Why, he risked his life to kill Goliath and save us all from the Philistines. Remember how proud you were of him then?"

Happily, Saul was moved by his son's plea and promised not to harm David. But another battle broke out and David's victory caused Saul to forget all his good intentions. His jealousy burned so intensely that David found out and realized that he must leave the city quickly. His wife, Michal, Saul's own daughter, let him through a window at night—and not a moment too soon, for Saul's men came looking for him. Clever Michal deceived them for awhile with an image the shape of a man that she had made and placed in bed. By the time they realized they had been tricked, David was some distance away, headed for Samuel's house at Ramah. *I Samuel 18:1–19:18*

TORN BETWEEN FATHER AND FRIEND

David's flight to Samuel in Ramah did not remain a secret long. When Saul heard of it, he sent messengers there to take David prisoner, never suspecting that the men would meet Samuel and fall into his spirit of prayer and prophecy, forgetting their evil mission. More guards were sent, but with the same lack of success. Samuel's noble spirit seemed to have more power over the men than Saul's orders.

Finally, Saul grew weary of waiting for his men to return. "I will go and get David myself," he determined.

But Saul found he had no more strength to resist God's spirit than his messengers had shown. At the sight of Samuel in his role of prophet and priest, the king himself forgot about capturing David and fell into an ecstasy. Like one possessed, he lay stripped naked on the ground all day and night.

By this time David was thoroughly confused. One moment Saul accepted him; the next, he tried to kill him. Where could he find an explanation for the king's strange behavior? There was one trustworthy source—the king's son and his best friend, Prince Jonathan.

In secret, he sought Jonathan and confronted him squarely: "What have I done to your father? What makes him want to kill me?"

Despite the unpleasant circumstances, Jonathan loved David as much as ever. In answer to these painful questions, he insisted that Saul had promised to do him no harm.

"I'm sure I would know if he intended to kill you," the prince went on.

"No, that's not necessarily true," David reminded him. "He's keeping his plans from you because he knows we're good friends."

"Then tell me what you want me to do," cried Jonathan. "Whatever it is, I'll do it."

So David revealed his plan. "Tomorrow," he said, "the king will begin a three-day feast in celebration of the new moon. Normally I would attend such a banquet, but this time I'm going to remain in hiding instead.

"When the king notices I'm gone and asks about me, say that I had to go to Bethlehem to my father's house. His reaction to this excuse will reveal his feelings about me."

"This whole situation greatly distresses me," Jonathan admitted. "I love you as much as ever and will do as you ask, yet my father is tearing us apart.

"If what you suspect is true, I won't even be able to meet you again and tell you of the outcome. You wait here in this field, and on the third day of the feast, I will signal to you whether or not it is safe for you to return to the palace.

"I will shoot three arrows over toward this rock where you will be hiding. If I call to my servant-boy, 'See, the arrows are on this side of you,' you will know you are safe. But if I say, 'Look, the arrows are beyond you,' there will be reason for you to flee for your life."

Then, with pledges of friendship and love, the two young men parted.

The next day, the feast was held as scheduled. Saul took his usual place against the wall with Jonathan opposite him and Abner, his general, by his side. No one mentioned David's empty chair.

On the second day of the celebration, however, the question came: "Where has David been for the past two days?"

"He had to make a trip to Bethlehem, Father."

Saul's eyes blazed in anger. "You wicked son! What do you mean—defending this son of Jesse? Don't you realize that he is going to keep you from ever reigning as king? Bring him to me. I'll kill him!"

Jonathan's anger matched that of his father. "Why should you kill David?" he shouted back. "What has he done to you?"

Saul answered by raising his javelin and hurling it toward his son. Furious, but not harmed, Jonathan ran from the table.

The next morning Jonathan went to the field at the time he had promised David. On the surface it appeared that he was merely practicing his marksmanship. He let three arrows fly through the air toward a certain rock.

"Run get them," he called to the lad who was with him. "They are over there, beyond you."

Then when the boy found them and returned, Jonathan handed him his bow, as well. "Here, take these back to the city. I'll follow right behind."

As soon as the boy was gone, David ran out to embrace his friend. Neither knew how long it would be before they could meet in safety again.

"Go in peace," said Jonathan. "The Lord shall be between us forever." Then they departed—Jonathan to the palace, David to an unknown exile.

I Samuel 19:18–20:42

A DESPERATE KING

After the meeting with Jonathan, David had no choice but to flee for his life. He was not welcome in the king's house; in fact, he knew he was not really safe anywhere in Israel. Yet, because he was forced to leave so suddenly, he found himself without food and weapons.

Along his route of escape, David passed the village of Nob where a tabernacle had been constructed after the one at Shiloh fell into ruins. Ahimelech, the high priest, was surprised to see a man of David's prominence appear alone and without notice, but David made excuses for himself that the man accepted. He even persuaded Ahimelech to give him the loaves of bread that were kept fresh on the table in the Holy Place; and just before he left, the priest presented him with the marvelous sword that had belonged to Goliath. Apparently it had been kept at the tabernacle as a kind of trophy, celebrating David's victory over the Philistine giant.

From Nob, David fled into Philistia and tried to pose as a madman; but he was discovered by the servants of the king and dared not stay there.

Next he came back across the border into the territory of Judah and found shelter in a great cave named the Cave of Adullam. Here he began to draw some followers—first his brothers and kinsmen, then others who were in trouble or discontented with King Saul's rule. With David as their captain, the band of outlaws amounted to about four hundred men.

Now Saul had spies all over the land, and they reported to him that David was collecting a small army for himself from among Saul's subjects. At this, he king became very angry.

"Listen here," he told his servants, "I don't like the things that are going on behind my back. You didn't even tell me that my son was in league with this son of Jesse."

Doeg, who was anxious to please, spoke up: "I was at Nob one day when David stopped at the tabernacle. The high priest gave him some bread and the sword of Goliath."

So Saul sent for Ahimelech, the high priest, and all those who served under him at the tabernacle.

"Why have you joined David to conspire against me?" he demanded of the priests. "You gave him bread and a sword so he could rise up against me."

"Why should we have suspected David?" Ahimelech asked. "There is none so faithful in your whole kingdom. He's your son-in-law, a captain in your army, honored in your household. I don't know what you're talking about."

But Saul at this stage was beyond reason. "You will die!" he screamed at Ahimelech. And Doeg, still his henchman, carried out his orders to kill all eighty-five priests and their families. Only Abiathar, the high priest's son, escaped and came to David's hideaway.

"I feel I am responsible for your family's death," David told him sadly. "I knew that day at Nob that Doeg would tell Saul.

"Now the king will seek your life same as mine. Stay with me and you will be safe." *I Samuel 21–22*

RETURNING GOOD FOR EVIL

Finally word came to King Saul that Abiathar, now high priest at his father's death, had joined David's army at Keilah, where they were fighting Philistine raiders. Gathering his own forces together, Saul rode in pursuit, but barely missed David and had to extend his chase into the surrounding wilderness. It seemed that his well-trained army was no match for David's "mighty men," however. Day by day the two groups followed each other through the hills, but David seemed divinely protected by the hand of God. At the one time when it appeared that Saul would close in, word came that the Philistines were raiding, and he had to abandon the chase.

While Saul was gone, David moved his men to the wild country near the Dead Sea. Here, at Engedi, he was hiding with some men in a huge cave when Saul returned with three thousand men to find him. Over the rough rock ledges the select soldiers climbed, but there was no sign of David. Saul himself finally grew weary from the effort and lay down to rest—at the mouth of the very cave where David and his men were hiding. From deep within, David sneaked up and cut off part of the sleeping king's robe; then he returned to his hiding place.

"Why don't you kill Saul now before he gets you?" his men whispered.

"No!" David answered. "I wouldn't harm God's anointed."

By and by Saul woke and, unconscious of what had happened, walked away. After he had gone a little distance, David ran to the mouth of the cave and called after him, "My lord, the king!"

When Saul looked around, David bowed to the ground to show he still respected him. "Why do you listen to those who say I want to hurt you?" he called to Saul. "Look, I had you in my power today, but I would not kill you. Here is a piece I cut from your robe, but I would not harm God's anointed. The Lord judge between us—you have no reason to fear me."

The sound of David's voice changed Saul into his former self for a moment. "David," he said, "is that you, my son?" Then he hung his head and the tears began to fall down his cheeks.

"You are a better man than I," Saul admitted. "You have been good to me, while I have tried my best to kill you. I know that you are going to be king some day. Promise me that you will not hurt my children when that time comes."

David promised all that Saul asked, but he and his men returned to their stronghold in the hills. He knew that Saul might still change his mind and turn against him, because it had happened before. In the best interest of peace, he eventually got permission for him and his men to settle in Philistia because he knew Saul would not follow him there. This solution proved satisfactory for more than a year.

Then the clouds that hovered over Saul began to darken once more. First, Samuel, the wise old prophet, died. Then the Philistines, with larger forces than ever before, gathered to attack Israel at Gilboa. The uncertain king felt truly frightened. He thought, "If only God were here to fight on my side. Or Samuel to pray on my behalf. Or David to lead my army."

But God had said, "Because you have not obeyed me, I have turned away from you and given the kingdom to another." Saul was all alone.

Indeed, it was a pathetic figure that had to face the Philistines in that episode. The whole Israelite army sensed their defeat from the beginning and turned and fled. In the slaughter that followed, Saul's three sons were killed, and Saul himself was wounded.

"Draw your sword and kill me before some Philistine comes!" he begged the armor-bearer that was beside him when he fell. But the servant would not kill his king. So Saul took his own sword and fell on it, killing himself.

In the rout that followed, the Philistines found the bodies of Saul and his sons and took them as prizes of victory; but the men of Jabesh-Gilead—remember that Saul rescued them in the beginning of his reign—took them in the night and buried them decently.

Thus ended the life of a truly tragic figure in Israel's history.

I Samuel 23–24, 28–31

CIVIL WAR

While Saul fought his dying battle, David was returning to his home in exile from a skirmish with the Amelekites. He was met by a weary man with dirty, torn clothes.

"Where have you come from?" David asked.

"I've escaped from the camp of Israel," the man replied.

"How did the fight go? Tell me."

"The Israelites have run away. Saul and Jonathan are dead!"

One might think that this news would have brought David relief—his years of danger and exile were over. But David's reaction was quite the opposite. He tore his clothes in anguish and wept over Saul, his king, and Jonathan, his friend. In memory of them he wrote a moving tribute, refusing to allow the injustice he had suffered to diminish his loyalty to "God's anointed."

> Saul and Jonathan, beloved and lovely!
>   In life and in death they were not divided;
> they were swifter than eagles,
>   they were stronger than lions.
>
> Ye daughters of Israel, weep over Saul,
>   who clothed you daintily in scarlet,
>   who put ornaments of gold upon your apparel,
>
> How are the mighty fallen,
>   in the midst of the battle!
>
> Jonathan lies slain upon thy high places,
>   I am distressed for you, my brother Jonathan;
> very pleasant have you been to me;
>   your love to me was wonderful,
>   passing the love of women.
>
> How are the mighty fallen
>   and the weapons of war perished! *–II Samuel 1:23–27*

With Saul dead, David was rightfully king; but there was no possibility of his stepping in and taking over the reigns of the kingdom. The defeat at Gilboa had made Israel a Philistine land once again. Also, Abner, the commander of Saul's armies, had set up Ishbosheth, one of Saul's remaining sons, as head of a rival government. They established their capital across the Jordan, out of reach of the Philistines.

The people of the tribe of Judah accepted David as their king, but some tribes of the north took Ishbosheth as their leader. Neither of these two small groups had much chance of facing the Philistines and bringing unity to Israel alone, so a civil war followed. From the first conflict at Gibeon it appeared that David would eventually win, but the struggle continued for about two years.

The real breaking point came when Abner and Ishbosheth quarreled, and Abner transferred his support to David. He sent messengers to David stating that he wanted to make a covenant. He also counseled the northern tribes, saying: "In times past, you wanted to make David king. Now, go ahead and do it, for the Lord has promised to deliver us from the Philistines by his hand."

David graciously received Abner at his capital at Hebron, but some of David's men mistrusted the general's motives. Had he really changed his loyalties or was he there to spy? Deciding that Abner was really on a mission of treachery, Joab, David's general, arrested him secretly and killed him.

When David heard of this, he was outraged. He cursed Joab and mourned for Abner, following his casket to the grave. "A prince and great man in Israel has fallen this day," he said.

So the people understood that David had not brought about Abner's death, and it pleased them, as everything he did pleased them. *II Samuel 1–3*

BUILDING A KINGDOM

With Abner gone, Saul's son Ishbosheth and his government had no power. His own supporters saw that there was no future in opposing David, so they decided to try to win his favor instead. One day when Ishbosheth was taking a noontime nap, two of them crept into his house and killed him. Then they traveled all night so they could give David the news.

"Ishbosheth, your enemy, is dead," the two soldiers reported. "We have avenged you of Saul and his family."

But David was not pleased, as they had hoped he would be. "As the Lord lives, when the man came to tell me that Saul was dead, I gave him the punishment he deserved. How much more you deserve it for killing a good man in his bed!"

And he commanded the men be killed.

Now nothing stood in the way of David's kingship. Representatives from all the tribes came to Hebron and said to him: "Even when Saul was king, you were the one who led us. Now take your rightful place as our king."

So they "made a covenant with him at Hebron, and King David made a covenant with them before the Lord, and they anointed David king over Israel."

With this covenant an excellent start, David set about to strengthen Israel within and without. First, he moved the capital from Hebron to the fortress city of Jerusalem, on Mount Zion. This selection was satisfactory to everyone because it was in the central part of the land. He renamed it City of David and settled there in newly constructed buildings.

Next, he set about to rid the Israelites of the Philistine menace. With the help of the Lord and the confidence and loyalty of all Israel, the old enemy was not nearly as great a threat as before. In just two encounters, David drove them completely out of Israel—this time for good.

Then he turned his thoughts to the whole reason for Israel's existence —her religion. Truly this side of life had been neglected by Saul, and his kingdom failed because of it. With King David, there would be a change. He determined that the center of government should also be the center of worship, just as it had been when Israel first came into the promised land. And there could be no center of worship without the Ark of the Covenant, that valuable chest that had been carved in the wilderness and had held the tables of stone on which the Ten Commandments were written. After Eli's death, the Ark had been stolen by the Philistines, but later returned. Ever since, it had been kept safely at the house of a man named Abinadab. David himself led a group to reclaim the Ark and bring it to its rightful home in Jerusalem. In an impressive parade they entered the city with their precious cargo. There was singing and dancing in celebration of the great event; and after the Ark was safely placed in the tent that had been prepared, King David offered sacrifices to God and blessed the people in God's name.

Still David was not content just to have the symbol of God's presence at rest in Jerusalem. Somehow it did not seem fitting to him that he should live in a fine house while the Lord of Hosts dwelled in a tent. He would build a grand temple in honor of the Lord!

But these were not God's plans. He did not want David to be concerned with a temple; he preferred that he build up the kingdom instead. "I will raise up your son after you," he promised David. "He shall build a house for my name, and I will establish the throne of his kingdom forever."

So David did not build a House of God, but he began making plans and collecting materials for his son who would. *II Samuel 4–7*

DAVID'S DARKEST HOUR

Once David had made Israel secure, he began to expand his territory. With more force behind him than Israel had ever been able to summon before, he completely conquered the lands of Moab, Edom, and Ammon. More important, he took new territory to the north, which made him ruler of a kingdom much larger than the original "Promised Land."

As a successful and powerful king, David then left more and more of the fighting to his commander Joab. One spring he sent Joab out against the Ammonites, and he remained in Jerusalem. Late in the afternoon, he walked out on the roof of the palace; and looking down, he saw a beautiful woman bathing in the courtyard of another house. The king inquired who the woman was and learned that she was Bathsheba, the wife of Uriah, one of his faithful soldiers.

This information did not please David. He had wanted Bathsheba for his own. In fact, his desire for her was so great that it led his thoughts in the most evil direction.

"I could have this woman if she were rid of her husband," he mused. "Let's see—he's out fighting the Ammonites now. What if he were killed in battle? That would take care of things and seem natural enough."

So David sent a letter to Joab: "Put Uriah in the middle of the fiercest fighting." When Joab obeyed these orders, the cruel strategy worked. Uriah was killed; and after a decent period of mourning, Bathsheba came to live in the palace as one of David's wives.

No one in Jerusalem suspected that there was anything amiss except for one person. He was Nathan, one of those men called prophets, who spoke for God and feared no man. When Nathan confronted David, he did not accuse him right away. Instead, he told this story:

"Once there were two men who lived in the same city. One was very rich and had many flocks and herds; but the other was very poor—he had only one lamb, and it was like part of his family.

"One day a visitor came to see the rich man. Instead of preparing one of his own animals to feed the stranger, he took the poor man's only lamb and killed it for the meal."

David was quite angry at the conclusion of Nathan's story. "That rich man deserves to die!" he fumed. "He must be made to give the poor man four lambs in repayment."

Nathan looked sternly at David. "*You* are that man," he accused the king. "The Lord made you king of Israel and rescued you from Saul. Why, then, did you kill to get what you wanted? You will be punished openly for what you did in secret."

Faced with his sin, David readily admitted it. He listened quietly while Nathan told him that as a punishment, his and Bathsheba's son would die.

Surely enough, the child did become very sick. Although he knew he deserved this punishment, David was grief-stricken. He fasted and prayed and lay on the ground for a week.

Then the child died. No one wanted to break the news to David. "He might harm himself if we tell him," the servants said.

But David noticed everyone whispering and understood what had happened. "Is it true my child is dead?" he asked.

"Yes," they replied. And to their surprise, the king got up, washed himself, and went to the house of God for worship. Then, for the first time since his son had fallen ill, he sat down to eat.

"While the child was alive," he explained, "I prayed, thinking God might let him live. But now that he is dead, I cannot bring him back to life. He can never be here with me again, but I know that some day I shall go to him."

Afterward, God gave David and Bathsheba another son. His name was Solomon.

II Samuel 11–12:25

A TRAITOROUS SON

When Solomon was born, David had other sons who were already grown. Among them, Prince Absalom was the most brilliant and handsome, and his father loved him very much. But Absalom committed a very grave wrong—he killed his brother Amnon in a quarrel. Even though he was the king's son, he knew what displeasure this would cause, and he fled the country.

For three years Absalom remained an outlaw, but David missed him and worried about him each day. Finally Joab, the general, played upon David's concern and begged him to permit Absalom to return to the capital city. David agreed to this with more relief than reluctance; but he refused to see his son, nonetheless.

For two years, the situation stood at this standstill, but Absalom was not pleased. He wanted the king's approval—not because he loved his father, but because his future plans demanded it. Therefore, he begged that Joab persuade his father to see him. It took a dramatic occurrence—Absalom's burning Joab's wheat field—to bring this about; but Joab was finally successful. Absalom was invited home and King David met him with a father's affection that had never been lost.

Absalom returned his father's embraces, but his was not really a loving heart. All this time he was plotting how to become king himself. Once he regained his father's favor, he put his plan into action. First, he needed people to notice him. This was not difficult to manage because he was the most handsome man in the land, with especially beautiful long hair. To draw further attention to himself, he rode around the city in a fine chariot, with fifty men running before him.

Next, he went out early in the morning to the city gates to meet the ordinary people who brought their complaints and disagreements to the king. He would greet them and put his arm around their shoulders, acting like he was their friend. "The king is too busy to see you," he would tell each one in confidence. "But if I were king, things would be different. I would take time to see everyone and act fairly toward them."

It is no wonder that Absalom completely stole the hearts of many of Israel's men within the four years that this continued.

Now David was not aware of all his son was doing. When Absalom came one day and asked permission to go to Hebron to worship, he granted it with no suspicion. Little did he know that Absalom was going there to declare himself king and gather his forces around him. It was a messenger who brought David the word; and it hit him with such shock that he seemed to lose control of the situation. Not knowing just what Absalom planned to do and not wishing to fight with his own son, he and his family withdrew to the banks of the Jordan River. Along the way some met them with tears and pledges of allegiance; another, a relative of Saul, with curses and threats.

Meanwhile, Absalom and his followers arrived in Jerusalem; and finding the palace empty, took it for themselves. Then they began to plan for the capture and surrender of David.

Absalom had two chief advisors. One of them, Hushai, was actually David's spy. When the other, Ahithopel, advised Absalom to strike swiftly and at night, Hushai proposed that this was not wise.

"David and his men are like bears robbed of their cubs right now," said Hushai. "Let me further remind you that they are experienced soldiers. You will have a better chance against them if you wait until you can gather a sizeable army and lead it in person." He knew that if he could convince Absalom to wait, he would give David more time to escape. Fortunately, Absalom looked upon the spy's advice with favor. Hushai took word of his success to the high priests and they sent the details of the plan on to David.

Although many of the Israelites had joined Absalom in Jerusalem, others refused to believe that David was not a good king. They saw Absalom for what he was—a disobedient son. These came to David across the Jordan and formed his army. As much as he despaired of the situation, David soon had no choice but to send these men out to meet Absalom's forces. David himself wanted to ride with them, but his generals would not hear of it. "You are worth ten thousand of us," they explained.

So David stood by the gate of the town and watched his men march off to battle. His parting words were those of a loving father: "Be gentle with Absalom for my sake."

The two armies met in a forest, and the rough countryside took its own toll during the day's fighting. Men were scattered from their comrades; and Absalom, riding upon a mule, came suddenly upon some of David's servants. As he turned and fled, his mule passed under a low-hanging branch. Absalom's head and hair became caught in the tree, and he was left hanging. A soldier went to tell Joab of the incident.

"Do you mean you left Absalom without killing him?" the general asked. "I would have given you a reward!"

"I heard the king's request, and I wouldn't have touched the young man for any prize," the soldier answered.

"I'm wasting time with you," Joab exclaimed. And he promptly went in search of the disabled enemy. Finding him hanging, but still alive, he thrust three darts into his heart. Then he blew on his horn, and the fighting ended.

David was still sitting by the city gates when he saw messengers coming from the direction of the battle. The first ran up, saying, "All is well! We have won the battle!" But David was not interested in the battle—he wanted to know how his son was. Then a second messenger arrived with news that Absalom was dead.

The king turned and made his way to an upstairs room. As he went, he shook his head and moaned, "O my son Absalom, O Absalom, my son, my son! If only I could have died for you!"

At that moment he was not a king who had saved his throne. He was, first of all, a father who had lost his son.

David's kingship never suffered another threat as serious as the one Absalom posed. The old ruler spent the last years of his reign in Jerusalem, guiding the nation toward its period of greatest strength. *II Samuel 13–16:14*

QUESTIONS: 1. *How did Samuel discover that David would be Saul's successor?* 2. *What coincidence first brought David to Saul's palace?* 3. *Discuss David's relation to the Psalms.* 4. *How did David come to fight the Philistine giant?* 5. *Why did Saul turn against David?* 6. *Discuss the friendship of David and Jonathan.* 7. *Where did David get food and weapons in his hurried flight?* 8. *How did he obtain an army?* 9. *Describe the scene in which David spared Saul's life.* 10. *How did Saul and Jonathan finally meet their death? What was David's reaction?* 11. *Which of Saul's sons challenged David's right to the kingship?* 12. *What changes did David make as king? How did this make the kingdom stronger?* 13. *Tell of David's greatest sin. What were its consequences?* 14. *How did Absalom gain support for himself?* 15. *Describe Absalom's defeat.*

Israel's Golden Age

AN UNDERSTANDING HEART

All along, David had expected his son Solomon to follow him to the throne; but at the end of his life, another son, Adonijah, tried to claim his right to succession. Nathan, the prophet, and Bathsheba, Solomon's mother, informed David of Adonijah's conspiracy.

"I swore to you before the Lord that Solomon would reign after me," David affirmed; "and he will!" Then he quickly set plans into motion that would make Solomon king at once and put an end to the dreams of Adonijah and his friends.

At his command, Solomon, Nathan, and Zadok, the high priest, formed an official procession. With Solomon riding on a donkey that was David's own, the group drew people's attention as they traveled from Jerusalem to a spring at Gihon. There Zadok took oil from the tabernacle and poured it over Solomon's head, pronouncing him king before God and the people. Then trumpets sounded, and the crowd shouted, "Long live the king!"

The celebration that followed proved that Solomon was clearly Israel's choice for king, as well as David's. Adonijah and his followers were left with no hope at all.

So David lived to see his son ascend to the throne, and he offered the new king this advice: "Be strong and show yourself like a man. Walk in the ways of the Lord, keeping all the commands given in the law of Moses, that the Lord may prosper all that you do and bless you wherever you turn." Then, having reigned for forty years, David died and was buried in his City of Peace.

Solomon, as a very young man, was left with an extensive and powerful kingdom. In his first few acts as king, he demonstrated his inherited power and swiftly rid himself of all possible enemies, including Adonijah, Abiathar, and Joab. Yet despite these acts of vengeance, he was basically a religious man, walking in the ways of his father. He realized the tremendous responsibility he had as the leader of God's people; and early in his reign, he sought the Lord's help in a service of worship and sacrifice at Gibeon.

After prayers had been offered and the sacrificial fires burned low, God appeared to King Solomon on that solemn occasion. "Ask me for any gift and I will grant it," he said to the young ruler.

There were many things Solomon could have chosen, but this was his answer: "Lord, you showed such kindness to my father David—no kindness greater than allowing me to serve as king in his place. But now, O God, I feel like a small child. I know so little, yet I am to rule this great nation. My request is for an understanding heart, that I might be able to decide between right and wrong and govern the people wisely."

God was pleased with Solomon's words. He told him, "Because you asked for this instead of long life or riches or victory in battle, I am going to grant your request. You shall have a wise and understanding heart like none before or after you.

"More than that, I am going to give you all the things for which you did not ask. You will have riches and honor; and if you serve me as your father did, you will have a long life, also."

Then Solomon awoke and found that it had all been a dream, yet a dream that came true.

I Kings 1–3:15

A TEST OF WISDOM

God gave Solomon all that he had promised—riches, honor, and the wisdom that had been the young king's first request. It was not long before Solomon's duties as king called for the use of this understanding heart, this uncanny ability to see clearly and swiftly the right and wrong concerning an issue. The first test was presented by two women, both of whom claimed to be the mother of the same baby.

One woman told the story: "Oh, my lord, this woman and I live in the same house. Both of us had babies at the same time, but she lay upon her child while she slept and it died. Before I awoke, she lay her son next to me and took my living child for her own. In the morning I could tell the dead baby beside me was not mine."

But the other woman said, "That is not true! The living child is mine." And they continued arguing back and forth.

King Solomon looked from one woman to the other. Then he turned to his servant and said: "Bring me a sword!" A sword was brought.

"Now," he continued, "give me the living baby. I will cut it in two and each of you shall have half."

At this, one of the women cried out and fell to her knees, "Oh, my lord," she begged, "do not kill the child. Give it to her, but let it live."

"No," the other woman said. "The king is right. Since we cannot both have it, neither of us shall have it. Divide it in half."

Solomon lay down his sword. He had heard enough. "Give the child to the first woman," he ordered. "She is its true mother because she could not bear to have it harmed."

The people were amazed by Solomon's wisdom. They knew it had to be a special gift from God.

I Kings 3:16–28

Loran Raymond Jones

CEDARS OF LEBANON FOR THE TEMPLE

I Kings 5:1–18

Loran Raymond Jones

THE QUEEN OF SHEBA MEETS SOLOMON

II Chronicles 9:1–12

Loran Raymond Jones

ELIJAH RUNNING IN FRONT OF THE CHARIOT

I Kings 18:41–46

Loran Raymond Jones

ELISHA REFUSING GIFTS FROM NAAMAN

II Kings 5:15–19

THE HOUSE OF GOD

David had given Solomon a large and peaceful Israel over which to rule. Therefore, Solomon had both the time and riches for pursuits that his father had had to deny himself. One of these pleasant tasks was the creation of a more impressive capital city. Solomon accomplished this with extensive building projects throughout Jerusalem. Over a period of years, he constructed an ornate palace for himself and another for his queen, a House of Cedars, a Hall of Pillars, and a Hall of Judgment. But his crowning effort was the great Temple, the House of God.

This structure had been the dream of David, and he had planned for it during his final years. He had even collected gold and silver and wood and stone to be used when it was built. All of these Solomon inherited, and in the fourth year of his reign he began to build.

Treasures from all over the world were gathered to add to those David had collected. Solomon's position as a powerful and peaceful king made it possible for him to deal with other rulers for valuable products from their countries. Especially notable was the cedar wood that Hiram, king of Tyre, furnished from the forests of Lebanon. Solomon sent men up to the famous forests to cut the trees into logs. Then these logs were tied into rafts and floated down the coast until they were taken ashore near Jerusalem.

Skilled workmen took these raw materials and carefully made each portion of the house of worship. Generally, its design was like that of the tabernacle Moses built, but it was much larger and more permanent. There was still an outdoor court with altars for burning sacrifices and pools for washing the gift animals. And there was another enclosed building containing two rooms, the Holy Place and the Holy of Holies. But these were built with cypress floors and cedar walls, inlaid with gold. The wooden surfaces were elaborately carved and inlaid with gold and precious stones, and the curtain before the Holy of Holies was embroidered in scarlet and purple. Two gold cherubim, with wings spread wide, guarded the precious Ark of the Covenant within this throne room of the Lord, the Holy of Holies. The whole structure was enclosed by a series of rooms where temple treasure was stored. On the outside, on either side of the entrance, stood two large bronze pillars. Altogether, it was a most impressive sight.

Seven years were spent building this house of God; and when it was finished, a great service of dedication was held. Solomon led a procession which brought the Ark from Zion, where David had placed it, to its new place under the sheltering wings of the cherubim. The priests, dressed in beautiful robes, sang in a chorus. The words of their songs praised God, "for he is good, for his steadfast love endures forever."

Then Solomon addressed the crowd in a wonderful sermon of God's acts of kindness toward Israel. He stood before the altar and prayed for the whole nation: "O God, the whole earth and heaven cannot hold you, much less this house I have built! But because we have called it by your name, hear us when we come here and pray."

Then the same cloud of glory that had hovered over the tabernacle filled the new house of worship with a heavenly light, and the people knew that it had been blessed and made holy by God's presence. *I Kings 5–8*

SOLOMON'S SPLENDOR

The temple Solomon built was only one example of the golden age Israel experienced during his reign. It was a time during which people lived in peace and prosperity they had never known before. With his great understanding in many areas, Solomon made the land of Israel one in which there was work for all, food to spare, and pleasant surroundings to enjoy.

David's son accomplished all this by making the country safe against those who might try to invade it. He built strong cities along the routes that enemies might travel and equipped them with thousands of chariots and horsemen. For years the Philistines and Canaanites had terrorized the Israelites with chariots; now King Solomon used them himself to keep a firm hold on the territory he had inherited from his father.

Besides maintaining peace with surrounding nations, Solomon also traded with them for profit. He and King Hiram cooperated in sending large ships to distant ports. Their fleet, sailing under the flag of Israel, brought gold, silver, ivory and precious stones back to Jerusalem. For curiosity and amusement, they included apes and baboons in their cargo.

The land of Israel was a natural crossroads for caravans traveling to the Near East, and Solomon managed to make this work to his advantage. He not only traded with these merchants, but also collected taxes from them in return for permission to pass through his land.

Much of the wealth that Solomon accumulated went toward maintaining his court in a luxurious fashion. A staggering amount of food was needed to feed his household every day. Within his palace, he sat upon an ivory throne, covered with gold. He ate only from golden dishes; silver became commonplace within his court.

No other ruler of the time lived amid more dazzling splendor than did King Solomon of Israel. Therefore, it is no wonder that stories of him were told even in faraway lands and that leaders of these nations came to see if the reports were true.

Among the curious was one called the Queen of Sheba. With a great train of camels, she and her companions made their way from their home in Arabia to Jerusalem, bringing gifts of spices, gold, and precious stones to Solomon. The queen came to hear his words of wisdom, as well as to see the luxury of his court. After she and Solomon had talked and the king had indeed given wise counsel on the questions that concerned her, the royal visitor was taken on a tour of the City of David. She saw the palaces and the temple, the beautiful clothes and delicious food, the servants, government officials, and all the rest.

Even a queen had never seen such marvelous sights. She said to Solomon: "Back in my own country, I heard about your wisdom and your greatness, but I could not believe the reports. Now that I've come and seen for myself, I realize that half had not been told me!

"Happy are your people! Blessed be your God, who made you king!"

And with a lavish exchange of gifts, she bid Solomon farewell and returned to her own country. *I Kings 4:20–34; 9:26–10:29*

A KINGDOM TORN

One method that King Solomon used to avoid conflicts with other nations was to form a "marriage alliance." He would take a member of the rival nation's royal family as his wife, and thus seal the peace between Israel and that country. Solomon knew that no king desired to attack the land where his daughter lived or to make war on his own son-in-law. By this method, he became the husband of many, many women, most of them from foreign lands. His harem included a princess from Egypt, from Moab, from Ammon, and other places.

As years passed, Solomon became more and more intrigued by these women in his household. He humored them and let them indulge in their foreign pastimes, including pagan religions. The day came when he even built shrines for their idol gods and worshipped at them himself!

When God saw this disobedience, he was sorely disappointed. Finally he told the wealthy ruler: "You have not kept my laws and commandments. Because you have turned your back on me, I will take the kingdom away from you and give it to another. For the sake of David, I will let it be yours for your lifetime; but your son will rule only two tribes."

From that time on, Solomon found himself in trouble. For the first time, neighboring countries began to resist his rule. Hadad led Edom in rebellion; Rezon caused an uprising in Syria. At home, the people began to grumble about the large amounts Solomon spent on himself and his projects. They were also dissatisfied with the way Solomon used them as nothing but slave labor to cut timber and stone for his buildings.

One of the commanders of these slave labor forces was a young man named Jeroboam. He was met one day on the road outside Jerusalem by one of God's spokesmen, Ahijah the prophet. Ahijah had on a brand new garment; but when he saw Jeroboam, he took it off and began tearing it until it was ripped into twelve pieces.

"Here," he said to the young man, "take ten of these pieces. They are the ten tribes which the Lord will tear away from Solomon and give to you, for he has worshipped idol gods and has not followed in the steps of his father David.

"His son shall keep two tribes for David's sake, but you shall have ten. You will be king of Israel; and if you keep his commandments, the Lord will build you a sure kingdom, as he did for David."

When Solomon heard this, he tried his best to kill Jeroboam. But the young man escaped to Egypt and remained there as long as Solomon lived.

I Kings 11

END OF AN AGE

The golden age had begun to tarnish before Solomon died. In all its extravagance, his court had grown idle and weak. Pagan gods had been introduced by the foreign women in his harem, and their shrines had begun to appear in the land. The ordinary people were heavily burdened with taxes and labor to maintain all the luxury of the court. Still, Solomon seemed successful, and the people remained loyal while he lived.

Then, after a forty year reign, he died and was buried in Jerusalem with his father David. His son Rehoboam immediately prepared for his own coronation, which would take place at Shechem. But before it could occur, news of Solomon's death traveled to Egypt, and Jeroboam returned to complicate the situation. He was in the crowd that assembled at Shechem for the ceremony. In fact, he came to Rehoboam as a spokesman for the people gathered there.

"Your father made our burdens too heavy," he told the new king. "Take away some of the taxes and work, and we will gladly serve you."

"I will give your request consideration," Rehoboam answered. "Return in three days and I will give you my decision."

So Jeroboam and the people stood aside to see what would result.

First, Rehoboam consulted the wise old men who had been Solomon's advisors. "The people have asked for some relief," he told them. "Should I give it to them?"

They replied: "If you will hear their plea and give them a good answer, the people will forever be loyal to you."

Then Rehoboam went to those of his own age who were his close friends. "Are the old men right? Should I grant the people their request?"

"Don't be weak and give in to your subjects here at the start," the young men urged. "Make them afraid of you. Tell them your little finger is bigger than your father's body."

To the foolish and impetuous young king, this advice made good sense. When Jeroboam and the people came for their answer, he stood before them and announced with a haughty air: "My father made your burdens heavy; I will make them even heavier. He struck you with whips; I will sting you with scorpions."

The people broke into an angry protest. "What rights do we have?" We don't have to remain loyal to David's family!

"Home to your own tents, you Israelites. Let Rehoboam take care of his own house!"

Then they all walked out on the new king, all but the tribes of Judah and Benjamin. The ten tribes that revolted chose Jeroboam as their king and set up a new capitol in the north. Rehoboam returned to Jerusalem, which remained his capital because it was in the land that belonged to the tribe of Judah. But his kingdom had been reduced to a fraction of its size and power.

With this incident, Israel's golden age ended. A kingdom divided could not endure for long. *I Kings 12:1–20*

QUESTIONS: 1. *How did David spoil Adonijah's attempt to take the throne?* 2. *As a young king, what gift did Solomon desire?* 3. *Did God approve of Solomon's request? What was his answer?* 4. *How did Solomon use his wisdom to solve the problem of the two women and the baby?* 5. *Where did Solomon get materials for the Temple?* 6. *What did the Temple look like?* 7. *Besides the building of the Temple, what made Solomon's reign a "golden age"?* 8. *How did Solomon become so wealthy? How did he maintain peace?* 9. *What special visitor came from a distant land to see King Solomon?* 10. *What were the "marriage alliances" Solomon made?* 11. *How did Solomon's many wives cause him trouble?* 12. *Why did the people grow discontented?* 13. *Who was Jeroboam? What did the prophet say about him?* 14. *Who tried to succeed Solomon to the throne?* 15. *What did the people ask Rehoboam? What was his answer?* 16. *What portion of the kingdom of Israel did Rehoboam receive? Which part went to Jeroboam?*

Troublers of Israel

A WIDOW'S GUEST

The kings who followed Jeroboam as rulers of the kingdom of Israel led the people even farther away from God than Jeroboam had. Each man seemed to be worse than the one before him, so that after many years the people had practically forgotten about God and about their role as his chosen people.

Ahab, who was the sixth king after Jeroboam, did more evil in Israel than all the kings before him. One of his worst mistakes was to marry a wicked woman named Jezebel, the daughter of a pagan king. She led Ahab and the people to turn away from God and worship the Canaanite gods Baal and Asherah. Could God allow the Israelites to go on in their evil ways and forget him completely?

At this critical time God began to raise up special representatives, whose task it was to declare the will of God to the people. These men were called prophets. One of the greatest of these prophets was Elijah.

Elijah was a rather stern and impulsive man, and when he received God's instruction to tell King Ahab that he would be punished for his wickedness and for teaching the people to worship idols, he went immediately to the palace. Ahab must have been surprised when he saw this strange-looking man dressed in animal skins and wearing an angry look on his face.

In a voice that resounded through the palace, Elijah announced, "As surely as the Lord God of Israel lives, there will be no more dew or rain in the land until I ask for it." And then he was gone.

Following this incident, God led Elijah to a hidden place beside the brook Cherith, and he provided food for the prophet by sending ravens twice a day with meat and bread for him. At first Elijah drank water from the brook. But when his prophecy that the land of Israel would have no rain proved to be true, the brook dried up.

"Go to Zarephath now," said the Lord, who had not forgotten his servant. "There you will find a widow who will feed you." So Elijah left the brook where the ravens had fed him and walked to the city of Zarephath. The trip was a long one, for God was sending him to a city outside the kingdom of Israel.

Now Ahab was very angry with the prophet by this time, and he blamed Elijah rather than God for the dead crops and dried-up river beds in his country. He sent men out into every kingdom and nation he knew, seeking for Elijah. When he found the prophet he planned to kill him, so Elijah was forced to travel in secret.

At last he arrived in the country of Sidon and entered the gate of the city of Zarephath. There he saw a woman, the widow of whom God had spoken, gathering firewood.

"Will you bring me some water to drink?" Elijah asked her. As the woman left to get the water, he called after her, "Bring me a little piece of bread, too."

"I'm sorry," replied the woman, "but all I have in my house is a little bit of meal and oil. I was just gathering sticks to build a fire and make them into a cake for me and my son. When it is gone, we will have to starve, because there is no more."

"Do not worry about that," said Elijah to the poor woman, "Go ahead and make a cake for me, and make some for you and your son, too. The Lord God of Israel says that your jar of meal and pitcher of oil will never be empty during the time that there is no rain."

The woman went to her house and cooked the cakes; and just as Elijah had said, meal and oil remained in the containers. The prophet stayed in the woman's house for many days, and never did either vessel become empty.

One day, while Elijah was still at her house, the woman's son became very ill and died. She knew Elijah was a man who had miraculous powers, so she thought he had something to do with the boy's death.

"Why did you cause my son to die?" she asked in tears. "Is it because of some sin of mine?"

"Give me the boy," was Elijah's reply. He carried the child upstairs to his room and put him on the bed. Then he cried to God, "Let this child's soul come into him again." He stretched himself over the boy three times as if trying to give him life through the warmth of his own body.

God heard the prayer of Elijah and caused the child's life to return. He began breathing again and Elijah could feel his heart beating.

Carrying him down to the mother, Elijah said, "Look, your boy is alive!" The happy mother took her son into her arms and gazed at the prophet with wonder in her eyes. She said, "Now I know truly that you are a man of God."

I Kings 15–17

TRIAL BY FIRE

Three years after Elijah had spoken the prophecy to King Ahab, no rain had yet fallen on the land of Israel. The fields were parched and the crops brown and withered from the heat of the sun. No water ran in the stream and river beds, and no grass could be found to feed the starving cattle. The hungry people, too, were running out of food. Every day they hoped to see a cloud or mist in the air; but each day dawned as hot and dry as the one before, and the country became even more barren.

King Ahab, who had searched in vain for the prophet he thought was responsible for the sad condition of the country, was becoming desperate. He called Obadiah, a servant of high standing in his household, and said, "Let us go out into the country where the springs flow and see if we can find enough grass to keep some of our animals alive." So they went out in opposite directions searching for water.

At this time God spoke to Elijah, who was still staying with the widow in Zarephath. "Go to King Ahab," he said, "for I am going to send rain again."

As Elijah was returning to Israel to see the king, he met Obadiah. Now Obadiah was a good man who still feared God. At one time, when Queen Jezebel had been looking for some of the prophets of God to kill them, Obadiah had hidden them away in safety. When he saw Elijah approaching, Obadiah fell to the ground and said, "Can it be that you are my lord Elijah?"

"I am," replied the prophet. "You must go to Ahab and say, 'Elijah is here.' "

"Oh, I dare not do that," said Obadiah fearfully. "Ahab has been searching everywhere for you. If I go now and tell him you are here, the spirit of the Lord may carry you away while I am gone, and he will kill me."

Elijah promised, "As the Lord lives, I will show myself to Ahab today." So Obadiah went in search of Ahab; and when he had found him, the two returned to meet Elijah.

"Is it you, you troubler of Israel?" demanded Ahab when he saw the prophet.

Elijah responded, "You, not I, are the troubler of Israel. You have brought this evil on your country by worshiping idols." Then Elijah challenged Ahab to a contest. "Gather all the people of Israel at Mount Carmel and bring also the priests of Baal and Asherah."

Ahab agreed to the contest readily, and he sent messengers out into the country telling the people to assemble at Mount Carmel. When all had arrived at the mountain, Elijah stood up before them and spoke loudly. With eyes flashing, he demanded, "How long can you go about with two opinions? If the Lord is God, you should follow him; but if Baal is God, then follow him." Some of the people were ashamed when they heard Elijah, but no one said anything.

"I am the only prophet of the Lord here," Elijah continued, "but there are four hundred and fifty priests of Baal. Let us both ask our gods to send fire from heaven, and we will worship the one who sends it."

The people agreed this was a fair test. A bull was prepared and placed on the altar of Baal, with wood beneath it. Then, as Elijah had said for them to do, the priests began calling on their god to send fire. "O Baal, answer us!" they cried loudly. From morning until noon they shouted to their god, begging for fire.

At noon Elijah began to mock them. "Cry louder," he said to the frantic priests. "Your god may be thinking, or perhaps he is on a journey; or he may be sleeping and need to be awakened."

The priests did cry louder. They were desperate because they were receiving no reply and angry because Elijah was mocking them. They cut themselves with knives and raved on through the afternoon. When they finally gave up their frenzied, useless attempt, the altar of Baal looked just as it had many hours before. The wood and the sacrifice had not been touched by fire; there had been no answer to their cries.

"Come near to me," said Elijah to the solemn crowd of people. They helped him repair the altar of the Lord that had been torn down when the people had turned to idols. The bull was prepared and laid upon the wood and a trench was dug around the altar. Then Elijah ordered the people to pour water all over the sacrifice. This was done three times, until the bull and the wood were drenched and the trench was filled with water.

Elijah began to pray, "O Lord, God of Abraham, Isaac, and Israel, let it be known today that you are God in Israel and that I am your servant and am doing this at your will. Answer me, O Lord, so that these people may know that you are God and have turned their hearts back."

The people seemed very moved at these words, and as they listened not a sound could be heard. Some of the old people were remembering the time when they had worshiped the Lord before they had turned to idol gods. Many who were younger had never heard a prayer to the God of Israel, and they were touched by the quiet and humble attitude of the prophet.

As Elijah finished his prayer, the fire of God fell suddenly from the sky and consumed the altar in flames. Even the stones and the dust were burned up in the hot blaze, and not a drop of water remained in the trench. The people fell on their faces with one accord at the sight and cried out, "The Lord, he is God! The Lord, he is God!" At Elijah's orders, the people seized the fleeing priests of Baal and killed them. When they had done this, Elijah once again went up on the mountain and prayed. Soon a small cloud could be seen rising out of the sea. It became larger and larger, dark and heavy with rain; then the sound of a gathering wind could be heard. The people hurried toward their homes as drops of rain began to fall. *I Kings 18*

IN A STILL, SMALL VOICE

Queen Jezebel, infuriated by what Elijah had done on Mount Carmel, was now even more determined to have him killed. She sent a messenger to tell him that he would not live beyond the next day. Elijah left the city to go off into the wilderness and hide, feeling very discouraged in spite of the victory on Mount Carmel. He felt that Israel would never turn back to God as long as wicked Ahab and Jezebel ruled.

Elijah sat down under a tree to rest. He felt that everything he had done had been of no use and he asked God to let him die. "I am no better than any who went before me," he said dejectedly. Then, tired and hungry after his journey, he fell asleep.

As he slept an angel touched Elijah and said, "Arise and eat." Elijah found beside him a cake of meal and a jar of water. He ate as the angel had instructed and then lay down again. A second time the angel touched him, saying, "Arise and eat, or else the journey will be too hard for you." Elijah ate and drank until he was satisfied, and then he got up to leave, refreshed by his sleep and the food.

For forty days Elijah traveled on the strength of the food the Lord had sent him. Finally he arrived at a cave where he would live in safety. The word of the Lord came to him in this place and asked, "What are you doing here, Elijah?"

"I have served you faithfully, Lord, but all the people of Israel have forgotten you, torn down your altars, and killed your prophets. I am the only one left, and they are trying to kill me too."

"Go and stand on the mountain before the Lord," came the voice of God.

Elijah went to the mountain. As he did so, a mighty wind arose. It was so strong and fierce that it blew great pieces of rock off the mountain. But the Lord was not in the wind. Then a great earthquake rocked the mountain under Elijah's feet, but the Lord was not in the earthquake. After the earthquake came a fire which roared and crackled before Elijah's eyes, but still the Lord did not appear.

Watching all these demonstrations of power, Elijah understood the great strength that the Lord commanded. He knew that not even Ahab and Jezebel could stand against the God of Israel. Then a still, small voice came into Elijah's ear, and he knew this was the Lord speaking to him. "What are you doing here, Elijah?" asked the voice.

Elijah explained once more that he had spoken for the Lord but could not make the people listen. He said that he was the only one left who was faithful to God.

God spoke words of comfort to Elijah, telling him that Ahab would not be king of Israel much longer, and that Elijah was to have another prophet as a companion, one who would take over his work when he was gone. Then God told his servant that he was wrong in thinking that he stood alone and that there was no one else faithful in all Israel. "There are still seven thousand who have not yet bowed to Baal," he reassured the tired and worried prophet.

Elijah could hardly believe these words, but he was greatly encouraged. He went off immediately in search of the man who would be his companion, the one who would follow him in the difficult task of speaking for God.

I Kings 19

NABOTH'S VINEYARD

The Lord blessed the Israelites while Ahab was king, though Ahab remained a wicked man and refused to obey. When Israel fought against the kingdom of Syria, led by King Ben-hadad, the poor Israelite soldiers were badly outnumbered. But the Lord still loved his disobedient people, and he helped them win the battle.

Beside the palace of King Ahab was a vineyard owned by a man named Naboth. Ahab wanted this vineyard; he wanted to make it into a vegetable garden because it was near his palace. So he said to Naboth, "Give me your vineyard and I will give you a better one in its place; or, if you prefer, I will pay you money for it."

But Naboth had inherited this land from his ancestors, and under the Law of Moses, it was supposed to be kept within the family. He refused to sell it, saying, "The Lord forbid that I should give you the inheritance of my fathers."

Ahab was so disappointed that he went into his room, lay on his bed with his face to the wall, and pouted. When his wife Jezebel came in and said that dinner was served, Ahab refused to eat. Imagine a king pouting like a child over a small piece of land!

"Are you not the king?" asked Jezebel irritably. "Why do you sulk this way? Get up and eat your dinner—I will get the vineyard for you!"

Jezebel, having come from a heathen country, had no respect for the Law of Moses. She thought it was the king's right to seize any land he wanted, no matter who owned it. So she laid a wicked plot to get the land. According to her plan a celebration was to be held honoring Naboth. During the celebration two men were to charge Naboth with cursing God and the king.

The plot worked just as Jezebel had planned. Naboth was set on a high place among the people; and as a great number gathered together, two men came in and told the lie concerning Naboth. Then, according to the law, the people took Naboth outside the city and stoned him until he died.

When Jezebel received word of it, she said to her husband, "Go up and take possession of Naboth's vineyard, for he is dead."

Ahab walked down into the vineyard which he had desired and which was now his. Suddenly he sensed the presence of someone else among the vines and he turned to see Elijah, whom God had sent.

"Have you found me, O my enemy?" asked the startled king, who knew that he had done wrong.

"Yes, I have found you," the prophet answered, "because you have done evil in the Lord's sight. Now evil will come upon you. The dogs who licked Naboth's blood will lick yours, too. All of your sons will be killed—those who die in the city will be eaten by dogs and those who die in the country will be eaten by vultures. Jezebel, too, will be eaten by dogs."

There was never a king more wicked than Ahab, never a man in Israel who angered the Lord more. But in spite of the fact that Ahab had submitted to his wife and led the people into idolatry, he still was an Israelite and he knew deep within himself that he was evil in God's sight. When he heard the prophecy of Elijah, he knew God was powerful enough to make it come true. He began to tear his clothes and refused to eat or talk.

God saw Ahab's sorrow, and he said to Elijah, "Do you see how Ahab is humbling himself before me now? Because he is doing this I will not cause this tragedy to come about during his lifetime, but after he is dead I will bring trouble to his sons." *I Kings 21*

A CHARIOT OF FIRE

Elijah served the Lord for many years, sternly rebuking the kingdom of Israel for its evil and trying to persuade the people and their rulers to turn back to God. After a time, wicked King Ahab was killed in battle; and, as Elijah had said, dogs licked his blood on the same pavement where they had licked the blood of Naboth. But the new king was also evil and the Israelites made no improvement.

One day as Elijah and his younger companion, Elisha, were walking together, the word of the Lord came to Elijah telling him that it was time for him to be taken away. Elijah told Elisha that he must go to another city, but Elisha replied, "As the Lord lives and you live, I will not leave you."

The young man followed Elijah from one city to another. He knew God was going to take Elijah away from the earth, though he did not know how. When they reached a certain place beside the Jordan River, Elijah removed his coat, rolled it up, and hit the water with it. The water parted and the two walked over on dry ground.

On the other side of the Jordan, Elijah asked, "What would you like for me to do for you before I am taken away?"

Elisha replied, "I ask that I may have a double share of your spirit."

"You have asked for a hard thing," replied the old prophet, "but if you see me when I am being taken away, you will receive that for which you have asked."

They were walking on, talking together, when a chariot of fire and horses of fire suddenly appeared to them, blazing a trail from heaven to earth. The fiery chariot landed between the two men. Elijah climbed into it, and as swiftly as the chariot had descended, it ascended back up into heaven in a whirlwind.

"My father, my father! The chariots of Israel and its horsemen!" cried Elisha as he watched the scene that flashed before him. And then he was alone.

Elisha slowly picked up the coat of Elijah which had fallen at his feet. His teacher, whom he had respected and loved, would not be with him any longer. Elisha was sad to see him go, yet he had been thrilled at the wonderful scene in which God had taken the old prophet to be with him in heaven. Elijah had not even had to die as other men do; only one man before him, the old patriarch Enoch, had been taken into heaven before death came.

As Elisha thought about this, he walked back to the Jordan and rolled up Elijah's coat. Then he struck the water with it, saying, "Where is the Lord, the God of Elijah?" The waters parted, just as they had before, and

Elisha knew that he had been given a double portion of the spirit of the great prophet Elijah. *II Kings 2:1-14*

THE WOMAN FROM SHUNEM

Elisha took the place of Elijah as a prophet in the kingdom of Israel, but he was a far different man. Elijah had served God in a time of great wickedness and idolatry; and because it so often seemed that the people had forgotten God altogether, Elijah was often very bold and angry with them. Somehow, with his great spirit and determination, he was able to keep the Lord's name alive when the worship of Baal threatened to kill it.

Elisha also insisted that the people worship God and turn away from their heathen idols, but he was of a gentler spirit than the stern Elijah. Elisha always tried to persuade the people more calmly, but he was just as great a spokesman for the Lord in the kingdom of Israel as Elijah was. He performed many miracles, most of them out of kindness for other people.

Elisha often passed through a city named Shumen. Whenever he did, a kind woman who lived there always gave him food and a place to rest. One day the woman said to her husband, "Since this man of God comes here so often, let us fix a room upstairs for him to use." The husband agreed to the plan, and the room was prepared.

One day as Elisha was resting in the room, he called the woman and said, "You have been so kind to me. What can I do to show that I am thankful?"

The woman, who was quite wealthy, replied that she needed nothing. Then Elisha spoke in private to his servant, Gehazi, asking what he could do for the woman.

"Her husband is old," answered the servant, "and when he is gone she will have no one. She has no children."

Elisha knew then that nothing would make the woman happier than to have a son. He called to her again and said, "This time next year, you will have a son."

The woman was afraid to believe these words at first, but surely enough, the prophecy did come true. The next spring, a baby boy was born to her and her husband. They loved him dearly and were grateful to Elisha for his kindness.

One morning, when the little boy had grown big enough to go with his father into the fields, he was standing among the reapers in the hot sun. Suddenly he grabbed his head and cried out to his father, "Oh, my head! My head!" The father knew that the child was really in pain, and had probably had a sunstroke. He called to a servant, "Quickly! Carry him in to his mother."

The anxious mother held her dear son in her lap all morning, but she was unable to help him and about noon he died. She carried him sorrowfully up to the room Elisha always used and laid him on the bed. Then she ran to her husband and said, "Tell one of the servants to get an ass ready; I am going to see the prophet."

Elisha saw the woman from Shunem coming from a distance, and he told Gehazi to run ahead and inquire about her and her family. But the woman did not want to stop and answer the servant; she wanted to see Elisha right away. When she reached him she fell down sobbing at his feet. At first she could hardly speak for her grief; but Elisha, seeing that she was in great distress, waited. Finally she was able to cry out, "Did I ask you for a son? Was I not afraid to believe you would give me one?"

Elisha knew something was wrong with the boy who had given so much joy to his parents, and he wasted no time in hurrying toward the house.

When he walked into his room and saw the lifeless child lying on his bed, Elisha must have felt almost as grieved as the mother. He closed the door so that he was alone and then he lay down with his body over the smaller one. As he stretched himself out with his hands on the child's hands and his face on the child's face, he felt the small body begin to grow warmer. He got up and walked about in the room and then stretched himself out on the child again. All of a sudden a sneeze came from the one who had lain so still and quiet, and then six more sneezes.

"Come and take your son!" Elisha called to the breathless mother. Entering the room with great joy, she saw her little boy sitting on the bed and looking about, the glow of health on his cheeks. She fell at Elisha's feet again, this time in great and unspeakable joy. Then she lovingly took up her child and went out. *II Kings 4:1–37*

SEVEN DIPS IN THE JORDAN

In the time of Elisha, the commander of the army of Syria was a man named Naaman. The king of Syria looked on Naaman very favorably because Naaman was a fine general and had led the army to many victories against the Israelites. The kingdoms of Israel and Syria bordered on one another, and often small fights would occur between groups near this border even when the two countries were not at war. Once when some Syrian soldiers had made a raid into the northern part of Israel, a little Israelite girl had been carried back to be a servant of Naaman's wife.

Naaman was a very kind and brave man, but he was losing his health and strength day by day because he had a disease called leprosy. It was a terrible thing when a person got this disease, because there was no cure for it. Sores would appear all over a person's body and, eventually, he would die. Other people did not want to be around lepers for fear they would get the disease themselves.

All of Naaman's family was disturbed because he had this disease, and when the little Israelite slave girl learned about it, she was sorry, too. One day as she was waiting on Naaman's wife, she said, "If only my master could see the prophet who is in Israel. I know this man could cure him of his leprosy."

Naaman's family was so distressed because of his illness that they became interested in finding out about this prophet. Although they had never heard of a cure for leprosy, they were willing to take any chance that might make Naaman well again. When Naaman told the king about the girl's statement, he, too, was anxious to try to find the prophet. He sent Naaman to the king of Israel with a letter and many gifts.

When Naaman arrived at the palace of Joram, who was the king of Israel at this time, he gave Joram the letter from his own king. Naaman did not know where to find the prophet of whom the little girl had spoken, but he thought that surely the king could direct him.

The king read the letter and could not understand its strange request. "Am I God, that I can cure such a disease?" he asked in anger. "I can see that the king of Syria is only trying to stir up a quarrel!"

But Elisha somehow heard about the visitor at the king's court, and he sent word that Naaman was to come to him. Naaman gathered all his horses and chariots and traveled across the country to the house where the prophet was staying.

Elisha did not even come out of the house to greet Naaman. He sent a messenger out who spoke to the general as he sat in his elaborate chariot surrounded by fine horses and servants. "Go to the Jordan River and wash yourself seven times and you will be healed," said Elisha's messenger.

These words brought an angry frown to the face of Naaman and he ordered the driver of his chariot to drive on. "I thought the prophet would do some wonderful thing to cure me!" he said as he left. "Why, the rivers of my own country are better than the Jordan River. What good could it do me to wash there?" He thought that a man of his dignity and position should have received better treatment than Elisha had given him.

The servants of the general were disturbed to see him so angry, for he was usually a very kind and courteous man. They said to him, "Sir, if the prophet had commanded you to do some very great and difficult thing, would you not have done it? Why not do this simple thing that he has said for you to do?"

Naaman reconsidered and decided that he had been rash and that his servants were right. He had only wished for the prophet to make a grand show of the healing because he thought of himself as important. He ordered his driver to take him back to the Jordan.

The great general walked down into the water and dipped himself once, then again and again until he had done it seven times. When he looked down at his body, he found his skin was as smooth and soft as a baby's!

Naaman hurried to the house of Elisha, where he thanked the prophet many times. "I know there is no God in all the earth except the God of Israel," he said. "Now please accept these gifts of thanks from your servant."

But Elisha would not accept the gifts and money that Naaman offered. He had only wanted Naaman to learn about God and to know that it was God who had healed him. He had received the only reward he wanted when Naaman said that he would no longer pray to any god but the God of Israel. *II Kings 5:1–16*

THE FALL OF THE HOUSE OF AHAB

Elisha performed many other miracles besides the healing of Naaman, but these were not the most important part of his work. Elijah had predicted that the royal family that descended from Ahab would be destroyed. Elisha made that predication become a reality.

The last king of this family was Joram. Elijah's preaching had had some effect on him and he had commanded the people to stop worshiping Baal, the idol god of the Canaanites. But he did not go far enough in his fight against idolatry. He made no attempt to stop the worship of the golden calves Jeroboam and set up when the kingdom divided after the death of Solomon. For a time, Elisha gave Joram advice that helped him remain free of neighboring kings who wanted to bring Israel under their control. Perhaps he hoped that Joram would turn even from the golden calves to the true worship of God. At any rate, the time finally came when he realized it was time to make Elijah's prediction of doom come true.

Elisha chose just the right moment to take action. Joram had been wounded in a battle with Syria and had retired to the royal palace at Jezreel to recover from his wounds. While he was there, his nephew Ahaziah, who was the king of Judah, decided to pay his uncle a friendly visit.

When Elisha learned the two kings were together, he knew there was no time to lose. Quickly, he sent one of the prophets who worked with him to the territory near Ramoth Gilead, where the army of Israel had camped after the battle in which Joram was wounded. Following Elisha's orders, the young prophet went straight to Jehu, the commander of the army. He told him that God had chosen him to be the next king of Israel and that it was his duty to "strike down the house of Ahab" and "avenge on Jezebel the blood of the prophets."

Jehu wasted no time in following the prophet's orders. With the full support of the army, he set out for Jezreel, driving his chariot as fast as he could make his horses go. When the watchman in the tower of Jezreel saw him coming, he guessed that it might be someone bringing fresh news from the battlefront and sent a rider out to meet him. When the rider asked Jehu what news he had, the commander evaded the question and kept on racing toward the city. As he and his men drew closer, the watchman decided that it must be Jehu, for no one in the kingdom drove a chariot as fast and furiously as did this general.

If Jehu himself was bringing news from the front lines, then it must be important. King Joram decided that he and Ahaziah should go out personally to meet the commander. When their chariots met, Joram asked, "Do you have news of peace, Jehu?" To this, Jehu answered, "How can there be peace in this land, as long as the sins of your wicked mother Jezebel go unpunished?"

Immediately, Joram saw what was happening. With a shout, he told Ahaziah to turn the chariot around and head back for the city. But it was too late. Jehu's bowmen filled the air with arrows. Joram was shot through the heart and died instantly. Ahaziah was fatally wounded, but he managed to escape to his own territory before finally dying.

Jehu's next victim was the wicked queen Jezebel, who had been living in Jezreel since the death of her husband Ahab. Even in the face of certain death, Jezebel demonstrated the fearlessness that had made her wickedness such a threat to the nation of Israel. Instead of going into a frenzy or panic, she calmly painted her face and fixed her hair while she waited for Jehu to arrive at the palace. As his chariot entered the gates, she leaned out of the window and called to him sarcastically, "Is it you, you murderer of your master?" Without bothering to reply, Jehu ordered two of the servants of the palace to throw her out of the upstairs window. Apparently without objecting, they did as they were told and the horses trampled her broken body. Then, showing that the blood in his veins ran cold, Jehu stepped over her broken body and went inside the palace to eat his lunch. Later, when they came out to bury her, all they found were her skull, her feet, and the palms of her hands. Just as Elijah had prophesied, the dogs had eaten the body of Jezebel within the walls of Jezreel.

Many would have been satisfied with killing two kings and a queen. But

Jehu was just getting started. The speed and cold-blooded efficiency with which he had killed Joram, Ahaziah, and Jezebel so shocked the people of Israel that they did not dare question anything he did. Like sheep, they joined with him and carried out every order he issued. Within a matter of days, seventy of King Joram's sons were slain. Then, everyone who had any close ties with the family of Ahab was slain, first in Jezreel, then in Samaria, the capital of Israel. Finally, Jehu summoned a great meeting of all the worshipers of the gods Jezebel had brought into the country. He pretended to be a worshiper of these gods himself, but once the worshipers had gathered, he commanded his soldiers to kill them with their swords as they knelt to praise their gods. At last, Jehu's bloody purge was ended and all traces of the evil reign of the family of Ahab had been removed. *II Kings 9–10*

QUESTIONS: 1. *Who was the king of Israel during Elijah's lifetime? What was he like?* 2. *How did Elijah survive the famine?* 3. *What brought Elijah back to Israel?* 4. *Who participated in the "trial by fire"? What was its outcome?* 5. *How did God comfort Elijah?* 6. *Who was Naboth? Why was King Ahab angry with him?* 7. *How did Jezebel do away with Naboth?* 8. *What punishment did Elijah prophesy would befall Ahab and his family?* 9. *Who became Elijah's companion and student?* 10. *How did Elijah leave the earth?* 11. *How did Elisha know that he was to take his teacher's place?* 12. *What service did the woman of Shunem perform for Elisha? How did the prophet repay her kindness?* 13. *How did Naaman hear of an Israelite prophet?* 14. *Why did Naaman seek the help of a prophet?* 15. *How was Naaman finally cured of leprosy? How did he react?* 16. *Who was chosen by God to replace Ahab's family as ruler of Israel?* 17. *How did Jehu accomplish the overthrow of the house of Ahab?*

Kings and Prophets

THE SHEPHERD OF TEKOA

After Jehu completed his dramatic and bloody purge of Ahab's wicked family, he took the throne of Israel for himself, establishing a dynasty that was to last almost a hundred years. In the early years of his reign, both Israel and Judah, the southern kingdom, were in desperate circumstances. Syria and Assyria attacked Israel and forced her to pay an enormous tax, or tribute. Although Judah was not bothered quite so much by foreign invaders, she was weakened by troubles within. By the middle of the eighth century B.C., however, Judah had settled her problems and Syria and Assyria had difficulties that made them release Israel.

These circumstances enabled both kingdoms to build up a level of prosperity that came closer to that which existed during Solomon's time. In Judah the king was Uzziah. The king of Israel was named Jeroboam II. Jeroboam did not abandon the worship of the calves the first Jeroboam had begun, but he was a most capable ruler in other ways.

Naturally, the people of both Israel and Judah felt that times were good. They were rich and growing richer, and they knew that God could be counted on to raise them to even greater heights. But not everyone felt that way. Two who strongly disagreed were the great prophets Amos and Hosea.

Amos was a native of the tiny village of Tekoa, on the edge of the wilderness of Judah, south of Jerusalem. He was not a preacher by profession. Instead, he was a herdsman and a "dresser of sycamore trees." The sycamore trees in Palestine bear a fruit that is something like a fig. These figs have to be punctured and pinched before they will ripen into a pleasant tasting food. This was Amos' job. Despite this, however, Amos was far from a "country bumpkin." His writings show that he had come into close contact with the large cities of Palestine and that he knew the habits and attitudes of the city dwellers he was addressing. But even more than that, they show that Amos was a man who was marvelously open to the will of God and who could relate that will to his hearers in a striking, vivid way.

Although he was a native of Judah, Amos did most of his preaching in the northern kingdom of Israel. When he first began to preach, the people of Israel were probably delighted at what he had to say, for he began by announcing that God was going to bring down severe punishment on several of Israel's neighbors. Then, as they began to nudge each other and smile smugly, he began to lash out at Israel.

He told them it was true that God had chosen them to be his special people. But this did not give them the right to do anything they pleased. On the contrary, it meant they had a special responsibility to do his will. Instead of saying, "Because you are my chosen people I will pay no attention to your sins and continue to bring you prosperity," God was saying, "Because you are my chosen people, I will punish you even more severely for your sins." To make sure no one misunderstood what he was talking about, Amos vividly described the sins of which they were guilty.

First of all, Amos attacked the mistreatment of the poor by the strong and the rich. He said to them, "You sell righteous men into slavery just so you can get a little more money in your pocket. You exchange a needy human being for a pair of shoes! While women and children starve in the shadows of your luxurious houses, you lie on beds of ivory listening to music and drinking wine."

The class of people who were most guilty of these heartless acts were the rich merchants of Israel. They kept the Sabbath, because it was "good business" to make a religious show, but they fidgeted all day long, hardly able to wait until they could get back to cheating their helpless customers. To make matters worse, their wives encouraged them in their dishonest ways. To them Amos said; "You cows are enjoying yourselves now, trampling the poor and goading your husbands into bringing you wine and jewelry, but the day is coming when God will lead you out of Isreal with hooks in your noses."

Next, Amos attacked their insincere religion: "You think God will be pleased by all your sacrifices and complicated rituals, but you are badly mistaken. Your worship is offensive to him, and will always be, as long as you continue to live as you are now living. Do not try to fool God with sacrifices and songs. Instead, let justice roll down like waters, and righteousness like an everflowing stream."

After Amos condemned the hypocrisy of the Israelites, he warned them that a day of judgment was coming. The prosperous days of King Jeroboam II and his sons were numbered. It was simply a matter of time until Israel would fall to an invader.

Eventually this kind of straightforward preaching got Amos into trouble. The priest at the temple at Bethel, where the prophet had spoken these words, sent word to the king that Amos was a part of a plot to overthrow the government. Probably because Jeroboam II instructed him to, the priest then told Amos to go back to his home in Judah. He also accused Amos of preaching for money. This made Amos angry. He was not a professional prophet, as some were. He was a sheepherder and a fig-grower. But when he saw how bad the situation had become in Israel, he could not help but speak out against it. Israel, he said, was like a basket of ripe fruit. Right now, it was pretty to look at, but it would not be long until it would be rotten and fit for nothing but the garbage heap. A day was coming when God would judge his people and unless Israel repented, and repented quickly, that day would be a terrible one for her.

But not all that Amos had to say was bad. Like the great prophets that followed him, he promised that even if the nation were destroyed, God would still keep the wonderful promises he had made to Abraham and his descendants. He would save a small "remnant" from destruction and would bring them back to the land of Canaan to be the beginning of a new nation. *Amos*

AN UNHAPPY MARRIAGE

Another man who was preaching God's word at this time was the prophet Hosea. God gave Hosea a much more difficult assignment than he had given to Amos. All Amos had to do was announce that God was going to punish Israel. Hosea had to explain why. The reason for the punishment that was coming was not that God hated Israel, or that he wanted to see her suffer. It was because he loved her! By punishing her, he hoped to win her back from the false gods she was serving. It was as if God were a loving husband and Israel were his unfaithful wife. He could not allow her to chase after other gods. Neither could he simply forgive her without punishing her. But he was always ready to welcome her back into his loving arms. Not many men could have preached this message and sounded like they meant it. The reason Hosea was perfectly suited for the assignment was because he had a wife like Israel.

Hosea was married to a woman who seems to have done everything she could to hurt him. Soon after they were married, she turned from him to other men. According to the Law, Hosea had every right to divorce her and look for a wife who would be faithful to him. Instead, because he loved her so deeply, he provided for her and protected her, even while she was seeking new lovers. Finally, her sin became so terrible that something simply had to be done. He still loved her, but before he would allow her to come back into his home, she would have to be punished for her sins. Hopefully, this punishment would make her see her error and cause her to realize how thankful she ought to be to her longsuffering husband.

It is easy to see how Hosea's marriage was very much like God's relationship with Israel. God had loved Israel dearly, and still did, for that matter. The early days of their "marriage" had been extremely happy, but those days had long since passed. Again and again she had forsaken the true God for idols of wood and stone. Again and again God had forgiven Israel and taken her back. But now, her sin was so great that there had to be a period of separation and punishment. When that was over, though, and she had renounced her worthless "lovers," the past would be forgiven and forgotten, and they could begin a new and much better life together.

Just a few years after Amos and Hosea stopped prophesying, their words came true in an awful way. The armies of the great Assyrian empire swept out of the Northeast and overran the northern kingdom of Israel. The Israelites fought bravely, but the capital city of Samaria was destroyed and over 27,000 Israelites were taken captive back to Assyria. There the Assyrian king mixed them in with people he had captured from other nations, and the ten tribes of the Northern Kingdom disappeared from the pages of history.

Hosea

AN UNWILLING PROPHET

During the time of Amos and Hosea, a new nation was arising in the East that was more powerful than any other nation had ever been. That nation was Assyria. As the mighty Assyrians began to swallow up the smaller and weaker nations around them, tales of the glory of the Assyrian empire began to circulate all over the world. Men talked of her bold military leaders, and her strange forms of religion. Nineveh, her capital city, became a symbol of power and might, of greatness and glory. And to those who feared they were about to be overtaken by the Assyrians, Nineveh became a symbol of evil. One man who thought of Nineveh in this way was the prophet Jonah.

One day God called Jonah, who seems to have been a prophet of the Northern Kingdom, and told him to go to Nineveh. "The people of Nineveh," God said, "have become so wicked that I can no longer accept their behavior. Go and preach to them. Tell them they must repent of their wickedness immediately or I will destroy them."

Some men might be happy to have an opportunity to serve the Lord, but not Jonah. Jonah could scarcely believe that God was going to give the Assyrians a chance to escape his anger. They deserved no such opportunity. They were wicked people, opposed to God and to his chosen people. At that very moment, they were probably planning to attack Israel. Surely God did not mean for Jonah to waste his time on people like that!

But deep in his heart, Jonah knew that God would not give such a command unless he meant it. His conscience began to trouble him. He did not want to disobey, but neither did he want to preach to the people of Nineveh. So, Jonah decided he would run away from God. He would go far away, to a place where God could not find him. Instead of going to Nineveh, he set out in the opposite direction, heading toward the Mediterranean Sea. When he reached the seacoast town of Joppa, he boarded a merchant ship that was sailing to a distant port. Surely God would not follow him there.

Not long after the ship left Joppa, God hurled a terrible storm over the sea. The ship tossed and rolled as great waves broke over its deck. The sailors feared that if this kept up much longer, the ship would begin to break apart.

Loran Raymond Jones

JONAH IN NINEVEH

Jonah 3:1–10

Loran Raymond Jones

HOSEA BUYS GOMER OUT OF SLAVERY

Hosea 3:1–5

Loran Raymond Jones

JEREMIAH'S GRIEF AT THE FALL OF JERUSALEM

Jeremiah 39:1–18

Loran Raymond Jones

DANIEL IN THE LION'S DEN

Daniel 6:4–23

In an attempt to prevent this, they threw all the goods overboard so that the load would be as light as possible. And, because they were religious men, at least in some sense of the word, they began to pray to their gods.

While all this was going on, Jonah was asleep in his room below deck. When the captain of the ship learned of this, he went down and woke him up roughly. "How can you sleep when all of our lives are in danger?" he asked. "Do your part, man! Pray to your God to save us. Perhaps he can somehow help us."

As the storm roared on, the sailors began to suspect that someone on the ship had committed a great sin, and that the storm was being sent as a punishment. To discover who the guilty person was, they cast lots, and the lots showed that Jonah was responsible for the storm.

"Who are you?" they demanded. "What is your occupation? Where do you come from? Who are your people? What have you done to bring this storm on us?"

Jonah explained to them that he was a Hebrew and that he was running away from a task God had given him. They asked him, "What shall we do to make the storm quiet down?" Jonah was ashamed that he had put their lives in danger, so he told them frankly, "You must throw me into the sea. Only then will God still the winds and the waves."

The sailors were good men. They did not want to kill Jonah just to save their own lives. They rowed hard to bring the ship back into land, but it was no use. Finally, as the sea grew even rougher, they threw Jonah over the side, after praying to God to forgive them if they were killing an innocent man. Almost immediately, the sea grew calm. At this, the astounded sailors fell on their knees and worshipped the Lord.

This was the end of the storm, but it was not the end of Jonah. As soon as he plunged into the water, God sent a great fish to swallow him alive. For three days and nights, Jonah lived in the wretched darkness of the fish's belly. Then, suddenly, the fish opened its huge mouth and vomited Jonah onto the dry land.

As he stood on the beach drying himself off and examining his body for injuries, Jonah heard God's voice coming to him again: "Go to Nineveh and tell the people there to repent." Jonah had learned his lesson. He would never try to escape from God again. He hurried as quickly as he could to Nineveh.

When he reached the great city, Jonah began to preach in the streets to anyone who would listen to him. "Unless you turn from your wickedness, the Lord is going to destroy your city."

Surprisingly, the people of Nineveh not only believed Jonah, they did something about it. They proclaimed a day of fasting and put on clothes usually reserved for mourning, to show how sorry they were for their sins. Even the king himself was affected by Jonah's preaching and joined in the public show of repentance.

When God saw that the men of Nineveh were sorry, and that they apparently wanted to change their ways, he also changed his mind and decided not to punish them.

All this would have delighted most preachers, but it made Jonah angry and sulky. He was disappointed that God wanted to save these foreign people. He said to God, "I knew you were a merciful God. I knew you would forgive them if they showed even the slightest signs of repentance. That is why I did not want to come to Nineveh in the first place. I would rather see Nineveh destroyed." And with this, he marched gloomily out of the city and built himself a little shack on the edge of town. There he sat down to wait and see what would happen to the city, perhaps hoping that God would decide to go ahead and destroy it as originally planned.

While Jonah sat there sulking, God taught him a valuable lesson. First, he caused a large plant to grow beside Jonah's little shelter. It had big leaves that threw a good shade over Jonah and protected him from the hot sun. Then one day, a worm attacked Jonah's plant and it withered and died. On that particular day, the sun was very hot and a sultry east wind made the day even more miserable. Jonah was so uncomfortable that he told God he would rather die than suffer any more.

Then God spoke to foolish Jonah: "How can you cry over a little plant that came and went in one day and then show no pity for a great city where thousands of children live?"

The story of Jonah ends with these words, but it is probably safe to say that what God said made Jonah realize that people are more precious than anything else in the world, and that God cares for every person, even those who have never had a chance to learn about him. Most of the Old Testament tells of God's concern for His chosen people, the Israelites, but the story of Jonah shows us that he is a God of all nations and that everyone falls under the scope of his love. *Jonah*

"HOLY, HOLY, HOLY"

As long as the kingdom of Israel was in existence, it received far more attention than the Southern Kingdom. Its rulers were more wicked, its sins more dramatic, its prophets more colorful. Now that the Assyrians had destroyed it and dragged its people off into captivity, the kingdom of Judah was thrust into the forefront. Its kings and prophets became the chief figures in the Biblical story.

The first of the great prophets of Judah was Isaiah. In sharp contrast to Elijah and Amos, Isaiah was a cultured gentleman who enjoyed a favored place at the royal court. As a result, he was constantly involved in political matters. He not only explained what was happening and foretold what was going to happen; he took a leading role in trying to make them happen.

We do not know just when Isaiah began to prophesy, but the experience that set him apart as the chief prophet in Judah occurred "in the year that King Uzziah died," a few years before the fall of the northern kingdom. One day while Isaiah was in the Temple in Jerusalem, he had a marvelous vision. He saw God sitting on a throne, "high and lifted up." The glory of the Lord filled the sacred temple and above him there were seraphim—fabulous creatures with heads of eagles, bodies of lions, and six wings. As Isaiah stared in awe, one of these creatures called out: "Holy, holy, holy is the Lord of hosts; the whole earth is full of his glory."

The creature's unearthly voice shook the foundations and caused the Temple to fill with smoke. The sights and sounds and smells and tremblings of this frightening experience completely terrified Isaiah, causing him to cry out: "Woe is me, for I am undone. I am a man of unclean lips, and I dwell in the midst of a people of unclean lips; and now my eyes have seen the King, the Lord of Hosts."

As if in reply to Isaiah's confession that he was a man "of unclean lips," one of the seraphim took a red-hot coal from the altar and touched it to the prophet's lips. This was a sign that his sins had been forgiven and that his lips were now purified for the task of speaking God's word to the people. Isaiah understood what was expected of him, for when the Lord said, "Whom shall I send, and who will go as my representative?", he answered, "Here am I; send me."

Isaiah 6

THE SIGN OF THE CHILD

Isaiah's first important assignment came during the reign of King Ahaz. This was still before the fall of Israel, and the northern kingdom had teamed up with the kingdom of Syria and was threatening to attack Judah. Naturally, Ahaz was worried. How could he possibly defend his kingdom against both Israel and Syria? Probably Ahaz was willing to listen to any advice he could get and was anxious to hear what Isaiah had to say. Unfortunately, when he heard the prophet's advice, it did not make much sense to him. Instead of advising him to hire the Egyptians to help him, or to try to make peace with Syria and Israel, Isaiah told Ahaz to "be quiet and fear not." God was going to destroy both Syria and Israel before they had a chance to harm anyone.

Ahaz wanted to believe Isaiah, but he could not. It was easy to trust in God during peacetime, but when the enemy was threatening, it seemed much safer to try to arrange for an army. Perhaps he should try to make some kind of agreement with the king of Assyria. When Isaiah learned of what Ahaz was planning, he confronted the king once more. "I want to prove to you that you have nothing to fear from Syria and Israel," he said. "Just ask for anything you would like the Lord to perform as a sign that he will protect you. No matter how difficult a thing you request, he will do it."

Ahaz replied, "I do not wish to put God to a test." This sounded good, but Isaiah knew the king was not being truthful. He did not want a sign from God because he did not want to follow Isaiah's advice.

Thoroughly irritated with the king, Isaiah said, "Well, you are going to get a sign, whether you want it or not. A young woman is going to conceive and bear a son. Before that child is old enough to know the difference between good and bad, both the nations you fear will be destroyed."

If Ahaz had waited, he would have found that Isaiah was telling the truth. But he did not wait. He simply did not have enough faith to keep calm and place his trust in the Lord. Instead, he stripped the holy Temple of its rich treasures and sent them to the king of Assyria, begging him to attack Syria and Israel. Not long afterward, the Assyrian army destroyed the Syrian capital of Damascus and, as we saw in the last chapter, overran northern Israel and carried its people into captivity.

Ahaz had escaped the disaster he feared, but he had paid a terrible price. He had not only stripped the Temple of its treasures; he had stripped Judah of its independence, for now he was at the mercy of the Assyrians.

In his stubborn refusal to listen to Isaiah, the king had also robbed himself of the prophet's valuable counsel. Isaiah was so disgusted over what Ahaz had done that he preached no more at the royal court as long as the stubborn king reigned. *Isaiah 7–8*

GOOD KING HEZEKIAH

When King Ahaz died, his son Hezekiah became king of Judah. Hezekiah was one of the best kings Judah ever had. He was thoroughly devoted to God and he was determined to do all that he could to regain the freedom his father had surrendered to the Assyrians. Little Judah was no match for the mighty Assyrians, but during the reign of Hezekiah, she gained much stature.

Soon after Hezekiah became king, a group of small nations around Judah decided to band together and rebel against the Assyrians. The king of Egypt, who was an enemy of the Assyrians, promised to send troops whenever the fighting started. Hezekiah must have been tempted to join these rebels; but Isaiah, who reentered public life after the death of Ahaz, convinced him that to do so would be foolish. Isaiah knew from past experience that the Egyptians were deceitful and would back down on their promise when the Assyrians struck. For the better part of three years, he walked around naked and barefoot, declaring that the Egyptians and those who trusted in them would be defeated by the Assyrians. Fortunately for Judah, Hezekiah listened to the prophet, for when the Assyrians attacked, Egypt did go back on its word and the rebellion was unsuccessful.

Hezekiah is best known as a great reformer. As early as the first year of his reign, he began to remove pagan practices that had crept into Judah's religion. During the reign of his father, Ahaz, things had gotten so bad that the Temple was not even being used anymore. Hezekiah appointed crews of workmen to clean out the Temple. They tore down all the idols and other pagan objects that had been brought into the Temple and threw them into a nearby brook. They wrecked the shrines of the Canaanite idols, Baal and Asherah.

When the Temple was thoroughly purified, services were begun once again, even though there were not enough faithful priests left in Jerusalem to fill all of the positions.

How thrilling the first service must have been! Musicians were stationed all around the temple. At the moment the burnt-offering was placed on the altar, the trumpet sounded and the people began to sing the psalms of David. They continued to sing until the offering was burned up. And then, the king and the princes, and the priests and the Levites bowed down and worshiped the Lord.

A few years later, the nations around Judah began planning another revolt. This time, Hezekiah was right in the middle of the planning. He knew the Assyrian king, Sennacherib, would be a tough enemy and he set about to strengthen Jerusalem in every way he could. He repaired the city walls and improved the defenses in key areas. He ordered a large supply of weapons made and organized the ordinary citizens into fighting divisions. He sent the people out into the hills and plains to stop up springs and brooks, so that the Assyrian army would have trouble finding water. And he made sure Jerusalem would have enough water by digging an underground tunnel to a large spring outside the city walls.

Isaiah was bitterly angry that Hezekiah had joined the rebellion, and he made his anger plain. "This agreement you have made with your neighbors," Isaiah said, "is a covenant with death. Even if the Egyptians deliver the help they are promising—and there is little reason to believe they will—you will not stand a chance against the powerful Assyrians. The Egyptians are men, not gods. You are foolish to think they can help you. Your only hope is to trust in God."

These biting words had little effect on Hezekiah. He was a righteous man, but he was so involved with the revolution that he rejected Isaiah's counsel. Unfortunately for Judah, Isaiah had been right again. In due time Sennacherib attacked the rebel forces. Surprisingly, the Egyptians did keep their promise this time, but it was no use. The Assyrians could not be stopped. Sennacherib did not destroy Jerusalem, but he trapped Hezekiah inside the city "like a bird in a cage" and forced him to pay him an enormous sum of money and to send many precious treasures, including Hezekiah's own daughters, back to the Assyrian capital.

A few years later, Sennacherib returned to Palestine and threatened once more to destroy Jerusalem. While he was busy attacking the nearby city of Lachish, the Assyrian king sent his chief assistant, who is called the Rabshakeh, to talk to the people of Jerusalem. When the Rabshakeh reached Jerusalem, he did not try to enter the city, but stood outside and shouted to the people who gathered on top of the walls.

"Why is Hezekiah so confident?" he asked. "Does he think bold words will defeat our powerful army? Is he so foolish that he is depending on Egypt? Egypt is like a rotten walking-cane that will splinter and pierce the hand of anyone who leans on it." Then the Rabshakeh began to poke fun at Hezekiah's army: "Sennacherib will give you two thousand horses free of charge if you can round up enough men to mount them." Then, in a claim that was certain to upset the people of the holy city, the Rabshakeh said, "You think that God is on your side, but I tell you that God himself has ordered Sennacherib to attack Jerusalem."

Hezekiah had not come out to listen to the Rabshakeh, but his chief assistants had; and they were horrified by what they heard and by the effect they feared these words might have on the people. They begged him to stop talking this way. But this merely urged him on, and he raised his voice once again. "Do not let Hezekiah deceive you," he cried to the people. "If you follow him, you will be utterly destroyed. If you want to live peaceably and enjoy a good, quiet life, then surrender right now. Do not depend on your God. He cannot help you now."

These words must have worried the people of Jerusalem a great deal. But they were loyal to their king and no one dared suggest that they surrender.

When his officers told him what the Rabshakeh had said, Hezekiah was terribly upset. He knew that much of what the Assyrians had said was true. Even if the Egyptians did help, there was little real chance they could defeat Sennacherib. Finally, Hezekiah decided that he needed to talk to Isaiah. Perhaps the prophet would know what to do.

Before this, you remember, Isaiah had always told Hezekiah that it was foolish to resist the Assyrians. But this time, surprisingly, he advised him to stand his ground and make the invaders come after him. The king of Assyria had gone too far when he boasted that not even God could stop him. Now God would show him he was still in control of the world.

Not long afterward, Sennacherib moved his troops into position to attack Jerusalem. That night, as the Assyrian army slept, a wave of death swept through the camp, killing thousands of the enemy soldiers. A poet has described the scene in this way:

> For the Angel of Death spread his wings on the blast,
> And breathed in the face of the foe as he passed.
> And the eyes of the sleepers waxed deadly and chill,
> And their hearts but once heaved, and forever grew still.

Sennacherib returned home without striking a single blow against Jerusalem. It was a stunning victory for God and his prophet. Hezekiah, the king, had trusted in the word of the Lord and the city of Jerusalem had been saved, just as Isaiah had promised. *II Kings 18–20*

IDOLS IN THE TEMPLE

Hezekiah, one of the best of the kings of Judah, was succeeded by his son Manasseh, who was one of the worst. Manasseh was only twelve years old when his father died. Perhaps Hezekiah had been too busy with the affairs of the kingdom to train the boy properly. Or it may be that the young king's advisers were wicked men. For some reason, Mannasseh seemed determined from the start to do things exactly opposite from the way his father had done them.

Manasseh encouraged the worship of practically every idol he could think of. He reopened the worship of Baal, the chief god of the Canaanites. He not only made an image of the Canaanite goddess Asherah, but he set this image up right in the Temple of God! In the courts of the Temple he built altars where people could worship the sun, the moon, and various stars. And worse than all these, he sacrificed his own son as a burnt offering to an idol-god named Moloch.

The Bible tells us that Manasseh shed much innocent blood. Probably, much of this blood belonged to faithful worshipers of God who criticized the young king for his sinful religious practices. The Bible does not go into detail on this matter, but the Jews had a tradition that said that one of Manasseh's victims was the prophet Isaiah. We can imagine that Isaiah must have opposed Manasseh. According to the tradition, Manasseh became angry with the old prophet and had his men place him inside a hollow tree and then saw him in two.

Late in Manasseh's life, the king of Assyria sent men to arrest him and bring him to prison in Assyria. We do not know what he had done to cause the king of Assyria to do this, but we do know that the event had a great effect on Manasseh. While he was in prison, Manasseh called on the true God to help him. Soon afterward, he was released from prison and allowed to return to Judah. This convinced him that he should turn from the idols to the Lord, and during the last years of his reign, he tried to undo the damage he had done earlier. But it was no use. The sins of his youth were too much to overcome. It was too late to win very many of the people back.

These years of Manasseh's reign were the darkest Judah had ever known. Assyria had controlled the land with an iron hand. Morals and religion had reached a low point. It seemed that Judah was about to become just one more idolatrous nation, like the nations about her. But suddenly, the picture changed dramatically. Assyria was attacked and finally beaten by the Medes and the Babylonians. And Judah got a new king. His name was Josiah.

II Kings 21; II Chronicles 33

THE BEST OF KINGS

Josiah was Manasseh's grandson, but he had nothing in common with his grandfather, except that he, too, became king at a very early age. Josiah was only eight when he took the throne. Naturally, he was much too young to rule a kingdom, so the actual work of ruling was done by his advisers. Unlike the men who had led Manasseh into idolatry, Josiah's advisers were righteous, god-fearing men who encouraged the young king "to seek the God of David his father."

As soon as he was old enough to have the confidence and support of the people, Josiah began to cleanse Jerusalem and Judah of everything that had to do with idolatry. An important part of this great reform was the cleaning out of the Temple of God, which Manasseh had turned into a place of idolatry. One of the priests who was helping with the cleaning was poking around in one of the many rooms of the Temple when he found a book. It was a book that contained the Law of Moses, telling the people how they should worship God. When Josiah read the book for himself, he was filled both with happiness and with fear. He was happy, because now he knew what God expected of his people. But he was afraid, because the book also told what God would do to his people if they did not obey his law, and Josiah knew they had not been obeying it. He was afraid the wrath of God might fall on Judah at any moment. When the book was shown to an old prophetess named Huldah, she told Josiah that he was correct in being afraid. Judah had been disobedient, and she would be punished; but, because Josiah was righteous and sincere, the kingdom would be spared as long as he lived.

Josiah began immediately to bring the people back to the worship of God. First he called them together and made a covenant with them in which they promised with all their hearts to keep the commandments found in the Book of the Law. Then, they finished the job of ridding Jerusalem of everything having to do with idolatry. They burned the image of Asherah that had been standing in the Temple and threw its ashes in a graveyard. They cleared the Temple court of all the articles connected with the worship of the sun, moon, and stars. They tore down shrines and altars that had been standing since the days of Solomon. And they destroyed the fireplace where children had been offered to Moloch. Finally, after the task at Jerusalem was completed, the zealous priests roamed all over Palestine breaking idols and tearing down shrines, including the shrine at Bethel, the place where Jeroboam had first set up the golden bulls.

For the rest of Josiah's reign, Judah enjoyed peace and prosperity, and the people loved their righteous king. Even when he had ruled for thirty years, he was still a young man, and they dreamed of many more glorious years. But then, tragedy struck. The Egyptian army was passing through

Judah on its way to fight the Babylonians. For some reason, Josiah decided to try to stop them. The Egyptian Pharaoh, whose army was much more powerful than the army of Judah, was not really frightened, but he did not want to have to stop and fight, so he tried to persuade Josiah to leave him alone. Unfortunately, Josiah would not listen. He attacked the Egyptians near the town of Megiddo. The battle was brief and, for the people of Judah, disastrous. An Egyptian arrow killed the finest king Judah had known. When he died, Judah also began to die. *II Kings 22–23*

A PERSECUTED PREACHER

We noticed, you will remember, that Josiah had been blessed with wise and righteous advisers. One of these advisers was the great prophet Jeremiah. Jeremiah was the chief prophet in Judah for over half a century. He began prophesying shortly after Josiah became king, and he continued to prophesy for almost thirty years after Josiah died. Jeremiah must have been pleased with many of the things Josiah did; in fact, he was probably partly responsible for many of them. But there was little to please him in the years after Josiah's death. These were years of extreme tragedy in Judah, and no one suffered any more than Jeremiah.

The first thing that made Jeremiah sad and angry was the attitude of Josiah's son, Jehoiakim, who became king after his father's death. Jehoiakim did not care whether his people had enough to eat, or whether they were worshiping God properly. All he cared about was enjoying the privileges of being king. Naturally, the people followed his example. If the king was not interested in worshiping God, why should they be?

Jehoiakim's attitude disgusted Jeremiah, and the courageous prophet wasted no time in telling him so. "You know nothing about being a king," he said. "You think the worth of a king can be measured by the size of his palace and the beauty of his robes. But you are wrong. The best king is not the man who lives in the finest palace or who wears the most expensive clothing. The best king is the king who truly cares for his people. Your father cared for the people, and when he died the streets of Jerusalem were filled with mourning. You care only for yourself; when you die, the people will weep for you no more than they would for a dead donkey."

Jehoiakim was not the only one Jeremiah attacked. He often went to the Temple and spoke to the crowds that gathered there. On one occasion he told them: "You think God will protect you because you have the book of the Law that Josiah found in the temple. Do not fool yourselves. Just having the book will do you no good. You must obey what it says. If you do not, then you will surely be punished."

Another time, he led the leaders of Jerusalem out to the city dump. There he took a clay pot and broke it into pieces. "The time is coming soon," he warned, "when Jerusalem will be like this clay pot—shattered beyond mending and good for nothing but to be tossed on the garbage heap."

Naturally, this kind of preaching did not make Jeremiah popular with the king or the people. He was beaten and put in stocks outside one of the gates of the Temple. His own relatives and many of his friends refused to have anything to do with him. Again and again Jeremiah regretted that God had ever called him to be a prophet. Finally, he became so downhearted that he cursed the day of his birth and charged God with tricking him into becoming a prophet just so he could torment him. But deep down, Jeremiah knew this was not true. He knew that God had chosen him because there was a job to be done and someone had to do it. And he also knew that no matter how much he had to suffer, he could not keep from preaching the word of the Lord. He said, "God's word is like a burning fire in my heart. I try to hold it in, but I cannot."

Because of the anger of the king and the people, Jeremiah did not dare go to the Temple in person. Instead, he preached his sermons to his friend and secretary, Baruch, who wrote them down on a scroll. When the scroll was filled, Baruch took them and read them to the people. When the princes heard these sermons, they were frightened by Jeremiah's warnings of doom and they decided that King Jehoiakim must also hear them.

Jehoiakim did not frighten easily. He agreed to listen to the reading of the scroll, but only to have a chance to show how little he cared about what Jeremiah had to say. As his servant unrolled and read a section of eight or ten inches, Jehoiakim would take his penknife and cut the section off and throw it into the fire. The princes urged him not to treat the word of God in this way, but Jehoiakim kept on cutting and burning until the entire scroll had been consumed in the flames.

It took a long time to write a scroll, and Jeremiah was sorry to have his sermons destroyed, but he was far from finished. Almost immediately, he dictated another scroll, which included everything the first had contained and a great deal more. In this second scroll Jeremiah made it clear that Jerusalem would soon be completely destroyed. "I saw a vision," he said. "The earth was waste, the heavens had no light, and the mountains were trembling. I looked, and I saw no man. The fruitful land had been turned into a desert, and the cities of the earth were lying in ruins. This is the way Jerusalem will look when the Lord attacks it in his fierce anger." In a very short time, these terrible words began to come true. *Jeremiah*

JUDAH'S LAST DAYS

In the years since the death of King Josiah, the Babylonians had defeated the Assyrians and were now threatening to conquer all the lands that had once belonged to Assyria, including Judah. Just after the beginning of the sixth century B.C., Nebuchadnezzar, the general of the Babylonian army, decided it was time to attack the little province. Shortly before he reached Jerusalem, King Jehoiakim died, leaving the nation in the hands of his eighteen-year-old son, Jehoiachin. After a brief battle, the young king surrendered the city to Nebuchadnezzar. Nebuchadnezzar did not destroy it at this time, but he crippled it so badly that it would never recover. It was customary for a conqueror to take home the treasures of the palace and the temple. But Nebuchadnezzar took home treasures that were even more valuable to the nation: ten thousand of her finest men. All that remained behind were the poor, the helpless, and the ignorant. To watch over those who were not good enough to be taken, Nebuchadnezzar appointed Jehoiachin's uncle, Zedekiah, to serve as king.

Zedekiah tried to be a good king, but he was a weak man who could not make up his own mind. If he had had wise advisers, he might have been able to prevent total destruction. Unfortunately, the men who might have given him good advice had been taken to Babylon and Zedekiah found himself surrounded by stupid men who knew little or nothing about either politics or religion. These foolish fellows advised Zedekiah to rebel against Nebuchadnezzar. Jeremiah realized this would bring certain disaster and he went to great lengths to convince Zedekiah and his countrymen that this was the case. "Our only possible hope," he pleaded, "is to keep Nebuchadnezzar's good will."

Zedekiah was willing to consider what Jeremiah had to say, but his advisers were angered by the prophet's words and threw him into an empty cistern, where he would have died if a servant in the palace had not rescued him.

A few months later, the Babylonian army struck Jerusalem again. The old city held out bravely for several months, but finally, the Babylonians broke through the wall and entered the city. They captured Zedekiah and put out his eyes, after forcing him to watch the death of his young sons. Then, to make sure Jerusalem would never give trouble again, they tore down its walls and burned its buildings, including the sacred Temple. Most of the people who survived the battle were taken to Babylon to join their country-men in exile. Jeremiah remained in the land a short while, lamenting over the destruction of his beloved city. Then, with a small group of refugees, he went down into Egypt, where he lived until his death a few years later.

Jeremiah

QUESTIONS: 1. *What occupation did Amos follow?* 2. *Which of Israel's sins did Amos describe?* 3. *What was to be the result of Israel's sinful state?* 4. *Why was Hosea's message especially meaningful?* 5. *What finally happened to the northern kingdom of Israel?* 6. *How did Jonah try to escape the task God assigned to him? Was he successful?* 7. *What was the result of his preaching in Nineveh? Was he pleased?* 8. *What lesson did God teach Jonah?* 9. *How was Isaiah called to be a spokesman for the Lord?* 10. *What did the "sign of the child" prove?* 11. *Why was Hezekiah known as a good king?* 12. *Who was the Assyrian king who attacked Jerusalem in Hezekiah's time? What was his end?* 13. *What marked Manasseh's reign as an evil one?* 14. *What did Josiah's men find while cleaning the Temple? What effect did its words have on Josiah and the people?* 15. *Why did Jeremiah attack Jehoiakim, Josiah's son? How did Jehoiakim react?* 16. *Who finally conquered Jerusalem? What did he take as a spoil of war?* 17. *Who was left in Jerusalem?* 18. *What finally happened to Jeremiah?*

Captives in Babylon

CREATURES AND WHEELS

As we have seen, when Jerusalem was destroyed, many of its citizens were taken captive to Babylon. In many ways, this period of the Babylonian exile, or Babylonian Captivity, as it is sometimes called, was one of the most important in the history of God's people. After the Babylonians overran Judah, the chances that the little nation would ever recover must have seemed awfully small. Her cities and towns lay in ruins. Her leaders had been killed or taken captive. The Temple of Solomon, the one thing that had always offered strength in troubled times, had been completely destroyed. Nothing was left to mark the spot but a heap of rubble and ashes. The nation of Judah had ceased to exist. But, of course, this was not the end. Judah did recover and the worship of God was once more established in Jerusalem. The exile played an important part in this recovery.

Life in exile was not particularly hard, as far as such things as food, clothing, and shelter were concerned. But Israel's faith was in serious trouble. The people of Israel had believed that God would never allow any real harm to befall Jerusalem or the Temple and that the day would never come when a descendant of David did not sit upon the throne. Now, both Jerusalem and the Temple were gone, and there was no throne for a son of David to sit upon. As the lonely days and weeks stretched into months and years, those in exile began to ask, "Why has this happened to us? How have we displeased God? How can we ever please him again?" One of those who tried to help find answers to these questions was the prophet Ezekiel.

Ezekiel is one of the strangest and most exciting figures in all the Bible. We know very little about his background and private life, except that he was a member of a priestly family, he was married, and he had been carried into Babylonian captivity about eleven years before the fall of Jerusalem in 586 B.C.

Ezekiel received his call to be a prophet after he had been in Babylon about five years. While he was sitting with the other exiles on the banks of the River Chebar in Babylon, Ezekiel saw a marvelous vision. In some ways, this vision reminds us of the one Isaiah saw in the Temple in Jerusalem, except that it was even more spectacular than Isaiah's had been. In the midst of a great dark storm cloud that flashed with thunder and lightning, Ezekiel saw four remarkable creatures. Each had the body of a human being and glistened like bronze. Each had four wings and four faces. The faces were those of a man, a lion, an ox, and an eagle. By the side of each of these creatures was a "wheel within a wheel" that enabled the creature to move throughout the heavens without ever pausing to change directions. Over these creatures and these wheels, on a platform of crystal and a throne of sapphire, the glory of the Lord appeared in the likeness of a figure of gleaming, fiery bronze.

When Ezekiel saw this vision, he did just what you and I might have done. He fell on his face in terror. But then, a voice ordered him to stand upon his feet. "I have chosen you to be my messenger," God told him. "I want you to preach to the exiles and to warn them not to try to rebel against the Babylonians. I have brought them here for a purpose. If they try to escape or resist the Babylonians in any way, they will be destroyed. If they remain here as peaceful captives, I will take care of them."

God did not try to fool Ezekiel into thinking his ministry would be easy. In fact, he told him that the exiles would not like his message and would probably not listen to him. "But," God assured him, "I will make your head as hard as flint, so that nothing they say to you will discourage you. Even if they do not heed your words, they will know that a real prophet has been in their midst."

This awesome vision so overwhelmed Ezekiel that he sat speechless among his companions for a full week. Then, the word of the Lord came to him, telling him that the time had come for him to begin his ministry as a prophet.

Ezekiel 1:1–3:15

SIGNS OF DESTRUCTION

Of all the great preachers of the Old Testament, none went to more trouble to call attention to his message than did Ezekiel. Instead of just announcing God's word to the people, Ezekiel acted out his messages in very dramatic ways.

To teach the exiles that God would not protect Jerusalem from Nebuchadnezzar and his Babylonian army, Ezekiel built a tiny model of a city with armies attacking it. Then, he put up an iron plate between himself and the model, as a sign that God had cut himself off from Jerusalem and would not help Israel resist the invaders. Finally, Ezekiel lay down beside this model for 430 days, almost fifteen months. He lay on his left side for 390 days and on his right side for 40 days. These numbers symbolized the approximate number of years the northern and southern kingdoms would be in exile; that is, Ezekiel expected Israel to be in Assyrian exile for 390 years, and Judah to be in Babylonian exile for 40 years.

As another striking sign of what God would do with his rebellious people, Ezekiel took a sharp sword and used it to shave his head and face. Part of his hair he threw into a little fire he built in the middle of his model of Jerusalem. Another part he scattered on the ground and beat it with a sword. The rest of it he tossed into the wind and struck at with the sword. These acts symbolized the various ways God would punish the people of Judah. Some would be consumed by disease and famine, others would die by the sword, and still others would be scattered throughout the world. Jerusalem was about to feel the terrible wrath of God.

Shortly after he completed this group of strange actions, Ezekiel was carried in a vision to Jerusalem. There he saw a sickening sight. An idol had been set up in the inner court of Solomon's Temple. Inside the Temple, the walls of the holy place were covered with pictures of various creatures the people had begun to worship. Ezekiel also saw women bowing down to the Babylonian goddess of agriculture and men worshiping the sun. This vision caused him to perform two more symbolic acts. First, he packed his bags and crawled through a hole in the wall, as a sign that the people would soon be going into exile. Then, he trembled and shook as he ate his meals, to symbolize the fear the men of Judah would have when the Babylonians attacked.

Not long afterward, word came to the exiles that Nebuchadnezzar had attacked the city of Jerusalem. This news came at a time when Ezekiel had just suffered a tragic personal loss. As we said before, he was a married man. On the day the message came that Jerusalem was under attack, Ezekiel's beloved wife died. In Palestine and the other lands of the Near East, it was, and is still, customary for people to make a great show of mourning by crying loudly and by tearing their clothing and covering their face and head with dirt and ashes. Ezekiel made none of these signs of mourning. Instead, he dressed and acted just as he would on any other day. The people knew that he loved his wife, and they could not understand his actions. When they questioned him, he told them that they would be so stunned when they heard the news that Jerusalem had finally fallen that they would not even be able to think about mourning in the customary ways. *Ezekiel 4, 5, 7, 9, 24*

VISIONS OF COMFORT

When news of the destruction of Jerusalem finally did reach the exiles, Ezekiel completely changed the tone of his sermons. Until this event, his message had been one of warning and doom. Afterward, Ezekiel became a prophet of hope and comfort.

In this later part of his ministry, Ezekiel continued to see visions. The most famous of his visions was that of the valley of dry bones. In this vision, God set Ezekiel down in the midst of a valley covered with thousands of dry, sun-bleached human bones. When God asked the question, "Can these bones live?" Ezekiel could give no answer. It seemed incredible that any life could ever come again to the heap of bones. Still, following God's instructions, he spoke to the bones and commanded them to "hear the word of the Lord." Suddenly there was a rattling sound and all over the valley, the bones rose and began connecting themselves to other bones until human skeletons were formed. Then, before Ezekiel's wondering eyes, sinew and flesh and skin began to cover the bones. Again at Ezekiel's command, the wind entered these human forms to give them the breath of life. "And breath came into them, and they lived, and stood upon their feet, an exceedingly great host."

The meaning of the vision was clear to Ezekiel and to those he told about it. As they understood it, the bones represented a slain and scattered Israel. In their present condition, as exiles in Baylon, it seemed impossible they could ever become a united people again. By the power of God's spirit, however, Israel would rise from her grave to live once again in her beloved homeland. *Ezekiel 37*

BRAVE YOUNG MEN

Among the many captives Nebuchadnezzar brought from Jerusalem to Babylon was a large number of princes and noblemen of Judah. Nebuchadnezzar hoped these intelligent young men could be useful in running the kingdom and he set up a special school to train them. Among those Jews he selected to attend his school were Daniel, Shadrach, Meshach, and Abednego.

For three years, these four young men were trained at the school until, finally, they were sent to the palace to serve the king. As a special reward for their excellent service, the king offered them the same rich food that he ate. But Moses had given the Israelites detailed laws about the kind of food they could eat, and the food the king offered was forbidden by these rules. Daniel and his three friends decided they could not disobey God by eating the king's food. So, they went to the Babylonian nobleman who was in charge and tried to explain their problem to him. The nobleman tried to be understanding, but he could not think of a workable solution. "If you do not eat," he said, "you will grow pale and thin. When the king sees you, he will blame me for your poor condition and will kill me for failing to take care of you. I simply cannot allow you to starve yourselves."

"Then let us try something," Daniel pleaded. "For a period of ten days, give us vegetables to eat instead of the king's rich food. At the end of that time, see if we do not look just as healthy as the young men who eat the king's food."

The nobleman could think of no reason why Daniel should try to trick him, especially since the young men were risking their own health, so he agreed to let Daniel and his friends try their plan. For ten days, the four faithful young Israelites ate nothing but vegetables. At the end of this period, the nobleman examined them and found them to be in better physical condition than any of the other young men who served the king. Soon afterward, when all the young men who had been training to serve in the Babylonian government were brought before the king, he chose Daniel, Shadrach, Meshach, and Abednego to take the most important positions in his court.

Daniel 1

THE KING'S DREAM

Not long after Daniel and his friends began to serve at court, King Nebuchadnezzar had a strange dream. In ancient times, men paid special attention to dreams. They believed their gods revealed secrets to them in dreams, and whenever they had unusual dreams, they tried to get someone to interpret their dream, to enable them to see into the future. Most Near Eastern kings had wise men in their courts who were thought to be especially skillful in the interpretation of dreams. Nebuchadnezzar had several of these wise men in his court and he asked them to explain the meaning of his dream. This task was always a difficult one, but Nebuchadnezzar made it doubly hard because he could not even remember what his dream was!

Naturally, the wise men were baffled. "If you could remember your dream," they said, "perhaps we could help you understand it. But if you cannot even remember what it was, how can you possibly expect us to tell you what it means?"

We would ordinarily expect Nebuchadnezzar to admit that he was asking an impossible thing, but he did not. Instead, he demanded, "Either you will tell me what my dream was and what it means or I will have you torn limb from limb."

The wise men did not know what to say. With hopeless fear written on their faces, they looked at each other, each one hoping that someone could save them by guessing the king's dream. The king grew more and more furious, but no one spoke. Finally, he ordered his guards to take them to the place of execution and kill them.

Now Daniel and his friends were also regarded as wise men, and the captain of the king's guard arrested them also, intending to kill them along with the Babylonian wise men.

"Why are you doing this? What have we done?" Daniel asked in surprise when he was arrested. Once the guard told him the story of the king's dream, he asked permission to speak to the king.

The king was still angry when Daniel was brought before him, but the young man begged, "O great Nebuchadnezzar, please do not kill the wise men yet. Give me a little time and I will ask my God to show me the mean ing of your dream." Surprisingly Nebuchadnezzar agreed to wait and named a time when Daniel would be expected to report to him on what he learned from his god. That night Daniel, Shadrach, Meshach, and Abed-nego prayed for a long time, asking God to tell them what the king had dreamed and to explain its meaning to them. Finally, God did speak and revealed to Daniel what he should tell the king.

When Daniel came before Nebuchadnezzar at the appointed time, he said: "O king, your dream was about a statue with a head of gold, breast and arms of silver, belly and thighs of bronze, legs of iron, and feet of clay mixed with iron. As you looked at this strange figure, a small stone struck the image on its feet. The force of the stone completely shattered the statue. It turned into dust and was carried away by the wind until no trace of it remained. Then the little stone grew until it became a huge mountain and filled the whole earth.

"Now the meaning of the dream is this. The various parts of the statue's body represent great kingdoms. The head of fine gold represents your kingdom. The other parts of the body represent other kingdoms that will arise after yours. The little stone represents a kingdom that God will set up. This kingdom, the Kingdom of God, shall never be destroyed. God has blessed you by letting you see what will happen in the future. This was your dream. This is the true interpretation of its meaning."

As the king listened to Daniel, he remembered that this had indeed been his dream, and he marveled that Daniel was able to give him the interpretation when his own wise men had failed. "Your God is God of gods and Lord of kings," he said in admiration, "and a revealer of mysteries, for by his power you have been able to reveal this mystery to me."

Then the king gave Daniel high honors and rich gifts and made him an important official over the whole province of Babylon, with special authority over the wise men of the court. At Daniel's request, he also placed Shadrach, Meshach, and Abednego in important positions in the kingdom. *Daniel 2*

THE FIERY FURNACE

When Daniel was able to interpret the unknown dream, Nebuchadnezzar realized that the young man's God was a mighty God. But he did not understand that he was the only God. He, like most people in ancient times, was used to worshiping many gods, and he thought the God of the Israelites was just another of these, even though he recognized that this particular god had marvelous powers the other gods did not have.

Since this was the case, Nebuchadnezzar did not consider it wrong to worship the other gods. One of these idol gods—the Bible does not tell us his name—was a special favorite of Nebuchadnezzar. To honor him, he set up a golden image almost one hundred feet high. He placed this enormous statue in a field and ordered all his subjects to bow down to it in praise and worship. At the dedication ceremony, a herald declared to the large crowd that had assembled: "When you hear the sound of the instruments of the royal musicians, you must fall down and worship the golden image King Nebuchadnezzar has set up. Whoever does not worship the image will be burned alive in a roaring furnace."

After that, whenever the music sounded, the people quickly bowed to worship the idol. But three men in the crowd did not bow down. They were Daniel's brave friends, Shadrach, Meshach, and Abednego. God had blessed them by keeping them healthy and by saving their lives when he revealed the king's dream to Daniel. They would not be untrue to him now by falling down before some statue that was not a god at all.

In the crowd with the three were several Babylonians who were jealous of the Israelites who had risen to such a high place in the Babylonian kingdom so quickly. When they noticed that Shadrach, Meshach, and Abednego did not bow before the image, they saw their chance to get even with them. As soon as they could, they hurried to Nebuchadnezzar and told him what they had seen.

"The Israelites you appointed as governors over the provinces are deliberately disobeying your command to bow before the golden image," they reported.

Their words had the effect they had hoped for. Nebuchadnezzar was furious. In a rage, he summoned the three offenders before him and said to them, "I will give you one more chance to obey me. The next time you hear the sound of the musical instruments, you must bow down before the image. If you disobey, even though you are my governors, I will cast you into a furnace. Then you will see that your god cannot help you."

The young men were not frightened. They answered the king calmly, "If our God wishes, O King, he can deliver us from your furnace. But even if he does not deliver us, we will still not worship your image."

This made Nebuchadnezzar even angrier than before. "Guards!" he cried, "Take these men and throw them in the furnace now! Make the fire seven times hotter than usual!"

The guards obeyed, and the fire was so hot that the men who threw the three Israelites in the furnace were killed by the intense heat.

Standing off at a distance, Nebuchadnezzar looked into the furnace. Then he looked again. "Did we not throw three men into the furnace?" he asked those beside him. When they told him this was correct, he asked, "Then why are there four men in the furnace now?" The men looked and saw that, indeed, there were four men in the furnace; and not only that, but they were walking around inside, unharmed by the flames. The fourth man had a marvelous appearance, "like a son of the gods."

Nebuchadnezzar realized what had happened. Approaching the door of the furnace, he called out, "Shadrach, Meshach, and Abednego, servants of the Most High God, come out of the fire and stand before me." At the sound of the king's voice, the three young men stepped from the furnace and walked toward him. The noblemen and counselors gathered around them to inspect the damage the fire had done. To their surprise, the young men were completely unharmed. Their hair was not singed, and their garments were not burned a bit. In fact, they did not even smell like smoke.

Nebuchadnezzar turned to the crowd and addressed them: "Blessed be the God of Shadrach, Meshach, and Abednego, who has sent an angel to protect them from harm when they refused to worship any other god. Hear this, O people of Babylon: anyone who speaks a word against the God of these three men shall be punished, for there is no other god who can do a thing like this." Then, Nebuchadnezzar promoted the remarkable young men to even more important positions than they had held before. *Daniel 3*

THE HANDWRITING ON THE WALL

Despite the fact that he worshiped idol gods, Nebuchadnezzar was a brilliant man and an excellent king. Unfortunately for the great nation of

Babylon, the kings who followed him were not quite so able and the nation grew weaker as time passed. Finally, a man called Belshazzar became king of Babylon.

Belshazzar enjoyed showing off his wealth and power by giving huge parties for his friends and for people he wanted to impress. On one particular night he gave a dinner for a thousand of the noblemen in his kingdom. To make the occasion seem very fine and grand, Belshazzar served his friends with the golden dishes that Nebuchadnezzar had taken from the Temple in Jerusalem when he destroyed the holy city.

While the guests were at the banquet, drinking wine from the cups that had been used to serve the One True God while they praised the gods made of wood and stone, a strange thing happened. High on the side of the wall a hand appeared, writing words no one could read or understand. As he saw the eerie hand moving slowly across the wall, King Belshazzar turned pale and his knees began to shake. In great alarm, he cried out, "Bring in the enchanters and the wise men! If any of them can tell me the meaning of these words, I will give him rich gifts and make him the third most important ruler in the whole kingdom."

When the order was announced, wise men from the city rushed to the banquet hall, each one hoping he would be able to explain the words and thus become a powerful ruler. They all looked closely at the strange words on the wall, but no one was able to read them.

The queen saw how troubled Belshazzar was and gave him some good advice. "There is a man in your kingdom," she said, "who has the spirit of the holy gods. Many years ago, King Nebuchadnezzar had a dream that neither he nor any of his wise men could interpret. But this man was called in and he was able to tell the king what his dream meant. The man's name is Daniel. If you will call him now, I am sure he will be able to read this message on the wall."

When Daniel was brought before Belshazzar, the king said, "Daniel, I have heard that you are a man of great wisdom and understanding. I have heard that you can give interpretations and solve problems. If you can tell me what this handwriting means, I will clothe you with royal garments and put a chain of gold around your neck and you shall become the third ruler in my kingdom."

"I do not want your gifts," Daniel told the king. "You may keep them or give them to someone else. But I will tell you the meaning of the writing on the wall.

"You are a great king," he continued, "but you have failed to give God the proper respect. My God has power over all earthly kings. It was he who helped Nebuchadnezzar become powerful, and it was he who raised up other kings to take his place. Now you have offended the Most High God by allowing your guests to eat and drink from the sacred vessels from God's Temple and by praising the gods of wood and stone and metal.

"Because he was offended, God sent the mysterious hand to write on the wall. The words the hand has written are: MENE, MENE, TEKEL, and PARSIN. This is God's way of telling you that your kingdom is about to come to an end. It will be taken from you and given to the Medes and Persians. God has tested you, O King, and you have failed the test."

Belshazzar was frightened by Daniel's words, but he was relieved to know the meaning of the handwriting on the wall and he rewarded him as he had promised. The royal robes were put on him and he was named the third ranking ruler in the kingdom.

But Daniel did not get to enjoy his role as a ruler for long. That very night, the sound of foreign soldiers was heard in the streets of Babylon. Suddenly the doors of the hall were thrown open and the Medes and Persians rushed in. The kingdom of Babylon ended with the invasion. In its place, the Medes and Persians ruled the world.

Daniel 5

IN THE LION'S DEN

The Persians appointed an old man named Darius to rule over Babylon. Darius was a good man and he chose Daniel to serve him as he had served King Nebuchadnezzar. The king was so pleased with the Israelite, who was now an old man himself, that he planned to give him even more authority in the kingdom. This made some of the princes and government officials jealous and they tried to find some way to keep Daniel from gaining the new post. They watched everything he did to try to find something bad to report to the king.

Daniel was such a righteous man that his enemies could find nothing evil to report; but they did discover that, three times every day, he opened his window toward Jerusalem and prayed to God. This gave them an idea for getting rid of him.

As the first step in their plan, the evil, jealous men went to the king and made a flattering speech, telling him how great he was. They said, "O King, you are such a wonderful ruler that you should issue an order that no one is to bow down to any god or man except you for a period of thirty days. Anyone who disobeys will be thrown into a den of lions, to be eaten alive." Darius was a good man, but he was also foolish and proud, and he allowed the men to convince him to issue such an order.

When Daniel heard about the law, he realized that his practice of daily prayer would violate it, but he still continued to pray. He believed it was more important to be loyal to God than to try to preserve his own life. When his enemies saw him pray as usual, they went to the king and told him what they had seen.

Darius now felt ashamed that he had signed such a foolish law, and he tried to find some way to save Daniel, but there was no way to do it. The law had been made and the Persians did not change their laws once they had been issued. So Darius sadly ordered his guards to put Daniel in the lion's den. In his heart, he hoped Daniel's great God could somehow save him, because he admired the Israelite and knew that he was a good man.

In those days, hungry lions were kept in a sealed pit to be used as a special punishment for criminals. When the guards led Daniel to the pit they could hardly hear the lions, because the opening to the pit was covered by a large stone. But when they moved the stone, the lions' roars came so loud and fierce that they quickly threw Daniel in and replaced the stone again.

All night the king worried about his former aide. In fact, he worried so much that he could not even sleep or eat his food. When morning finally came, he hurried to the lion's den and called out in a worried voice: "Daniel, was the God you serve so faithfully able to save you?"

From deep inside the darkness of the pit, Daniel called back, "O King, do not worry. My God sent an angel during the night and he shut the lions' mouths so that they did not hurt me. He knew that I had done no wrong, and now, great king, you can also know that I did not mean to show disrespect for you by praying to my God."

The relieved and happy Darius had Daniel taken from the pit. Then, realizing that the jealous princes had tricked him, he commanded his soldiers to throw them in the pit with the lions. This time, there was no angel to shut the mouths of the beasts and the evil men were killed.

For the rest of his life, Daniel served at the royal court, assisting the king and foretelling the kingdom of God that was to come. *Daniel 6*

QUESTIONS: 1. *Why were God's people in exile in Babylon?* 2. *What happened to Jerusalem?* 3. *Where did Ezekiel do his prophesying?* 4. *With what vision*

Loran Raymond Jones

ESTHER EXPOSING HAMAN'S PLOT

Esther 7

Loran Raymond Jones

EZRA AND ASSOCIATES IN JERUSALEM

Ezra 10:6–14

Loran Raymond Jones

NEHEMIAH PLANNING JERUSALEM'S RESTORATION

Nehemiah 2:12–20

Loran Raymond Jones

JOB AND FRIENDS

Job 32:1–15

did God summon Ezekiel to his ministry? 5. *Describe the messages Ezekiel taught with the model of Jerusalem.* 6. *What was the meaning of Ezekiel's shaving his head and face?* 7. *Why did Ezekiel not mourn for his wife?* 8. *What did the vision of dry bones symbolize?* 9. *What kind of school did Daniel, Shadrach, Meshach, and Abednego attend?* 10. *Why did they refuse to eat the king's food?* 11. *What was Nebuchadnezzar's dream and its meaning?* 12. *Why were Shadrach, Meshach, and Abednego put into the fiery furnace?* 13. *Who was in the furnace with the young men?* 14. *Describe the feast given by Belshazzar.* 15. *What message did the handwriting on the wall bring?* 16. *Who was the Persian king served by Daniel in his old age?* 17. *How did the princes trick Darius into punishing Daniel?* 18. *How was Daniel saved from the lions?*

Jerusalem Rebuilt

THE CAPTIVES RETURN

In the last years of Belshazzar's rule, the people of Babylon had grown quite discontent with his leadership. Therefore, when Cyrus the Persian entered the city with his troops, even though he was a foreign conqueror, the people spread green twigs in his path and welcomed him with rejoicing.

Afterward, Cyrus treated the Babylonians with the wisdom that had made him master of the greatest empire the world had even known. His soldiers strolled through the streets without their weapons, under strict orders not to steal anything or to harm or frighten the citizens in any way. And this was only the beginning. Cyrus set about immediately to provide better housing for the poor and to repair portions of the city that had become run down. The king himself worked with the people as they repaired the broken wall of Babylon.

When we see how Cyrus treated the people he conquered, it is easier to understand the marvelous gift he offered to the Jewish exiles he found in Babylon—the gift of freedom. Only one year after he conquered Babylon, Cyrus issued a decree in which he declared that any Jew who wished could return to Jerusalem and rebuild the sacred Temple. Thus, the lowly remnant of Israel had the official support of the world's mightiest power to reestablish her religion in the holy city of Jerusalem.

Not every Jew wanted to return to the homeland. By this time, many of them had come to feel quite at home in Babylon. No one under forty-five could remember any other home, since all the Jews under that age had been born in exile. Why should they be anxious to trade a comfortable life in a great world center for one of hardship that was about to meet them back in Judah? Others were willing to go, but wanted someone else to make the trip first. But a sizable number caught the vision of a New Israel, and they were ready to return to Judah.

As these brave pioneers prepared to leave, their friends and relatives who had chosen to remain behind gathered round to tell them goodbye and to give them gifts for themselves and offerings for the new Temple. At the same time, the royal treasurer of Babylon, following the instructions of Cyrus, brought out the sacred vessels Nebuchadnezzar had taken from the Temple and presented them to the group.

The leader of the hardy band was a man named Sheshbazzar, who seems to have been the son of King Jehoiachin, one of the last kings of Judah, whom Nebuchadnezzar had carried to Babylon as a prisoner a few years before the destruction of Jerusalem. Sheshbazzar's title was "governor," which probably means that he had full authority to set up the new Jerusalem community as he saw fit, just as long as he did nothing to threaten the welfare of the Persian empire.

Back in Israel, the group found their existence a hard and disappointing affair. The usual troubles of pioneer communities were made even worse by locust plagues, drought, and famine. In addition to these, their neighbors to the north continually caused them trouble. These people were called Samaritans.

The Samaritans were irritated because the Jews had moved in on land that had previously belonged to them, but that was not the major reason for their opposition. When the Assyrians had conquered the northern kingdom of Israel, they had carried many people away with them into captivity. In Assyria, these Israelites had married people from the other nations the Assyrians had conquered. The Samaritans were the result of this mixture. Although they still worshiped the One True God, the Jews who returned from Babylon did not consider them pure Jews and would have nothing to do with them.

The first trouble with the Samaritans arose over the rebuilding of the Temple. In the first year or two after the exiles returned, Sheshbazzar died, leaving the leadership of the community in the hands of Zerubbabel, who served as governor, and Jeshua, the high priest. The first thing these new leaders did was to bring the people together to build the Temple. When the Samaritans heard about the project, they approached Zerubbabel and Jeshua to ask their permission to share in the building. The two leaders, together with other important men in the community, answered them flatly: "No. You have nothing to do with building a house to God. We will build it by ourselves."

Naturally, this angered the Samaritans and they decided that if they could not help with the building, they would do what they could to see that it did not get built. They mocked and threatened the Jews. They hired people to try to frustrate them in every way they could. Also, they wrote letters to the Persian king, warning him that if the Jews were allowed to complete the Temple, they would use it as a center for planning rebellions. All of these things together finally accomplished their purpose, at least temporarily. Sometime before the death of Cyrus, the Jews abandoned work on the Temple, after finishing only the foundation and the altar of burnt-offerings. For almost twenty years, these abandoned beginnings stood as a reminder of the despair that filled the hearts of the struggling little group. Then, interest in the project was raised by two prophets, Haggai and Zechariah.

Ezra 1–4

PROPHETS OF ENCOURAGEMENT

By the time Haggai came on the scene, the people of Jerusalem had grown indifferent about rebuilding the Temple. They were building fine houses for themselves, but they were saying there was no hurry about building a house for the Lord. Haggai attacked this attitude with biting words: "You have been troubled by locusts and plagues and famine. These have not been accidental. They have been God's way of punishing you for your laziness."

Haggai's words were so effective that less than a month later the work of rebuilding the Temple was begun anew. But as the people worked, they realized that the new Temple was going to be poor in comparison to Solomon's magnificent building. Haggai comforted them, telling them that God was pleased with their efforts and would bless them with good harvests and prosperity.

Haggai's co-worker in this task of encouraging the people to continue the rebuilding of Jerusalem was Zechariah. Zechariah described a number of colorful visions he had had, which indicated that the day of small things was over and that God would soon come to dwell again in the midst of the city as he had in the days of David and Solomon.

Before long, word spread that the Jews were working on the Temple again. Several officials in the Persian government tried to halt the project, but the Jews told them that Cyrus himself had authorized it. A check of the royal records was made and Cyrus' original decree was found. The new king, whose name was Darius, demanded that Cyrus' order be honored and not only told the Jews they could go ahead with their building, but offered to furnish whatever supplies and money they needed.

With all problems removed, work on the Temple progressed rapidly from this point and was finished within a few months. At the joyous dedication ceremony, hundreds of animals were sacrificed as burnt-offerings and the Temple was officially reopened. Shortly afterward, the Passover was kept. At last, it was possible to say that Israel had truly been rebuilt. And it would stand until another son of David, who was called the Christ, arose to announce that the Kingdom of God was among men. *Haggai; Zechariah*

QUEEN OF PERSIA

As we have seen, not all the Jews returned to Judah when Cyrus gave them the opportunity. Many of them had been living in Babylon so long that they preferred to remain there. One of these was a man. He lived in the city of Shushan, which was one of the capitals of the Persian empire. Living with him was his beautiful young cousin, Esther, whose own parents were dead.

The king of Persia at this time was Ahashuerus. During a great feast Ahashuerus gave for his princes and noblemen, he asked his wife Vashti to come before the men and display her beauty. When Vashti refused, he grew quite angry with her and decided that she would no longer be his queen. To find a woman to take her place, he held a contest to find the most beautiful girl in the kingdom.

Among the young girls brought to the palace to appear before Ahashuerus was Mordecai's beautiful young cousin, Esther. As soon as the king saw her, he knew that she would be his choice. He could see just by looking at her that her heart was as pure and lovely as her face. So Esther, who was a Jew, became the queen of Persia.

Mordecai had come to think of Esther as a daughter, and he missed her greatly when she went to live in the palace. Although he could not see her. he did stay in touch with her by sending messages.

One day Mordecai overheard two men plotting to kill the king. Immediately, he reported what he had heard to Esther in one of his messages. When she told the king, he ordered his soldiers to capture the men and punish them. Then, he wrote down Mordecai's brave deed in the official book of records.

The greatest man in the kingdom at this time, besides the king himself, was a man named Haman, who was chief of all the princes. No one was more impressed with his importance than Haman himself. He loved to see the people bow before him as he passed through the streets. But Mordecai, who was a strict Jew, worshiped only God and refused to bow down when Haman passed by. This made Haman quite angry. When he found out who Mordecai was and that he was a Jew, he decided to take out his anger not just on Mordecai, but on all Jews.

Haman told the king that the Jews were causing trouble in the empire by refusing to obey the laws of the nation. Somehow, he managed to convince Ahashuerus that what he was saying was true. The king did not know much about the Jews. In fact, he had no idea that his own queen was one. So, he gave Haman permission to kill all the Jews in the kingdom.

A decree was made calling for the death of all natives of Judea. Copies were sent throughout the kingdom and the day for the massacre was set. When Mordecai and his fellow Jews learned about the decree, they put on torn and ragged clothes and roamed about the city protesting the terrible law. Esther heard that Mordecai was acting strangely and sent a messenger to find out what was wrong with him. Mordecai told the messenger about the terrible command and sent Esther a copy of the decree as proof that what he was saying was the truth. He also asked her to go to the king and try to persuade him to spare her people.

When Esther received Mordecai's pleading message, she was greatly troubled. She quickly sent a message back to him, saying, "No one in the kingdom can go to the king unless the king sends for him. If I suddenly appear in the court without an invitation, the king might kill me, even though I am his wife. I am particularly afraid to go at this time because he has not sent for me for thirty days, and I fear he might be angry with me."

But Mordecai did not give up easily. He sent word back: "Remember that you are also a Jew. Do not think you will be safe just because you are in the palace. Perhaps the very reason God raised you up as queen was so that you could save his people at this time."

This convinced Esther. She wrote back to Mordecai that she would go before the king in three days, and she asked him and the Jews to pray for her.

On the third day, Esther put on her most beautiful robes and walked through the palace halls to the entrance to the throne room. As she stood trembling in the doorway, the king, sitting on his throne across the room, smiled and held out his scepter to her. "What do you want, Esther?" he asked. "I shall give you anything, up to half of my kingdom."

Esther did not tell the king what it was that she really wanted. This might have made him angry at her. Instead, she asked him to come to a special dinner and to bring Haman with him.

Haman was delighted when he found out that he alone had been invited to dine with the king and queen. As soon as the meal was over, he hurried home to tell his wife and friends about it and, of course, about how well the king and queen had treated him. On the way, however, he saw Mordecai on the street. As usual, Mordecai refused to bow down as he passed, and this spoiled Haman's happy mood. Immediately, he ordered a gallows made on which he could hang Mordecai.

That same night the king was having trouble going to sleep and asked one of his servants to read the chronicles, the book in which the official records of the kingdom were kept. While reading, he found the record of the occasion when Mordecai had saved his life by reporting the plan of two men to kill him. He remembered that he had never rewarded Mordecai for his loyalty and decided to do so the very next day. On the following morning, he asked Haman if he had any ideas as to the best way to honor a man who had pleased the king greatly.

Haman was vain enough to think the king was talking about him and happily suggested that the man be dressed in fine clothing and paraded through the streets on the king's own horse, with a leading nobleman walking ahead of him to proclaim the man's loyalty and bravery to the people. This pleased Ahashuerus, and he said, "That is an excellent idea, Haman. The man I want to honor is the Jew named Mordecai. And I want you to be the one to walk through the streets before him."

We can imagine how this must have astonished Haman! He could hardly raise his head as he walked about the city, singing Mordecai's praises. How humiliating it was for him, the chief prince of Persia, to be praising the man who was causing him such misery, the same man he had been planning to hang.

After the embarrassing experience, Haman again went to dine with King Ahashuerus and Queen Esther. During the dinner, the king looked at his beautiful wife and was pleased with her. "Tell me, Esther," he said, "is there anything you would like for me to do for you?"

Esther replied solemnly, "Yes, my king. I ask you for my own life and for the life of my people. We are all about to be killed."

"What do you mean?" demanded the king. "Who would dare threaten you or your family?"

At this, Esther turned to the chief of the princes and said, "Our enemy, this wicked Haman!"

Haman saw that his plot had been exposed, and he began begging for his life; but the king was too angry to listen. He declared that Haman should be hanged the next day on the gallows that had been built for Mordecai.

On that day Mordecai took Haman's place as the chief of the princes. The law for the destruction of the Jews could not be changed, but Ahashuerus did make a new law that allowed the Jews to fight back against anyone who tried to kill them. Most of the Persians made no attempt to fight the Jews, and the ones who did were quickly destroyed.

Thus, the day on which the Jews were all to be killed turned out to be a day of great victory for the people of God. In thanksgiving for their deliverance, they celebrated a great feast. Jews today still celebrate that feast, which is called the feast of Purim. When they do, they remember the beautiful queen who saved their people.

Esther

A WALL OF SAFETY

Life in Judah in the years that followed the dedication of the Temple continued to be discouraging. With no wall to restrain attackers, Jerusalem had to suffer repeated raids from her hostile neighbors. In addition to this, Judah's enemies wrote letters to the king of Persia telling him that the Jews were planning to start a rebellion against the empire. Gradually, the religious zeal Haggai and Zechariah had stirred up began to die down. The people began to hold back the offerings they were supposed to give and to offer their weak and sickly animals as burnt offerings, instead of the best animals which the Law of Moses demanded. Judah was badly in need of reform. This came with the work of Nehemiah and Ezra.

Nehemiah, although he was a Jew, was the cupbearer to Artaxerxes, the king of Persia. The cupbearer was the king's most trusted servant and was able to talk to him each day when he brought him his food. One day, Artaxerxes noticed that Nehemiah was looking particularly sad and troubled. When he asked what was the matter, Nehemiah told him that he wanted to return to Jerusalem and help his people rebuild the wall of the city.

Earlier in his reign, Artaxerxes had forbidden the Jews to rebuild the wall of Jerusalem, but he trusted Nehemiah so much that he agreed to let his favorite servant journey to Jerusalem for a few years to help his people. Not long afterward, Nehemiah set out for Jerusalem under the protection of a royal bodyguard.

As soon as he reached Jerusalem, Nehemiah made a secret inspection of the city wall under cover of darkness. This convinced him that it was absolutely necessary to rebuild the burned and broken structure. So he called the leaders of the people together and told them his plans. They agreed with him wholeheartedly and "strengthened their hands for the good work."

Not everyone was pleased with the news that Nehemiah was planning to rebuild Jerusalem. Almost immediately, the leaders of the nations surrounding Judah began thinking of ways to stop him. The most important of these enemy leaders were named Sanballat, Tobiah, and Geshem. They liked being able to bully Judah whenever they felt like it, and were determined not to let the Jews grow strong enough to strike back at them.

First, they told Nehemiah that they would tell King Artaxerxes that he was planning a rebellion. This lie had convinced other kings, but Nehemiah did not worry, because he knew Artaxerxes would not believe that his favorite servant would be disloyal to him. Next, the enemies tried to discourage the Jews by poking fun at the wall. "What are you feeble Jews doing?" they asked. "Do you really think you can make a wall out of burnt stones and rubbish? Your little wall will be so weak that if a fox runs upon it, it will crumble under his weight." But despite their jeers, the wall grew higher and higher, "for the people had a mind to work."

When words failed to stop the Jews, the enemies decided to resort to force. Secretly they plotted to attack the city by surprise and kill the workers. Fortunately, a Jew who lived in enemy territory found out about the plot and warned Nehemiah. From that day on, Nehemiah made sure that his people would be ready for a surprise attack. The work force was divided into two crews. While one crew worked, the other stood guard. Even the workmen carried their weapons by their side, ready to drop their tools and begin fighting at a moment's notice. They were determined the Samaritans would not keep them from rebuilding the wall.

When Sanballat, Tobiah, and Geshem saw that nothing could stop the Jews as long as they had Nehemiah to spur them on, they tried to lure him out of the city so they could kill him. But Nehemiah was far too clever for them and refused to leave the protection of the city. Then, a spy who pretended to be Nehemiah's friend told him that some of the people were planning to kill him and that he should hide in the Temple, where he would be safe. Nehemiah knew that this, too, was a trick. "If I hide in the Temple," he said, "the people would think I am a coward and would no longer do what I ask them. I will not go in!"

In less than two months, Jerusalem had its wall. This success caused the people to have even greater confidence in Nehemiah and he was able to bring about many other badly needed reforms in the business, moral, and religious life of the city. One of the things that troubled him most was the fact that many Jews were beginning to intermarry with those from neighboring nations. The practice of intermarriage with these pagans had grown so widespread that many of the children did not even know how to speak Hebrew any longer. This made Nehemiah so angry that he cursed the people, beat some of them, and even pulled their hair. "Do you not remember that our fathers always had trouble when they began to accept the ways of other people? Even wise Solomon was led astray by his foreign wives. You must stop marrying people who are not Jews."

The people made some improvement under Nehemiah, but they did not put away all their foreign wives until the time of Israel's next great reformer, Ezra, the scribe.

Nehemiah 1–6

THE GREAT REFORMER

Ezra came to Judah while Nehemiah was still governor. He had been living among the exiles in Babylon and had received permission from King Artaxerxes to return to Judah to reorganize the community of God's people on the basis of the Law of Moses. Ezra knew the Law from beginning to end and loved it with all of his being. Artaxerxes not only gave Ezra permission to teach the Law; he gave him the legal authority to enforce the law. If a man refused to obey Ezra's commands, he could be executed for his disobedience.

Shortly after Ezra arrived in Jerusalem and told the people of his plans, a group of leaders came to talk to him about the problem of marriages between Jews and their pagan neighbors. When Ezra learned that many Jews had done this and that children were growing up who did not know the law and could not even speak or read Hebrew, the language in which the scriptures were written, he was greatly upset. Quickly, he called for all the men of Judah to assemble in Jerusalem.

Three days later, the men of the nation gathered in the large square in front of the rebuilt Temple. A heavy rain was falling, but no one dared suggest that they postpone the meeting. Soon, Ezra stood up to speak: "You have sinned and married foreign women. You must confess your sin to God and promise to do his will. If you do not want God to punish you, you must separate yourselves from the people of the land and put away your foreign wives." The men were ashamed and admitted that they had done wrong and would try to do what Ezra suggested. In less than three months, all who had married foreign women and who wished to remain a part of the Jewish community had divorced their wives and sent them away with their children. The first step to a pure community had been made.

Sometime during the first year of Ezra's work, the people gathered again in a large square in front of one of the large gates leading into Jerusalem. They had come to hear Ezra read from "the Book of the Law of Moses" that he had brought from Babylon. What a thrilling moment this must have been! A high wooden platform had been built for Ezra. As he opened the sacred book, the entire congregation rose in respect and reverence for the holy word. Then Ezra began to read. He read from early in the morning until noon. As he read, several Levites explained the meaning to the people, so that everyone in the crowd was able to understand it.

It had been a long time since the people had thought seriously about God and his law. Now, as they heard Ezra read about the exodus and the giving of the law on Mt. Sinai, their hearts began to ache with a mixture of sadness and joy, and tears welled up in their eyes. Ezra and Nehemiah urged them not to weep but to think of the day as a time for great rejoicing. Finally, the people stopped crying and began to eat and drink and to talk excitedly about what they had been hearing.

For seven days Ezra continued to read from the holy book. Later that month, the people made a new covenant with God. In grateful thankfulness for the blessings he had given them, they agreed "to walk in God's law which was given by Moses and to observe and do all the commandments of the Lord God." With the work of these reformers, the Old Testament narrative ends. One more prophet, Malachi, speaks of a time when the Lord himself will return to the Temple. It is with that event the next portion of the Bible begins.

Ezra

A PROBLEM OF SUFFERING

Besides the books of narrative which deal with the history of Israel as God's chosen people, the Old Testament contains other material which is classified as "wisdom literature." Wisdom, to the Jewish people, was thought of as the ability to apply one's knowledge and experience in obtaining a good and happy life. *Psalms, Proverbs, Ecclesiastes, Song of Solomon,* and *Job* pursue this theme in various ways. Some are written in prose; some, poetry; some, both. *Proverbs* reveals an optimistic outlook; it consists of short sayings that express in a memorable way the fact that good will be rewarded and evil will be punished. *Job* and *Ecclesiastes,* on the other hand, question the meaning of life and suffering, sometimes pessimistically.

The story of *Job* is written as a dramatic poem, one of the greatest pieces of literature of all time. An unknown writer places its setting in the land of Uz. Its main character, Job, is an extremely rich man and a good one, as well. His wealth includes great herds of cattle, sheep, and camels and a large family composed of seven sons and three daughters. He worships God with sacrifices and prayer each day. Not only does he pray for himself, but Job also prays for his children. "It may be that one of my sons has done wrong and has not asked God to forgive him yet," he reasons.

According to the common belief, Job should have prospered because of his goodness, but the drama is built around the fact that he suffers instead. His goodness seems rewarded with nothing but affliction.

The reason for the sorrow in Job's life begins in a heavenly council between God and Satan. "Have you noticed my servant Job?" the Lord questions his enemy. "There is no one on earth as good as he, so careful to turn away from evil and do right."

"No wonder Job is so faithful," Satan returns. "He has every reason to be so. If something bad were to happen to him, he would probably turn away from you."

"Try him and see," the Lord urges. "Do anything you wish to anything he has, only do not hurt him." So the contest begins. First a servant comes running to Job and says: "Master, we were out plowing with the oxen a while ago when the Sabeans came and took them. All of the other servants were killed in the fight—I am the only one who escaped!"

The servant has hardly finished telling his bad news when another runs up, looking very excited. "Lightning from the sky just struck all the sheep and the servants who were watching them," he cries. "I am the only one still alive!

The another comes to Job with this word: "The Chaldeans made a raid upon our camels. They took the animals and killed the servants who were with them."

If this were not enough, another servant comes in with the worst report of all. "Job," he says, "your children were all having dinner together at your oldest son's house when a great wind blew the house down and killed them all."

Poor Job! In one day he loses his children, his servants, his flocks and herds—everything he owns. He tears his clothes and falls upon the ground in mourning, but he says nothing against God. "The Lord gave them all to me, so they are his to take away. I still bless his name."

Satan hardly knows how to react to Job's attitude. He complains to the Lord: "Job has not turned away from you yet because he himself has not been harmed. If that were to happen, he would curse you, I know."

"You may try to find out," the Lord replies, "only do not take his life."

So Satan causes terrible boils to break out on Job's skin. The sores cover him from the top of his head to the bottom of his feet. In any position he turns, he seems to press against an infected place. He is in such pain that even his wife agrees that it would be better for him to die.

Then three of Job's friends enter the scene. They try to tell Job that God is sending him these troubles because he has done something wrong. They try to get Job to confess to his sin. Back and forth they argue, with Job insisting that he has done nothing to deserve his affliction.

This dialogue continues without coming to a conclusion until it is abruptly interrupted by the voice of God. In a whirlwind he speaks for himself, claiming that he has complete power in the world. With beautiful poetry he confronts Job with all the marvels of the universe. Where was Job when the world was formed? What are its measurements? Does he know the origin of light and darkness? Did he put the stars in the sky?

Job is completely awestruck with the magnificence of God. He still cannot understand his suffering, but he realizes that it is just one of the many mysteries of the universe to which only God holds the key. He confesses that he must wait in peace before the greatness of God.

At the conclusion of the drama Satan stands convinced that Job will not turn against the Lord. Because he has proved himself a faithful man in the face of all adversity, Job's good fortune is restored twofold. *Job*

QUESTIONS: 1. *How did Cyrus treat the Babylonians when he captured their city?* 2. *What favor did Cyrus grant the Jews?* 3. *Did all the Jews in Babylon return to Jerusalem? If not, why?* 4. *Who led the band back to Judah?* 5. *Why was there conflict with the Samaritans?* 6. *Why was the Temple left unfinished for almost twenty years?* 7. *Which two prophets encouraged the Jews to complete the Temple?* 8. *How did Esther chance to become the queen of Persia?* 9. *Why did Haman hate Mordecai?* 10. *How did Haman arrange for a massacre of the Jews?* 11. *Describe Esther's encounter with the king in the throne room.* 12. *How did King Ahashuerus honor Mordecai?* 13. *What became of Haman?* 14. *Why did Jerusalem need a wall so badly?* 15. *Who led in rebuilding the wall?* 16. *Why did Ezra hate the practice of Jews marrying pagans from other nations?* 17. *What effect did Ezra's reading of the Law have upon the people?* 18. *What is the "wisdom literature"?* 19. *What did Job discover about the problem of suffering?*

The Messiah Comes

BETWEEN THE TESTAMENTS

The Old Testament stories end following the work of Nehemiah, Ezra, and Zerubbabel; the New Testament begins four hundred years later with the coming of the Messiah. It is natural to wonder what were God's chosen people doing during that time.

Probably most of the Jews lived and died in the countries to which their fathers had scattered when Jerusalem was destroyed. Some of these married natives of the nations that they had adopted as their home; and in the years that followed, they lost their "separateness" as Israelites. Others who found themselves far away from Jerusalem tried harder than ever to remain God's distinct people. Since they could not go to the Temple for worship, they built synagogues in the cities where they were grouped together. Synagogues were buildings where worship services were held and the Law read and taught.

The Jews who had returned to Jerusalem after the Babylonian exile were also caught in the world struggles of the period. First, Alexander the Great ruled the area; then, after his death, it fell into the hands of first the Egyptians, then the Syrians. Some of the Syrian rulers were very harsh with the people of Jerusalem. They plundered the city and the Temple and punished those who were caught keeping the commands of the Law. Finally a family known as the Maccabeans arose and led the Jews to victory as the old hero-leaders had done. The father of the family, Mattathias, and then his sons after him stood before the Jews as both warriors and priests, and threw off Syrian oppression. They also restored the Temple, which had been damaged, and the feast days, which had been discontinued.

Then Rome became the greatest world power, and the Jews could not maintain their freedom against the might of the Roman armies. The city of Jerusalem was captured by General Pompey and placed under Roman military rule. A man named Herod was made king of the area of Palestine, and he ruled as the Caesar in Rome directed.

Bondage to Rome was very difficult for the Jews to accept. It is true that they were allowed to worship as the Law of Moses directed, but the high-priest was controlled by the Romans, so even their freedom of worship was limited. Then there were the high taxes all Jews were made to pay to the Roman government; these were a cause of irritation.

The whole situation was a frustrating one to a nation that prized freedom as highly as did the Jews. It is no wonder that many of them thought their only hope depended on the coming of the promised Messiah. They pictured his entering the scene and driving Herod and the Romans out of Palestine. Then he would reestablish the rule of David's family, as had been promised; and the nation of Israel would be as respected and strong as it had been when David's family originally ruled.

Indeed the time for the Messiah's coming had arrived, but those with hopes of his being an earthly deliverer of the Jews were to be disappointed. He was, it is true, to bring a great victory, but it would be a victory over sin, rather than Rome. In God's wisdom, he was to reign as a triumphant king, but over a kingdom that would include heaven and earth for all time, rather than Palestine of the first century.

With the unfolding of this life that would fulfill the promises to the chosen people and change the history of the world, the New Testament begins.

AN ANGEL AT THE ALTAR

In the days when Herod the Great ruled Palestine and Rome ruled the world, Temple services were held in Jerusalem according to the ancient custom. One day, it fell the duty of an old priest named Zacharias to enter the Holy Place during the service and burn incense upon the golden altar. While the people stood praying in the court, he stepped into the dimness of the sacred room and touched fire to the fragrant substance that lay upon the altar. The contact of fire and incense immediately filled the room with a cloud of sweet smoke; and to Zacharias' surprise, an angel appeared in the midst of the smoke.

The first reaction of the priest was one of fear; but the angel said, "Don't be afraid, Zacharias. Your prayer for a child has been heard. You and your wife Elizabeth are finally going to have a son. When he is born, you will name him John.

"His birth will bring you gladness and joy; in fact, many will rejoice because of it. God's spirit will be with him in a special way, giving him the power to lead the people back to righteousness and to prepare them for the Messiah's coming. His work will be like that of the prophets of old."

Zacharias could not believe what he had heard. "How can I know this is true?" he asked. "My wife and I are old, too old to have children."

"I am Gabriel and have come from the very presence of God to bring you this good news," the angel replied. "In order for you to believe it is true, you will not be able to speak until it has come to pass."

Now the people worshipping outside had begun to wonder what was keeping Zacharias inside the Holy Place for so long. When he finally came out to them, he could not speak and had to motion with his hands that he had seen a vision.

Luke 1:5–23

GABRIEL'S SECOND VISIT

North of Jerusalem in a little town called Nazareth, nestled in the hills ot Galilee, there lived a maiden named Mary. She was a cousin of Elizabeth, the wife of Zacharias. Mary's fellow Galileans longed deeply for the Messiah to come and rescue them from the power of the Romans. Perhaps Mary herself had thought about his appearance, never dreaming the role she would play in that great event. Her immediate attention was upon her engagement and approaching marriage to a good man named Joseph.

Then God came into the life of this pure, young Jewish woman. The angel Gabriel appeared suddenly to her one day, as he had six months before to Zacharias. "Hail, O favored one; the Lord is with you," he greeted her.

Mary was at once puzzled and troubled by the presence of the holy creature; she wondered what his words meant.

Then the angel spoke again: "Do not be afraid, Mary, for God has chosen you. He is going to give you a son who will be his own Son, as well. You shall call him Jesus, and he will rule over a mighty kingdom that has no end."

But Mary was still a little confused. "How can I have a baby," she asked, "when I am not married?"

"Your child will not have an earthly father," the angel explained. "His Father is the most high God, who dwells in heaven."

"Let it happen just as you have told me," Mary said softly.

Before he left, Gabriel told Mary that her cousin Elizabeth was also going to have a son, a special child from God. Then he disappeared as suddenly as he had come.

Mary's head was whirling when the angel left—she had so much to think about, and she needed to talk to someone she could talk with. Elizabeth was the answer! As quickly as possible, she made the trip to her cousin's home.

No sooner had Elizabeth heard Mary's voice than she guessed her wonderful secret. "How wonderful that the Lord has chosen you among all women!" Elizabeth greeted her young cousin. "What a blessing this child you will bear will be! And how fortunate for me that the mother of my Lord has come to visit."

Then Mary's soul was so filled with joy that she broke out into a song of praise, sometimes called the *magnificat*.

My soul praises the Lord,
I rejoice in God my Savior,
For he has given honor
To his humble handmaiden.
In years to come, people will call me blessed,
Yet the great thing was done
By he who is mighty.
Holy is his name.
His mercy has lasted from generation to generation.
With his strong arm
He has put down the proud and mighty,
He has fed the hungry.
Now he has remembered Israel,
As he promised Abraham
And Abraham's family forever.

For three months Mary remained with Elizabeth and Zacharias; then she returned to her home in Nazareth. *Luke 1:26–56*

A BOY NAMED JOHN

Shortly after Mary's visit, Elizabeth gave birth to a son, as the angel Gabriel had promised. According to Jewish law, she and Zacharias took him to the Temple when he was eight days old to dedicate him to the Lord and to name him. Many of their friends and relatives, rejoicing with them, came along.

"I suppose you're going to name the child Zacharias, for his father," several in the crowd suggested.

"No," Elizabeth said. "This baby is going to be named John."

"Why call him John?" they asked. "There is no one named John in your family."

Now old Zacharias had not spoken a word since the day when he had seen the angel by the side of the altar; but at this point, someone noticed that he was trying to say something with his hands. Finally, they saw that he wanted a tablet. When one was brought, he took it and simply wrote, "His name is John."

At once, he was able to speak again; and to the amazement of his relatives and neighbors, he poured out his joy and praise to the Lord:

Blessed be the Lord God of Israel,
Who has visited his people
And has planned their salvation,
As he promised long ago.
That we should be safe from our enemies,
Free to serve him without fear,
In holiness and righteousness,
All the days of our life.

You, my child, will be the prophet of the Most High,
To go before him and prepare the way,
To tell the people of salvation,
Of forgiveness of sins,
Through the tender mercy of God
When his daylight dawns,
Giving light to our darkness.

The crowd was impressed with these words of Zacharias and with the hopeful thoughts expressed. They asked each other, "What will this child really be?" and they watched with interest as the years passed and John grew to be a fine boy, strong in body and in mind. *Luke 1:57–80*

THE MESSIAH ARRIVES

Before Gabriel appeared to Mary, she was engaged to be married to a man named Joseph. However, when Joseph found out that she was expecting a child, he had some misgivings about their marriage. While he was trying to decide what to do, an angel appeared to him in a dream, saying, "Joseph, go ahead and marry Mary as you had planned. The child she is going to have was given by God to save his people from their sins."

So Joseph took Mary to be his wife.

About the same time, Augustus Caesar, the Roman emperor, commanded that a census be taken throughout all the provinces where he ruled. He had decided to collect a new tax, and all his subjects had to go to their home cities to register. Not one name was to be missing from the lists the Roman officers held.

Although Joseph lived in Nazareth, he was from the family of David, whose ties were in the city of Bethlehem, near Jerusalem. He had no choice but to go to Bethlehem and be counted in the census, even though the trip was a difficult one for Mary, whose baby was due to arrive very soon.

When the two reached Bethlehem, they found it already packed with travelers and were unable to find even a room at the inn. As a last resort, they bedded down for the night in a stable; and while sheltered there in the darkness of that shed, Mary gave birth to a son. She wrapped him up warmly with soft cloths and laid him to sleep in the only bed she could find—a manger filled with hay.

In a little wooden feed trough in a stable behind an inn lay the promised Messiah, and no one knew about it—at least not yet. But the angels around the throne of God knew, and before long they had spread the word to others. The first to hear the glad tidings were some shepherds who were guarding their sheep on the hills around Bethlehem. From out of the starry sky, one of the angels suddenly appeared, shining with the glory of the Lord's presence.

The shepherds were frightened; but the angel said, "Behold, I bring you tidings of great joy, which shall be to all the people. For there is born this day in the city of David, a Savior, which is Christ the Lord."

The angel added that they could find the child in Bethlehem in a stable. Then a great chorus of heavenly beings appeared, filling the silent night with the most beautiful music:

> Glory to God in the highest
> And on earth peace
> Good will among men.

When the angels were gone, the shepherds hurried into the city to see the child. Finding him with Mary and Joseph, as they had been told, they were more amazed than ever. At length they returned to the fields, thanking God for what they had seen and heard.

On the eighth day, like John, the child was named by his parents. They decided to call him Jesus, as the angel had suggested before he was born. Then, when he was forty days old, they brought him to the Temple in Jerusalem; and according to the Law of Moses regarding the first child born into a family, they made an offering of two pigeons.

At this time, there was an old man named Simeon living in Jerusalem. He was so anxious for God's promised One to come that the Lord had permitted him to live long enough to see Jesus with his own eyes. On the day that Mary and Joseph came to make their sacrifice, the Spirit of God led Simeon to the Temple, also. In fact, he was already there waiting when they arrived. When he saw the child, he took him from Mary and held him fondly while he thanked God. "Now I am ready to die," he said, "for with my own eyes I have seen the one God has sent to be the glory of Israel and the Savior of the whole world."

While Simeon spoke, an old woman named Anna, eighty-four years old, came in. Through God's Spirit, she, too, recognized the Christ child and gave thanks for his coming.

Mary and Joseph looked at one another happily and stored up in their hearts the words Simeon and Anna had said, just as they remembered the shepherds' description of angels singing on the night Jesus was born. It was wonderful, yet puzzling, to realize that their infant son was also God's Son who had come to live on earth. *Matthew 1:18–25; Luke 2:1–38*

FOLLOWING A STAR

In a country east of Jerusalem and Bethlehem, there lived some wise men who spent their time studying the stars. They hoped to discover in the movement and pattern of the constellations the answers to many questions about life and God. One night, as they searched the sky, they noticed a star that was unusually bright. Because it shone over Judea, they decided that a new king had been born there; and they came westward to find him.

Upon reaching Jerusalem, the men stopped to ask directions. "Where is the new King of the Jews?" they inquired, thinking everyone would know about him. "While in the East, we saw his star; and we have come to worship him." To their dismay, no one seemed to know what they meant.

Now Herod, the Roman ruler in Jerusalem, heard about the wise men and their questions. Talk of a new king was unpleasant for him to consider, so he called in the teachers and priests of the Jews.

"Who is this Christ, for whom your people are looking?" he asked. "Where is he to be born?"

And because the Jewish scholars knew the words of the prophets, they were able to give him an immediate answer: "The book of Micah tells us that he will come from Bethlehem."

Next Herod sent for the foreign wise men and questioned them about the strange star they had followed. He directed them to Bethlehem, saying, "Go and find this king of the Jews; then come and tell me where he is so that I may worship him, also." Actually his plan was to kill the child.

So the wise men turned toward Bethlehem. Suddenly the unusual star appeared overhead once more and guided them to the very house where Jesus was. They went inside; and when they saw the little one, with Mary, his mother, they knew this was the child born to be King. They knelt before him in worship; and from their treasures, they brought forth royal gifts of gold and precious perfumes called frankincense and myrrh.

But they did not return to Herod. In a dream God warned them to bypass Jerusalem and return home by another route.

Joseph, too, had a dream, in which an angel of the Lord told him to take the infant Jesus to Egypt, for Herod was trying to find him and destroy him. It was the middle of the night, but Joseph got up and awakened Mary. He told her to get ready for a journey. Quietly they gathered up their things, wrapped the baby warmly, and left for the faraway country of Egypt.

King Herod waited and waited for the wise men to return. When he finally heard that they had tricked him and gone home another way, he became very angry. He decided he would find the new king without them! Quickly he dispatched soldiers to Bethlehem with orders to kill every male child there under two years of age. But his cruel plan did not succeed, for by this time, Jesus was safe with his parents in Egypt.

Not long afterward, Herod died, and God told Joseph that it was safe to return to Israel. But because Herod's son was ruling in Judea in his place, Joseph did not stop in Bethlehem this time. He kept traveling northward with his family until they came to Nazareth, his and Mary's home when they first married. Here Joseph worked as a carpenter, and he and Mary provided the home in which Jesus grew to be a man.

Matthew 2

IN HIS FATHER'S HOUSE

The Bible has very little to say about the years Jesus spent as a boy in Nazareth, but we can imagine that his life was much like that of other Jewish boys of his day. His home was probably a very simple, country cottage, with Joseph's carpenter shop close by. His school was the village synagogue, or place of worship. Here he and others his age learned to read and to quote long passages from the Law of Moses and the writings of the prophets. They were also taught the stories that surrounded the well-known characters of Jewish history—Abraham, Moses, David, and all the rest.

On the Sabbath day there was no school held at the synagogue, but Jesus returned with his family and all other faithful Jews of Nazareth for worship. Once more the Law was explained and read, so it is no wonder many boys like Jesus knew much of it by memory.

To Mary and Joseph, the most important event of the year was Passover. They and other Jews from all over the world made it a point to return to Jerusalem at this time to celebrate the sacred feast that was first eaten by their ancestors on the night they left Egypt. When Jesus reached the age of twelve, he was considered old enough to become a "son of the Law" and to enter the Temple with other men for worship; so his parents let him accompany them to Jerusalem for the first time. Together with others from Nazareth, they traveled the sixty miles to David's city. Some walked and some rode donkeys in a large caravan. For two or three days they traveled—talking, singing, greeting old friends, and making new ones.

Finally they saw Jerusalem spread out on the hills before them. It was an impressive thing for the boy Jesus to first glimpse the great city so bound to his people's history. No doubt he was deeply moved when he caught sight of the splendid Temple, when he worshipped within its walls with the other men, and when he ate the simple Passover meal with his family. He lingered over the experiences, as though he could not be satisfied.

When the seven-day celebration was over, Mary and Joseph started for Nazareth with the rest of their group. They traveled all one day without sight of Jesus, thinking he was walking along with others his own age. But when evening came and he had not joined them, they began to look for him among their friends and relatives. No one had seen him all day.

There was nothing for the worried parents to do but return to Jerusalem in search of their son. They found him still in the Temple, discussing the Law with the greatest teachers of Israel. These wise men seemed intrigued with a lad who could ask such thoughtful questions and also respond to their questions with answers that showed an understanding beyond his years.

Mary could not resist a little scolding: "Son, why have you done this to us? We have been looking everywhere for you. Didn't you know that we would worry?"

"Why did you have to look for me?" Jesus replied. "Didn't you know that I would be in my Father's house?"

Neither Joseph nor Mary understood, but Mary remembered his answer and thought about it afterward.

This time Jesus obediently returned with them to Nazareth and to the life he lived as the eldest son of their humble family. As years passed by, he grew "in mind and body, more pleasing to God and to men." *Luke 2:39–52*

QUESTIONS: 1. *Why were synagogues first built?* 2. *What was the name given to the family that led Israel in throwing off Syrian oppression?* 3. *Who controlled the world when Jesus was born?* 4. *Why did the Jews resent the rule of Rome? What did they think was the answer to their frustrating situation?* 5. *What did Gabriel tell*

Zacharias? Why did Zacharias lose his voice? 6. *What did Gabriel tell Mary?* 7. *What relation were Mary and Elizabeth?* 8. *How did Zacharias regain his voice?* 9. *Why did Joseph and Mary have to go to Bethlehem?* 10. *Where was Jesus born? Why?* 11. *Who first heard about the Messiah's birth?* 12. *Who were the two people that saw Jesus when his parents brought him to the Temple?* 13. *How did the wise men find their way to Judea?* 14. *Why did Herod also want to find Jesus?* 15. *Where did Joseph take Mary and the child?* 16. *Where did they settle when they returned to the land of Israel?* 17. *What did Jesus study in the synagogue?* 18. *Why did Jesus go to Jerusalem with his parents? How old was he?* 19. *Where did Mary and Joseph find Jesus when they thought he was lost?* 20. *What was Jesus' explanation for being there?*

Kingdom Beginnings

A NEW PROPHET

Practically nothing is known concerning the life of Jesus from the time he visited Jerusalem at the age of twelve until he left Nazareth as a man of thirty to begin his Father's work. We can assume that outwardly he lived a normal existence, because his neighbors saw nothing unusual about him; but we know that inwardly his mind was active, always observing the lives of those around him.

For one thing, he was forced to watch the Roman government use its power over his people. This experience was bound to have made him aware of how weak and helpless the kingdom of Israel had become. Surely he noted that the only time a spark of hope shone in the eyes of the people was when they spoke of a leader, a Messiah, who would deliver their nation. These things must have caused him to think and to communicate with God, as no other man before him could. He was the Messiah. How could he save? Where should he lead?

Meanwhile, John, the promised son born to Zacharias and Elizabeth had also grown to manhood. From an early age, he, too, had known that God had a special purpose for his life; and he had gone into the desert alone to consider his future. The rough country suited this brooding young man, and he grew to prefer the simple life he found there. Like Jesus, his thoughts were on the people and their need for a saviour. He considered how Israel had always failed to meet God's demands. Then, in response, he felt the call to make the nation aware of its sin, to prepare it to follow a deliverer.

So he came out of the desert, a strange figure of a man who wore rough robes made from camel skins and ate food of the desert, locusts and honey. By the Jordan River, not far from Jerusalem, he began preaching his message about the new King and his Kingdom.

"Get ready! The new kingdom will come and you will be too sinful to be a part of it," John said. "Give up your evil ways, and do what is right."

It did not take long for word to travel that a new prophet was speaking beside the Jordan River. For years there had been no one to speak with the authority of God, and the people flocked out to hear him. They listened spellbound while he pointed out their sins. Then he called for them to be baptized to show that they wanted to be clean and pure, fit for God's kingdom when it came.

"We know we need to change," the people agreed. "What can we do to show it?"

"You can share your food and clothes with those who have none," John replied.

"Those of you who are tax collectors should take no more money than the law allows. You, soldiers, should be gentle to the people and be sure that you are right before you make accusations. Be content with the money you are paid."

But of those Jews who felt that they were already good enough and needed no improvement, John was outspoken in his scolding. "You brood of snakes!" he said to them. "How do you think you are going to escape that which is coming? Don't think that you can claim Abraham as your father and be saved. Being Abraham's children will not account for a thing if there is wickedness in your lives."

Loran Raymond Jones

THE NATIVITY

Luke 2:1–20

Loran Raymond Jones

THE FLIGHT INTO EGYPT

Matthew 2:13–15

Loran Raymond Jones

THE CARPENTER SHOP

Luke 2:51–52

Loran Raymond Jones

THE BOY JESUS IN THE TEMPLE

Luke 2:41–52

Loran Raymond Jones

JESUS IN THE WILDERNESS

Matthew 4:1–11

Loran Raymond Jones

WATER MADE INTO WINE AT CANA

John 2:1–11

Loran Raymond Jones

NICODEMUS VISITS JESUS

John 3:1–13

Loran Raymond Jones

JESUS AND THE SAMARITAN WOMAN

John 4:5–30

Such crowds came to John and were baptized by him in the Jordan River that the fire of hope was fanned among the people. They asked him, "Are you the Christ? Will you be the one who delivers us?"

John was quick to reply. "No," he said; "I am not the promised One of God. He is so much greater than I that I would not even be good enough to stoop down and fasten his sandal. I have baptized you with water, but he will baptize you with the Spirit of God."

To the north, in Galilee, Jesus heard of the new prophet and his sermons. Sensing that the time had come for him to begin his work, he came south and joined the people who presented themselves to John for baptism. But when John saw him, he hesitated. He knew that he had come face to face with one greater and holier than he.

"Why have you come to me?" John asked the Christ. "I should be baptized by you."

"Let it be so," Jesus replied. "It is part of God's plan."

So Jesus and John walked out into the water, and John baptized him just as he had all the others. When Jesus came out of the water, he was radiant with God's presence within him. At that moment, the Father's spirit, in the form of a dove, rested on him; and he heard a voice from heaven, saying, "You are my Son, and you have pleased me greatly."

Matthew 3:1–17, Mark 1:1–11, Luke 3:2–22, John 1:19–24

A STRUGGLE WITH SATAN

After Jesus was baptized by John, he went off alone into the deserted country west of the Jordan, a place so barren only wild animals lived there. In this setting, he spent more than a month in thought and prayer. He knew that he needed to understand perfectly the tasks he would perform on earth as Savior and Deliverer. He needed to face them openly and receive God's strength to help him carry them out. All of this was not easy. There was always the temptation for him to reject his calling, to fail in his duty because he was a man.

Yes, he had an opportunity to choose the wrong path, just as all men do. Satan came and offered it to him.

During his time of meditation in the wilderness, Jesus had been so intent upon his thought that he had not eaten; and when it was over, he found himself weak and starving. Knowing this, Satan suggested to him: "Use your power as God's Son to change these stones on the ground into bread."

Jesus felt that he had the power to perform such a feat, but he realized that his power was not to be used merely to give material things to himself or to others. Comforts of life impressed people, but there were other things of greater value. To show what he meant, he quoted from the Law of Moses he had learned so well as a boy: "Men cannot live on bread alone; he needs to live by the words God speaks to him."

But Satan does not give up easily. He tries all of us over and over, seeking to have us turn from God's will and follow his own. He next sought to tempt Jesus by showing him a view of the kingdom in its days of glory. "Israel could rise among the nations of the world again and you could lead her to it," Satan urged. "You would only need to submit to me."

But Jesus was not willing to give in to the pride and ambition and other sorts of evil it took to obtain power and glory on earth, for it, like Satan's other gifts, was of little worth once it was gained. On the other hand, God's rewards had an eternal value. So he said, quoting again, "The Law of Moses commands that I serve God and God alone."

Still Satan would not go away. From a point high on the Temple, he asked that Jesus throw himself down and let God send angels to save him. Perhaps he was trying to make Jesus feel that he should forsake his trust in God if harm ever came his way. Or he might have been suggesting that Jesus perform spectacular miracles to attract the attention of the people.

In truth, Jesus knew that his power was not to be used just to amaze the crowds. And his faith in God was not the sort that failed when he was made to suffer. Instead, it would help him overcome the dangers and trials he might face. So he answered: "I will not test God's power in this way."

At this, Satan left, realizing he had been defeated. He had made Jesus face the temptations that would stand in the way of his work on earth, and the Christ had mastered them all. *Luke 4:1–13*

FISHERS OF MEN

After the period of thought and trial in the wilderness, Jesus was ready to begin his work. He journeyed from the Jordan Valley back to Galilee—not to Nazareth, but to Capernaum, a fishing village on the Sea of Galilee. Here he began the preaching, the healing, the signs and wonders that proclaimed to the people that he was appointed of God and had God's power working in him to win the hearts and minds of other men.

At the very beginning, he selected several men to assist him in spreading the good news about the coming of God's kingdom. One might expect him to have gone to the synagogues of Galilee and chosen the teachers of the Law, but he did not. Those men could not give the people the message Jesus wanted them to hear. Instead, he walked down by the Sea of Galilee and mingled with the fishermen. Two of them were brothers, Simon and Andrew, who had gone to hear John and already knew something of Jesus. In fact, John had pointed Jesus out to Andrew one day; and immediately Andrew had gone to get Simon.

"Come with me!" he said excitedly to his brother. "I have found the Messiah!"

So Simon returned with Andrew to the place where Jesus was staying. Before any introductions were made, Jesus recognized him. "Are you not Simon, Jona's son?" he asked. Then he added: "Some day people will call you Peter, a Rock."

Therefore, when Jesus met the brothers fishing by the Sea of Galilee, they were not strangers. All it took was an invitation from Jesus—"Come with me and you will become fishers of men"—to make them leave their nets and follow him.

Further down the shore he found two more brothers, James and John, mending nets with their father Zebedee. At Jesus' call, they, like Peter and Andrew, came immediately, leaving Zebedee and the servants in the boat, wondering what had happened.

Soon afterward Jesus found a man named Philip who answered his summons with the same willingness the others had shown. Like Andrew, Philip could not keep his discovery of the Messiah, or Christ, to himself. He went to his friend Nathanael and said, "I have found the deliverer spoken of by Moses and the prophets. He is Jesus of Nazareth, the son of Joseph."

Now Nathanael himself lived not far from Nazareth, and he knew that it was only a small village. It was hard for him to believe that someone famous had come from there. "Can anything good come out of Nazareth?" he asked.

"Come and see," Philip replied.

So the two went to Jesus. As they were walking toward him, Jesus looked up and saw them. "Here comes an Israelite with a truly pure heart," Jesus said, speaking of Nathanael.

The man blinked with surprise. "How did you know about me?"

"Before Philip ever called you, I saw you standing under a fig tree," Jesus explained.

This impressed Nathanael. "You must be God's Son," he admitted. "You know more than a man could know."

"Have you believed in me just because I said I saw you under the fig tree? You will see much greater things than that," Jesus told him.

Another of Jesus' helpers was found among the tax collectors, a more unlikely group than fishermen. These hated Jews had turned their backs on their own people to assist the Roman government, and one would scarcely think they would have had an interest in the gospel, or "good news" about the kingdom. Yet when Jesus called one named Levi (later known as Matthew), he was drawn to leave all and follow.

Altogether, Jesus chose twelve such special helpers, whom he called "apostles." Besides the seven already mentioned, there were Thomas, another James who was the son of Alphaeus, Thaddaeus, Simon the Canaanite, and Judas Iscariot. With this band who had turned aside from everything to come with him, Jesus began the work that changed the world. *Matthew 4:18–22; 9:9–13, Mark 1:16–20; 2:13–17; 3:13–19, Luke 5:1–11, 27–32; 6:12–16, John 1:35–51*

THE WEDDING FEAST

Mary, the mother of Jesus, was attending a wedding in nearby Cana; and she sent word to Jesus and his new followers to join her. "You will all be welcome," she assured them.

Now in those days a wedding was followed by a great feast, sometimes lasting all night, or even a day or two. Mary and Jesus and the disciples were only a small part of the huge crowd that was present at the celebration following this particular wedding.

During the middle of the party, Mary came and called Jesus off to one side. "They have run out of wine," she whispered to him. "The servants don't know where to turn."

Somehow Mary knew that Jesus could do something to help. She gave him a pleading look and then turned to the servants and said, "Do whatever he tells you."

Jesus looked about the room. His eyes lighted on six huge jars, about the size of barrels. They were of a sort commonly used in Jewish homes to keep water for washing before meals, as commanded in the Law.

"Fill those jars with water," Jesus said.

So the servants filled them with clear water to the very brim.

"Now," Jesus went on, "take some of the water out and let the ruler of the feast taste it."

Into a jar, one of the servants dipped a ladle and brought it out, dripping and full. But it was not full of water! It held a delicious wine!

The one in charge of the food took the ladle and tasted it. "This is wonderful!" he exlaimed. "Where did it come from?"

Then he called the bridegroom over. "Taste this," he said. "Usually people serve their best wine at the beginning of the party, but you have saved the finest until now."

This was the first time Jesus demonstrated his power in Galilee, and it made the disciples who were with him believe even more fully than before. *John 2:1–11*

A NIGHT VISITOR

During the time that Jesus lived, there were leaders of the Jews who felt that they alone were keeping God's law. Many of these, particularly a group called the Pharisees, disliked the fact that Jesus had not chosen them to be his special helpers. They disapproved of his spending his time to serve the poor, feeling that if he were really the Messiah, he would come to them and work most with them. After all, they tried hardest to live after God's commands.

What these Jews failed to realize was that they were not being true to the real meaning of the Law. In his work, Jesus was pointing out to them its true values, the ones that would stand when God's kingdom came. Unfortunately, most of them could not admit that they had been wrong; therefore, they never believed in Jesus.

One exception was a leader in the Jewish council named Nicodemus. Realizing that most of this associates were not in sympathy with the Christ, he came to see him in secret during the night.

"Master," Nicodemus said, "I know that you have been sent by God. No one could do the things you do if God were not with him."

When Jesus saw that this man was interested in his work, he began to speak to him about the kingdom he had come to introduce. "If you want to be a part of God's kingdom, you will have to be born again."

This sounded confusing to Nicodemus. "Born again?" he asked. "How can this be? Can a grown man become a baby?"

"You are speaking of man's body; I am talking about his spirit," Jesus explained. "Everyone in the kingdom will have a reborn spirit, a clean spirit, like new.

"It should not be too hard to understand. You can tell when the wind is present although you don't know where it came from or where it is going. In the same way, you will know that your heart is changed, but not how it was done."

Then he went on with some more of the kingdom's most important concepts: God loved the world so much that he sent his own Son into the world to live. Everyone who believes in him will not die, but live forever. His reason for coming to earth was not to find fault and condemn, but to show people how to live—to let the light of truth shine in the darkness of their sinful lives. *John 2:23–3:15*

"LIVING WATER"

Between Judea, where Jerusalem and Bethlehem were located, and Galilee, where Nazareth and Capernaum were found, there lay a province called Samaria. Normally, Jews traveling from Judea to Galilee avoided Samaria, choosing to make their journey unnecessarily long rather than pass through its borders. They based their long-standing hatred on the fact that the Samaritans were descendants of the ten tribes of Israel who broke away from the kingdom after the death of Solomon and intermarried with foreigners. Through the years, their worship of God had differed from that of the tribe of Judah, who had remained loyal to the succession of kings from David. For one thing, they had built their own temple on Mount Gerizim and ordained priests from among their number to serve in it. The Jews in Jerusalem considered them half-breeds and refused to let them worship at the Temple there.

But Jesus had a love for all people that prevented him from making such distinctions between nations. When he wanted to travel from Judea to Galilee, he did not hesitate to pass right through the heart of Samaria. About noontime, he sat down beside an old well that Jacob had dug centuries before and sent his friends into the nearby town to buy food. While he was there, a Samaritan woman came out from town to fill her water jar at the well.

"I have no way to draw water," Jesus admitted to the woman. "May I have a drink from your jar?"

She gave him a strange look. "Are you, a Jew, asking me to give you a drink? I'm a Samaritan."

"If you recognized me and knew what I had to give, you would ask me for a drink, and I would give you living water," Jesus told her.

"What do you mean?" the woman asked, rather confused. "You have no bucket to draw any kind of water, and this well is deep. Where are you going to get 'living water'?"

"If you drink water from this well, you will get thirsty again," Jesus replied. "But the water I'm speaking of is different. Once you drink it, you will never thirst." He was referring to her thirst, or need, for a better understanding of God.

At first, the woman had thought that he meant to give her some magic kind of water that would keep her from having to return again and again to the well. But the more he talked, the more impressed she became.

Finally, she ventured, "Sir, I think you are a prophet. Tell me, you Jews say that men ought to worship in Jerusalem, but my people worship right here on this mountain. Who is right?"

"The time is coming when people will not have to worship at any particular place," Jesus answered. "They will see that God is a Spirit; and when they have this Spirit in their hearts, they will be worshiping in the true way."

"Yes, I know. A Messiah is coming who is going to tell us all these things."

Jesus looked up at the woman of Samaria. "I am the Christ," he said quietly.

Just then, the disciples arrived with food from the village. In the confusion, the woman forgot all about her water jars and ran back into town. "Come with me!" she said to her people. "Come and see a man who knows everything. Do you think he could be the Promised One?"

A crowd gathered around the woman and followed her back out to the well. When they saw Jesus and talked to him, they were convinced that he was God's son. They begged him to remain with them, which he did for two days. During that time, many came to believe in him.

"At first, we believed because of what you told us," they said to the woman who had gone to the well. "But now we have seen for ourselves that he is the Savior of the world." *John 4:5–42*

A PROPHET WITHOUT HONOR

From the Jordan, from Cana, from Samaria, came word that one named Jesus was speaking with great authority and performing wonderful miracles. The people of Galilee were particularly interested in these stories because they knew him to be a native of their own province. Curious to see if what they had heard was true, they welcomed him in every city and synagogue of their land.

Among these Galileean villages, Jesus chose to proclaim his message in Nazareth, the place in which he grew up, where his family still lived. Arriving there on a Sabbath Day, he entered the synagogue at the time of worship, as he was accustomed to doing.

Because Jesus now had a reputation as a teacher, he was called upon to read the lesson from the prophets. Standing, he took a scroll, opened it to the words of Isaiah, and read:

> The Spirit of God is upon me
> Because he has chosen me to preach good news to the poor:
> He sent me to set captives free,
> And make the blind see,
> To liberate the mistreated,
> To proclaim that the time of the Lord has come.

When he had finished the passage, he rolled up the scroll and handed it back to the ruler of the synagogue. Then he said: "Today you are seeing these words come true."

The people sat up and began listening with interest. Jesus continued: "You have heard of the deeds I have done in other places; now you are probably going to demand that I perform the same wonders here.

"I tell you, a prophet is usually honored everywhere except in his own home. Take the example of Elijah. During his lifetime, there was a famine that lasted three and a half years, and many in Israel needed help. But did God send Elijah to any of them? No. Instead he sent him to a widow in the region of Sidon. And Elisha—he could have cured lepers in Israel, but he chose to heal only Naaman, the Syrian leper."

At these words, the mood of the congregation changed. They did not like Jesus to imply that the promises of God were to be granted to outsiders.

"What right does he have to say these things to us?" they demanded. "Why is he any wiser than the rest of us? Isn't he the son of Joseph, the carpenter? Don't his brothers—James, Joseph, Judas, and Simon—live here among us?"

And they became so overwrought that they forced him to leave the city with very little good accomplished. Disappointed, but not defeated, he moved to Capernaum, the larger city on the Sea of Galilee. In the next several months, it became the center of his blossoming public ministry.

Matthew 13:54–58; Mark 6:1–6; Luke 4:16–30

QUESTIONS: 1. *What kind of man did John grow to be?* 2. *How did John make his appearance to Israel? What was his message?* 3. *How did the people respond to John's preaching?* 4. *Describe the baptism of Jesus.* 5. *Why did Jesus retire to a lonely place following his baptism?* 6. *In what three ways did Satan tempt Jesus to turn aside from his God-given mission?* 7. *How did Jesus answer Satan each time?* 8. *Why did Jesus not choose his helpers from among the Jewish leaders?* 9. *Describe the men chosen to be apostles.* 10. *What celebration did Jesus, his mother, and his friends attend?* 11. *How did Jesus first demonstrate his power?* 12. *How did Jesus describe the "new birth" to Nicodemus?* 13. *Why did the Jews avoid Samaria? Why didn't Jesus avoid it?* 14. *What was the "living water" Jesus offered to the Samaritan woman?* 15. *What was Jesus asked to do when he visited Nazareth?* 16. *Why did the Nazarenes resent his teaching?* 17. *What place did he choose for the center of his now-public ministry?*

The King Shows His Power

A BUSY SABBATH

The city of Capernaum, located on the Sea of Galilee, became the center of Jesus' activity following his rejection in Nazareth. Capernaum was already the home of some of his most faithful friends, the fishermen Simon, Andrew, James and John. Here, as in other towns with a large Jewish population, Jesus found favorable audiences whenever he went to the synagogue. The common people who heard him at such services could immediately tell the difference between the way he spoke and the way in which they were used to hearing the priests and teachers talk. Those men always pointed out the things other people had said about God, and they made the Law of Moses a burden. Jesus, on the other hand, spoke about God as one who knew Him well and had a way of making religion become a blessing.

At one such synagogue service, a man in the crowd suddenly stood up and shouted: "What are you trying to do, Jesus of Nazareth? Destroy us? I know who you are. You're God's Holy One."

Jesus took one look at the distraught man and he knew what was wrong. "Peace," he said quietly. Then, "Come out of this man, you evil spirit of Satan," he ordered.

With a convulsive cry, the evil spirit left the man. His sane self was restored, and the difference was so striking that the crowd assembled was amazed. "What is this?" they asked each other. "Jesus has authority over Satan himself." And they quickly spread the story all through the region of Galilee.

From the synagogue, Jesus went with Simon, Andrew, James and John to Simon's home. There they found that the mother of Simon's wife had become ill with a very, very high fever. When Jesus heard of it, he went into the room where the woman lay. Touching her by the hand, he helped her to sit, then to stand. Immediately, her fever left, and she felt so well that she began serving food to those in the house.

This incident was spread as quickly as the one that had occurred at the synagogue; and it is no wonder that by evening a crowd had gathered around Simon's house. With new found hope, people from all around brought their loved ones who were sick to the place where Jesus was. When he saw the large group waiting for him outside the door, his heart was filled with compassion. He stepped out into their midst and laid his hands upon them, making them well. *Matthew 8:14–17; Mark 1:21–34; Luke 4:31–41*

A HOLE IN THE ROOF

The busy Sabbath Day, filled by synagogue services and the incidents at Simon's home, left Jesus drained and weary. Early the next morning, he got up and went out of Capernaum to a deserted place, where he refreshed himself in prayer with his Father. But Jesus could not remain alone now. He had become a public figure. Before long, Simon and the others came to get him. "Everyone is looking for you," they said. "Come back into Capernaum."

Jesus answered, "Let us go into other towns, that I may preach there too. This is the work I have come to do." So the apostles followed him through all the cities in that part of Galilee, hearing him spread the news of God's kingdom and seeing him heal all kinds of illness. He even dared to touch and cure the wretched body of a man with leprosy, a man no one else would come near. Because the crowds were demanding more and more signs of healing, Jesus asked the former leper not to say anything to anyone, but the man was so excited that he told the story to everyone he met. Just as Jesus expected, the crowds grew to such size that he could not even get into the cities, but had to move toward the open fields. Even there, people flocked from every direction.

Eventually Jesus and his band of close followers returned to Capernaum. When it was reported throughout the city that he was at a certain house, the people gathered there in great numbers, filling the house itself, and overflowing into the yard all around. Four men who had brought a palsied friend to be healed found that they could not even get near Jesus. Still, they were so concerned for their friend, whose arms and legs shook and could not support him, that they refused to be discouraged. Finding an outside staircase, they climbed up onto the flat roof and began opening up a hole. When it was large enough, they lowered the man by the four corners of his bed to the spot where Jesus was standing.

No doubt Jesus was amazed when the sick man appeared through the roof, and he was impressed with the determination and faith that the man's friends had shown. He looked down at the man and said, "My son, your sins are forgiven."

Some of the Jewish Pharisees who suspected and doubted Jesus were present in the crowded room. When they heard what Jesus had said to the palsied man, they began whispering among themselves. "What right does he have to speak that way?" they asked. "He has no power to forgive sins—only God can do that."

Immediately Jesus sensed the resentment the Pharisees felt; and looking their way, he said, "Which is it easier to say—'Your sins are forgiven,' or

'Rise and walk'? To show you that I indeed have the power to forgive sins," (he turned once more to the sick man), "Rise, pick up your bed, and go to your house."

At once, the palsied man felt a steadying strength surge through his body. He stood up, rolled up the mat that had served as his bed, lifted it, and walked out of the house, praising God with every step. The crowd that was left behind shook their heads in disbelief. Those who trusted in Jesus as the Messiah believed more than ever in his promises and claims. Even the critical Jewish leaders could not dispute what had happened, but this made them despise Jesus more than ever. *Matthew 9:1–8; Mark 1:35–45; 2:1–12; Luke 4:42–44; 5:12–26*

JESUS VERSUS THE PHARISEES

The most religious Jewish men of Jesus' day, the ones who studied the Law of Moses, were very disappointed in Jesus. He was nothing like the Messiah they had anticipated. For one thing, he had ignored them and chosen common working men—even a tax collector—to be his closest friends. He spent most of his time in the province of Galilee with the poorest, most ordinary folk.

These men who thought themselves so religious decided, therefore, that Jesus was not what he claimed to be because he did not fit their image. They still came out to hear him, but merely for the sake of finding fault and proving to themselves that he was not sent from God.

Sometimes they came right out and asked him questions about the Law to try to trick him. This was especially true of the Pharisees, because they felt that no one knew the finer points of the Law better than they. One day they challenged Jesus: "Why don't your disciples fast on the Sabbath Day? John's disciples did, and we Pharisees do."

Jesus explained: "While the bridegroom is at the feast, everyone is happy; there is no reason to fast and mourn. When the bridegroom goes away—that is the time for fasting."

At another time Jesus was in Jerusalem for the Passover, and men of this same type were following him around there to see what he would do. Not far from the Temple there was a pool called Bethesda where sick people gathered. According to popular belief, the waters of the pool bubbled at certain times; and when this happened, the first sick person to reach the pool would be cured.

As Jesus passed by Bethesda Pool on a Sabbath Day, he stopped to speak to a man who had been crippled for thirty-eight years. "Would you like to be well?" he asked.

"Oh, yes," the cripple replied, "but I have no one to carry me over to the water when it bubbles. Someone else always reaches it first."

"Get up. Pick up your bed and walk," Jesus told him.

Immediately, the man was cured. With ease, he rolled up his mattress and walked away. But some of the Pharisees were nearby; and when they saw him, they said, "You're not supposed to be carrying that mat. It's the same as working, and we are commanded not to work on the Sabbath."

He answered, "The one who cured me told me to pick it up and carry it away."

So the self-righteous Pharisees confronted Jesus later. "Why did you heal that man on the Sabbath?" they demanded to know.

"My Father and I work to do good on all days," Jesus replied. But this answer only made them angrier than ever. Not only had he broken the Sabbath; he had also referred to God as his Father.

This was only the beginning of the controversy Jesus was to carry on with the Jewish leaders concerning the Sabbath Day. It was all brought to the front on another occasion when Jesus and his disciples walked through a cornfield and plucked some of the ears of corn to eat.

"Stop!" said the Pharisees present on that Sabbath. "It is against Jewish law for you to do that."

"What do you mean?" Jesus answered them. "Don't you remember what David did when he was hungry? He went into the sanctuary and took some of the holy bread to eat. I tell you, one greater than the Temple is here now, and he is Lord even of the Sabbath."

Then, on another Sabbath, he was going into the synagogue for worship when he passed a man with a withered hand. Knowing that they were watching, Jesus turned back to look at the Pharisees. "Would it be breaking the Sabbath for me to heal this man?" he asked them. Then he posed some more questions for them to consider: "Which of you, if you had one sheep and it had fallen in a pit on the Sabbath, would not go and rescue it? Well, this man is worth far more than a sheep. You need to realize that it is always right to do good on the Sabbath.

"Now, stretch out your hand," he said to the handicapped man. And when the man obeyed, he found his once-withered hand as well and strong as the other.

But nothing Jesus had said convinced the Pharisees that he was God's Son and that he was showing them the true meaning of the Law. Instead, they began to plan how they could be rid of him.

Matthew 9:14–17, 12:1–14; Mark 2:18–28, 3:1–6; Luke 5:33–39, 6:1–11; John 5:1–18

SERMON ON A MOUNTAIN

No doubt many were attracted to Jesus because of his healing power; but once they realized that this was only a demonstration of God's power that lived within him, they were drawn to him as their Savior. They believed in him, proclaimed that he was King in their lives, and wanted to know how they could become subjects in his kingdom.

The kingdom was one of the most difficult things Jesus tried to explain. During the years of his ministry he used many different illustrations to try to reveal its unusual nature. The longest explanation he gave is written in the book of Matthew and known to us as the Sermon on the Mount. It begins with a description of the lasting qualities subjects of the kingdom would demonstrate:

> Blessed are the poor in spirit: for theirs is the kingdom of heaven.
> Blessed are they that mourn: for they shall be comforted.
> Blessed are the meek: for they shall inherit the earth.
> Blessed are they which do hunger and thirst after righteousness: for they shall be filled.
> Blessed are the merciful: for they shall obtain mercy.
> Blessed are the pure in heart: for they shall see God.
> Blessed are the peacemakers: for they shall be called the children of God.
> Blessed are they which are persecuted for righteousness' sake: for theirs is the kingdom of heaven.
> Blessed are you, when men shall persecute you and say all manner of evil against you falsely for my sake.
> Rejoice and be exceedingly glad: for great is your reward in heaven.

Then Jesus went on to explain the effect that the members of his kingdom would have on the world. Their example would shine like the lights of a city that was set on a hill. Others, seeing their "light" would want to become part of the kingdom also.

He showed how the laws of his kingdom would differ from the Law of Moses. Rather than merely performing or abstaining from certain acts, a member of the kingdom of God would have a deeper understanding, one that called for a pure heart and mind behind all actions. In this way, he would fulfill the real issues of the Law—the love and justice that the Pharisees failed to see in all their rule-keeping.

All subjects of the kingdom were to put God foremost in their lives. They were not to be overly concerned with the things in the world around them lest these become more important than God and eternal matters. In turn, God was going to see that the physical necessities of life were supplied. "Don't worry," Jesus said, "about what to eat or drink or wear. Look at the birds—they don't plant and harvest crops. Yet God feeds them. And think about the lilies of the field—they are not concerned with the way they look, yet God has clothed them with more beauty than Solomon possessed when he wore his most splendid robes.

"Now if God cares that much for the birds and the flowers, don't you believe he will take care of you?" he questioned his listeners. "After all, you are of much more value in his sight, and he knows that you need these things."

"Will there be many in the kingdom?" some wanted to know.

Jesus replied, "Not everyone who calls me 'Lord, Lord,' will be included, but the ones who do the will of my Father. Many will try to belong, but only a few will be able to enter in because the others will find it too hard. They will think that it is too difficult to live after God's rules instead of their own."

"If it is so hard to enter into the kingdom, how will we ever succeed?"

"Ask God's help, and it will be given to you. Look for him and you will find him. Remember that God is your Father. Since you understand that fathers on earth know how to take care of their children, can't you believe that God, in the same way, knows how to care for you?"

The crowd nodded in agreement. The kingdom was taking on meaning.

Matthew 5, 6, 7; Luke 6:17–49

"PEACE, BE STILL"

The crowd that gathered to hear the Sermon on the Mount was just one of many that pressed close to Jesus day after day. In every town throughout Galilee, and even in the open fields between, he healed the sick who came or were brought and spoke of his Father in heaven. Many times his lessons were taught from the banks of the Sea of Galilee, located in the middle of the province. In fact, it was here that Jesus engaged in such an intensive ministry that he grew very tired and asked the people to leave. Still they lingered, however, begging for his healing touch or his life-giving words.

When he saw that there was no other way to rest, Jesus said to his closest disciples, "Let us get in a boat and row to the other side of the lake."

Soon a boat was found, and Jesus' friends rowed him out into the lake away from the crowds. Exhausted, the Savior himself went to the front of the boat to rest on a cushion. Within a few moments, he had fallen fast asleep, not noticing the dark clouds that were swiftly covering the sky.

The disciples began to worry when they saw that the clouds were heralding a fierce storm. The wind began to blow, stirring up the waves and causing the boat to rock; but they rowed along in silence, knowing how much Jesus needed the undisturbed rest. Then the wind began to blow stronger than ever, and the mighty waves beat against the boat and lifted it high. Some broke over its side and filled the bottom with water.

At this point, the disciples were not only worried; they were terribly frightened. They grabbed Jesus and shook him to wake him. "Master, we are about to be drowned!" they cried. "Help us, save us!"

Jesus sat up and looked about at the raging storm. All he had to say was, "Peace, be still." At once, the winds ceased and the water grew calm. The dark clouds passed by, and the little boat rocked gently on untroubled water.

"Why were you so afraid?" Jesus asked the disciples. "Why did you get so worried when I was here all along? Do you not believe in my power?"

The men looked in amazement at the still water, then at Jesus, and finally at one another. They shook their heads as if they could not believe what they had seen. What kind of man was this who could control even the wind and the water? How could anyone fail to believe that he was the Son of God?

Matthew 8:23–27; Mark 4:35–41; Luke 8:22–25

A SLEEPING MAIDEN

When Jesus and his friends returned to Capernaum from their trip across the Sea of Galilee, they found another crowd already assembled and waiting for them. Jesus had no sooner stepped from the boat than a man moved in front of the rest and came and knelt down before him. This man was Jairus, an important figure in the city because he served as leader in the synagogue. On this occasion, however, Jairus did not feel like a proud person. He was humble and distressed as he pled with Jesus: "My little girl is about to die. You must come—just lay your hands on her—and I know she will get well."

Jesus smiled at Jairus. "I will come with you," he agreed. "Lead me to your house." So the two started toward Jairus' home, but the whole crowd moved along with them. There were so many trying to walk down the narrow streets with Jesus that he could not cover much distance.

One of the people in the throng was a woman who had been sick for twelve years. She had been to many doctors and spent every cent she owned, but she got no better. No one paid any attention to her now and she pushed and pushed to get close to Jesus. "If I could only touch the bottom of his clothes," she thought, "that would be enough to make me well."

At last the woman reached Jesus' side. Reaching out her hand, she timidly touched the bottom of his robe. Immediately, she began to feel better and knew that she was healed.

Then Jesus wheeled around and asked suddenly, "Who just touched me?"

"What do you mean?" replied one of the disciples with a laugh. "Why, there are people pressing against you and touching you on every side."

But Jesus had felt a special touch and knew that his power had gone out to help someone.

The woman still stood back in the crowd, afraid that she had done something wrong. As Jesus looked her way, she came forward, shaking and frightened. She fell down on the ground before him and admitted what she had done. In reply, Jesus comforted her by saying, "Daughter, you have been made well because you believed that I could heal you. There is no reason to be afraid. Go in peace."

While Jesus took the time to speak with this woman, Jairus remained at his side, waiting anxiously to hurry on. He knew that his daughter could not live long. But before he and Jesus could progress any further, a messenger arrived from his house. "You need not trouble the Master any further," he whispered to Jairus. "Your daughter is already dead."

"Don't be afraid," Jesus said quickly. "Just believe in me and your daughter will yet be saved." Then they hurried to Jairus' home as fast as the crowd would permit.

Already the house was full of relatives who had come to comfort Jairus and his wife. They stood around weeping and wailing for the little girl. "Don't cry," Jesus said, as he passed them at the door. "She is not dead—just sleeping." But they looked at him with disbelief. They had seen the girl and they knew she was dead.

So Jesus cleared them all out of the way, and took only Jairus, his wife, and three disciples into the room where the little girl lay. He bent over the child and took one of her cold hands in his own. "Little maiden, get up," he called gently.

As he spoke, the girl opened her eyes. She sat up and threw her legs over the side of the bed. Then she stood and walked to her father and mother.

"Now she will need something to eat," Jesus said. And as the mother hurried to find food for her daughter, he and his three friends walked out of the house and back to the crowd that was waiting for them.

Matthew 9:18–26; Mark 5:21–43; Luke 8:40–56

A PICNIC SUPPER

Around the villages of Galilee Jesus traveled once more. With him went the twelve disciples, as well as other friends who provided money for food and lodging. In every place Jesus spoke to the crowds that flocked to hear him and healed the sick that were brought; yet it seemed that he was only beginning to accomplish the task that was set before him.

"There is so much to be done," he admitted to his disciples, "and so few of us to do it. Pray that God will send more workers."

He decided that one way to accomplish more was to share his work with his closest companions, the "apostles." Calling the twelve around him, he gave them a portion of God's power so that they could teach and heal as they had seen him do.

"Go forth, now, and preach to the Jews in every city," he charged them. "Tell them that the kingdom of God is very near. Heal their sick; cast out the devils that live within them. Up until now, you have received every blessing from God's hand. Now it is time for you to share with others.

"On this journey, you are not to take money or extra clothes. You will earn enough as you go along.

"Search out those who are anxious to hear your message and spend your time with them. If you find people unwilling to listen, move on to the next town."

So the men went out in pairs and did as Jesus had commanded them. After a while they returned with a report of their experiences. Again and again Jesus tried to give them his attention and listen to the things they had to say, but the crowd around him made it impossible.

"Come, we must get away and rest for awhile," he said to his weary friends. And he climbed into a nearby boat with them and began rowing across the Sea of Galilee to a quiet spot on the other side. The people, however, saw what Jesus planned to do and they hurried around the Sea by land. In fact, they made the trip faster than Jesus and his friends and were already waiting to meet the boat when it touched shore. When Jesus saw them, his heart was touched. He could not resist their need, and he stayed to speak until late in the day.

No doubt the apostles did not welcome the intruding crowd. As evening came on, they called Jesus to one side and made a suggestion: "Lord, it is getting late and there is nothing here for the people to eat. Send them away now, so they will have time to reach a village and buy some food before dark."

"There is no need to send them away," Jesus replied. "You can feed them."

Now the apostles had had a tiring day, and they were growing a little impatient. Philip answered for them: "It would take a great deal of money to buy enough bread for all these people, and we have no money at all."

"Why don't you see how much bread is already here?" Jesus suggested patiently.

Andrew searched the crowd and came back with the answer. "There is a little boy who brought a supper of five small loaves and two fishes. He is willing to share this small amount."

"That will be plenty," Jesus answered. "Ask the people to sit down upon the grass."

So the apostles walked through the crowd and urged everyone to stay and eat. Soon they had the people seated in orderly groups, waiting to see what Jesus was about to do. They all grew quiet as Jesus took the loaves and fishes the boy had brought and gave thanks to God. Then he broke the food in pieces, dividing it among his helpers so they could distribute it to the people. At Jesus' touch, the food seemed to multiply. The more he broke it, the more there was. Finally, the apostles reported that everyone present—about five thousand—had been served and that there was food to spare. In fact, when the meal was finished and they passed through the crowd to collect the scraps, they filled twelve baskets! They had seen another example of the King's power. *Matthew 9:35–10:14; Mark 6:30–44; Luke 9:10–17; John 6:1–13*

WALKING ON WATER

After feeding the five thousand from the boy's small supper, Jesus dismissed the crowd and ordered his apostles to start back across the Sea of Galilee without him. He planned to remain alone on the shore for a time and join them later.

In the faint light of dusk, the men began their journey. Then night fell, and with the coming of darkness, the wind began to blow. No matter how hard they rowed, the men seemed to have no control over their small boat. It rolled helplessly on the mounting waves.

From his position on shore, Jesus could see his friends vainly fighting the stormy sea. Through the darkness, he went out to meet them, walking on the water as though it were dry ground.

Already the apostles were frightened by the rocking boat, but when they noticed a figure moving toward them across the water, they began screaming with fear.

"It's a ghost!" they cried when they could think of no other explanation.

Then they heard a familiar voice, saying, "Don't be afraid. It is I."

Peter called out, "Lord, if it really is you, let me come to you."

"All right," Jesus answered. "Come on."

So Peter climbed over the side of the boat and tried to take a few steps. Surely enough, the water was firm under his feet. With his eyes on Jesus, he began walking toward him.

But the sound of the wind rushed past Peter's ears, reminding him of the storm. He took his eyes from Jesus and looked at the leaping waves. In that moment, he started sinking.

"Master, save me!" he cried.

Jesus immediately stretched out his hand and caught Peter's. He helped him to his feet again. Then he said, "Peter, you have so little faith in me. Why did you become afraid when you knew that I was with you?"

Peter had no answer to give. He hung his head in shame.

Once the two reached the boat, the stormy wind stopped as suddenly as it had come. Those present were again impressed with the power of the one who had called them to follow. They bowed before him and said, "Truly you are the Son of God." *Matthew 14:24–33; Mark 6:47–52*

GLORY ON THE MOUNTAINTOP

One day when Jesus and his disciples were traveling to some towns north of the Sea of Galilee, Jesus gave them a question to answer.

"Who do people say that I am?"

"Some say that you are John the Baptist; others say that you are Elijah or Jeremiah or one of the prophets come to life again," they answered.

Then Jesus said, "Who do *you* say that I am?"

"You are the Messiah, the Son of God," Peter spoke up.

"Peter, you will be blessed for saying that," Jesus replied. "My Father has given you the faith to believe in me."

About a week later, Jesus took Peter, James, and John with him upon a mountain to pray. While they were there, the face of Jesus began to shine like the sun and his clothes became a dazzling white. A heavenly glory seemed to beam from him. Then two men appeared and talked with Jesus—they were Moses and Elijah.

The three apostles stared at the wonderful sight before them. Not knowing what else to do, Peter spoke up. "Lord, it is so good for us to be here. Let us set up three places of worship—one for you, one for Moses, and one for Elijah."

But before he had finished speaking, a cloud swept down and covered all of them there on the mountain. A voice came out of the cloud and said, "This is my beloved Son. Listen to him."

The glorious vision, the cloud, and the voice made the three men fall to their knees and hide their faces. They hardly knew what to think. Then they felt a tender touch.

"Get up," Jesus said. "Do not be afraid."

Timidly, the men raised their eyes. There was Jesus, all alone. His glory could not be seen any more, but Peter, James, and John would never forget how he had looked. To them, more than ever before, he was the promised Messiah, the Son of the Living God. *Matthew 16:13–17:8; Mark 8:27–9:8; Luke 9:18–36*

QUESTIONS: 1. *Discuss the events that occurred on the busy Sabbath.* 2. *Did Jesus minister only to the people of Capernaum? Where else did he go?* 3. *Why did some men cut a hole in the roof of the house where Jesus was staying?* 4. *Why did the Pharisees not approve of Jesus?* 5. *Name the things that Jesus did on the Sabbath of which the Pharisees disapproved.* 6. *What did the Pharisees want to do with Jesus?* 7. *What kind of qualities of life would members of God's kingdom show?* 8. *What would be most important to subjects of the kingdom? Why were they not to worry about other things?* 9. *How did Jesus sometimes escape the crowd that always pressed close to him?* 10. *How did he handle the storm that arose while he slept in the boat?* 11. *Why couldn't Jesus and Jairus travel any faster to aid the sick girl?* 12. *What happened before they arrived at Jairus' home?* 13. *Describe Jesus' actions in the young girl's room.* 14. *Why did Jesus call on his apostles to help him in his work?* 15. *What did the crowd do when Jesus tried to escape them in a boat again?* 16. *How was the crowd by the seaside fed?* 17. *How did Jesus join his disciples, who were already out at sea?* 18. *What happened to Peter when he tried to walk on water?* 19. *What experience did three apostles have on the mountaintop?* 20. *What did all these demonstrations of Jesus' power lead his disciples to conclude about him?*

The Kingdom Explained

LIKE LITTLE CHILDREN

Jesus performed his miracles to show that God was bringing forth his kingdom. He was breaking into the world through his Son in a more forceful way than he had acted through the patriarchs, kings, or prophets. Even though Jesus proclaimed this with his healing and other mighty works, he had to add considerable teaching concerning the kingdom. His instruction often took the form of sermons and explanations of scripture; but perhaps his most memorable remarks were the parables he told. These were short, fictitious stories about something that might occur in real life. They were especially helpful because they were easily understood. For instance, Jesus explained the growth and effect of the kingdom by saying that it was like mustard seed, a very tiny object that in time becomes a large tree. Another comparison was with a little bit of yeast hidden in some dough. It works quietly, but soon affects the whole lump of dough.

The subjects of the kingdom would show their willingness to serve God in the humble quality of their lives. The disciples could not understand this. In every kingdom of which they had heard, the most important members were the highest-ranking officials. One day, Jesus found them bickering over the positions they would hold once his kingdom was established. Each wanted an important, impressive role.

From a group standing nearby, Jesus called to a little child. When the youngster had come, he lifted him into his arms and turning to the disciples, said, "The most important subjects of my kingdom will be like this child—they will realize they are weak and trust in God rather than themselves.

"You see," he went on, "to rank first in the kingdom, you will have to be willing to become the servant of all.

"Doing good for a little child is the same as doing good for me. But a terrible punishment is reserved for those who teach children to do wrong. Why, these little ones have angels before God's throne who watch over them."

Later on, mothers began bringing their children to Jesus to be blessed by him. The disciples felt that this was a task that he should be spared. His time was already filled, so they explained to the women, "Our Lord is too busy. He cannot possibly see all of you."

But Jesus said, "Do not turn the little children away. Let them come to me. And remember that the kingdom of heaven belongs to them and to those like them."

Matthew 13:31–33; 18:1–5; Luke 18:15–17

THE UNFORGIVING DEBTOR

As we can see, the nature of the kingdom was difficult for even Jesus' closest companions to understand. Sometimes he would enlighten them by giving them a special, deeper explanation of a story he had told to a larger group. Or he would relate a parable just for their benefit.

One day the apostle Peter sat listening to Jesus speak of the necessity of one's forgiving those who commit some wrong against him.

"Lord," he asked, "how many times should I forgive someone who sins against me? Seven times?"

"Seven times would only be a beginning," Jesus replied. "Seventy times seven would not be too much." Then he told this story:

There was once a king who decided to settle his accounts with all those who owed him money. One subject was brought in who owed him the huge sum of ten million dollars. There was no way he could possibly raise enough money to pay off his debt to the king.

"Since you cannot pay," the king said, "you and your family will have to be sold as slaves and the money from the sale given to me as payment."

The man fell on his knees at this pronouncement. "Have patience and let me have a little more time," he begged. "Eventually I will repay you."

So the king, being moved with compassion, agreed to forgive the man of his debt.

On his way home, this same servant of the king happened to meet a friend who owed him a small debt of about twenty dollars. Grabbing him by the throat, the man demanded that he repay the loan immediately.

"Give me a little time," the friend asked. "I will pay you soon."

But the man would not listen to any excuses. He had the friend locked up in prison until he was able to pay.

When news of this reached the king, he summoned the man to reappear in court. "You wicked servant!" he accused the debtor. "I forgave you a large debt when you asked it of me. Why didn't you show the same forgiveness to your fellowman? Now you, too, shall go to prison until you repay every cent!"

Then Jesus added, for Peter's benefit, "That is the way God will feel toward you if you fail to forgive those who wrong you. He has already forgiven you of so much; surely you can forgive a little." *Matthew 18:15–35*

A REAL NEIGHBOR

Another aspect of the kingdom that caused some misunderstanding and brought forth many questions was that of eternal life. Jesus had promised

Loran Raymond Jones

"FOLLOW ME"—CALLING OF MATTHEW

Matthew 9:9

Loran Raymond Jones

JESUS AND THE PHARISEES IN THE CORNFIELD

Matthew 12:1–8

Loran Raymond Jones

THE SERMON ON THE MOUNT

Matthew 5—7

Loran Raymond Jones

THE TEMPEST STILLED

Mark 4:35–41

Loran Raymond Jones

THE TRANSFIGURATION

Matthew 17:1–13

Loran Raymond Jones

BLIND MAN AT THE POOL OF SILOAM

John 9

Loran Raymond Jones

JESUS AS THE GOOD SHEPHERD

John 10:1–18

Loran Raymond Jones

THE GOOD SAMARITAN

Luke 10:25–37

that the kingdom would last forever and that its members would continue to live with God in heaven after they had ceased to exist on earth. This concept led one of the experts of Jewish law to ask: "Master, what should I do to have this eternal life that you speak of?"

"You know the Law," Jesus said. "What does it tell you to do?"

The scholar was surprised that Jesus had answered him with a question, but he replied, "It commands that I love God with all my heart, all my soul, all my strength, and all my mind. And I am also to love my neighbor as myself."

"What you have said is correct. If you obey it all, you will be able to live forever."

This did not satisfy the lawyer, for he was one of those who doubted Jesus' claim to be the Messiah. He had hoped to make Jesus look foolish with his questions, so he asked another: "The Law says I am to love my neighbor —just who is my neighbor?"

This was the answer he received:

One day a man was taking a trip from Jerusalem to Jericho. The road between these two cities is a dangerous one because it is bordered by great rocks where thieves often hide. As this man was traveling alone, he was overtaken by a band of these robbers, beaten, stripped of his clothes and his money, and left beside the road to die.

Now that day a priest, one who served in the Temple, chanced to be making a trip along the very same road. Although his life was supposed to be dedicated to the service of God, he did not stop to help the dying man. Instead when he saw him, he made a special effort to pass by far on the other side of the road.

Later on, a Jew from the tribe of Levi—the tribe set apart to lead in the worship—also came by. But he, too, merely glanced at the suffering man and continued on his journey as though he had seen nothing unusual.

Finally, a Samaritan, one of those hated half-breeds to whom the Jews considered themselves superior, came along. Seeing that the injured man was a Jew, the Samaritan could have felt that he had every right to leave him lying in the ditch; but instead, his heart was touched by one who was in trouble. He stopped and cleaned the man's wounds with some oil he had in his baggage. Then, after bandaging them as best he could, he lifted him onto his own horse and led the beast to the nearest place of lodging. All night he sat beside the sick man's bed, doing what he could to relieve his patient's suffering.

The next day, it appeared that the injured man would live; and the Samaritan decided to continue with his journey. Nevertheless, before he left, he went to the innkeeper with some money. "Use this to care for the man I brought here," he instructed. "If you have to spend any more, I will repay you when I come back by."

When the story was finished, Jesus turned to the lawyer and asked, "Now which was a neighbor to the man who was robbed—the priest, the Levite, or the Samaritan?"

"The one who helped him, of course," the lawyer answered.

"Then go, and do the same," Jesus replied. *Luke 10:25–37*

THE GOOD SHEPHERD

In order for the people to understand his own role in the kingdom more clearly, Jesus often spoke of himself in terms of a shepherd. A shepherd was a familiar figure to the people among whom Jesus lived and taught, as it had been for generations in that part of the world. From the time of Abraham, the Jewish people had maintained flocks of sheep, although the shepherd boy David was probably the most famous of those who had followed the profession.

"A thief tries to sneak into the sheepfold to steal and destroy," Jesus explained. "But as a shepherd, I have come to give life, and to give it abundantly. I stand at the door of the sheepfold and call, and my sheep recognize my voice because they know me well. They come readily and follow me as they would follow no stranger.

"I am the Good Shepherd; the good shepherd will lay down his life for his sheep. If a hired shepherd saw a wolf coming, he would run away and leave the sheep to be snatched by the wild beast. But a good shepherd, one who knows his sheep, will stay with them and lay down his own life, if necessary, to save them."

There was another time when Jesus used the shepherd figure to make his point. On this occasion he was being criticized by the Pharisees for associating with people of all kinds, even those who were known to be leading sinful lives. The self-righteous Jews felt that a respectable person—and certainly one who claimed to speak for God—would not waste his time with sinners. To explain his own actions, Jesus asked the Pharisees: "Which of you, if you had a hundred sheep and lost one, would not leave the ninety-nine that are safe and go in search of the stray? You would go out into the wilderness, looking high and low for it. Then when you found it, probably wounded or caught in a dangerous place, you would lift it gently to your shoulders and carry it home. Once you arrived there safely with the sheep, you would call your friends and neighbors together to celebrate with you, saying, 'Rejoice with me, for I have found my sheep that was lost!'

"In the same way, there is more rejoicing in heaven when one sinner changes his life than there is over the fact that ninety-nine never needed forgiving at all."

And to prove the same point, Jesus added another little parable: "There was a woman who had ten silver coins and lost one of them. In an effort to find it she lit lamps throughout her house, and she swept in every corner.

When it was recovered, she went to tell her friends and neighbors of her good fortune.

"I tell you," Jesus said in closing, "this woman's joy is like that of the angels of God when one sinner asks for forgiveness." *Luke 15:1–10; John 10:1–18*

THE LOST BOY

The parables of the lost sheep and the lost coin were told by Jesus to defend his associating with people whom the Pharisees considered to be sinful. In telling them, he tried to show that God's love extended to the lost, for they needed his grace more than anyone else. The most famous story which illustrates this point is one concerned with a lost boy. We know it as the story of The Prodigal Son:

There lived a man who had two sons. One day the younger of the two came to him and said, "Father, I want my share of your fortune right away that I can spend it as I please." So the father divided up all that he had and gave the son his rightful portion. Happy with his new wealth, the young man gathered up his things and left for a distant country.

In the faraway land, the youth found many things of which to spend his money—gambling, gifts for friends, rich foods, and wine. Before long, he found himself with all of it gone. Those who had pretended to be his friends while he had the money now deserted him. He saw that he would have to find a job in order to feed himself.

Then a famine came upon the country, and food became very scarce. There were no crops to tend, and no jobs to be had. In desperation, the young man persuaded a farmer to let him feed pigs. By this time, he was so hungry that he would have eaten some of the husks that were intended for the pigs, but no one gave him any.

Among the smelling, grunting animals, the young man could not help thinking of the home he had left and the fact that the servants who worked for his father were better off than he was. He made up his mind: "I will return to my father and admit how wrong I have been. I know I do not deserve to be his son any longer, but perhaps he would let me live at home as a hired servant. That would be enough."

Immediately he set out for home. For many days he traveled, until finally he saw the familiar buildings in the distance. Then he noticed someone standing there, waiting—it was his father! The two began running toward each other and fell into each other's arms.

"Father," the son began, "I am not fit to be your son." But the father could not stand to hear his boy speak that way. He turned to a servant and said, "Bring a fine robe for my son, and put a ring on his hand and shoes on his feet. Then kill a fat calf and prepare a great dinner. It is time for a celebration!"

Now during the time the younger son had been away wasting his inheritance, the older one had stayed at home, helping his father. He had never asked for his money, and he was disturbed when the father seemed to place so much importance on the return of his brother. He refused to attend the celebration dinner, and the father found him sulking outside instead. "Son," he said, putting his arm around the older brother, "this does not mean that I love you any less. You have been good to stay with me. But now we should be glad that your brother has returned. He that was lost has been found!" *Luke 15:11–32*

THE COST OF DISCIPLESHIP

In the Sermon on the Mount, Jesus had pointed out that membership in the kingdom of God would often prove costly because it would call for the disciple to make all other aspects of his life of less importance. If there were distractions which began to turn his attention and interest away from God, they had to be removed or forgotten. This lesson was brought forcefully to the mind of a rich young man who came eagerly seeking Jesus one day.

"Master," he asked, "what shall I do to inherit eternal life?"

"Do you know the Commandments—you shall not kill; you shall not steal; honor your father and mother?"

"Oh, yes," the young man insisted. "I've obeyed all of these things since I was a child. Is there anything else that I lack?"

Looking at the man, Jesus loved him, for he knew that his question sprung from an earnest desire to do that which was right. "If you would be perfect," he answered, "there is one more thing you must do. Go and sell what you have and give the money to the poor. Then your treasure will be in heaven, and you will be free to come and follow me."

But the young man's face fell as he heard these words, for he was very rich. With a heavy heart, he walked away, unwilling to pay the price discipleship demanded of him.

Jesus turned to his disciples. "It will be very difficult for a rich man to enter this kingdom," he explained. Then, when they displayed some amazement at his statement, he added: "It will be hard because their trust is in riches, rather than in God. A camel can more easily pass through the eye of a needle than a man of wealth enter into the kingdom of God."

This caused even more astonishment among the group of Jesus' closest friends. "Then who will be saved?" they asked.

"Things that are impossible for men are possible with God," was the Master's reply.

Peter quickly reminded Jesus that he and the other disciples had left everything to follow him.

"Any man who leaves family or home for my sake shall receive a hundred fold in the life to come," Jesus assured him. "Many who are last now, shall be first then." *Matthew 19:16–30; Mark 10:17–31; Luke 18:18–30*

FROM DEATH TO LIFE

Many of Jesus' disciples had given up their family attachments and the comforts of home to follow him; but the Master himself had also forfeited earthly ties and possessions. On one occasion he admitted that while foxes had holes and birds had nests, he had no home of his own. Instead, he ate and slept in the homes of his friends, some of whom he visited again and again when he returned to their villages.

One such family, whose home was always open to Jesus, was composed of a man, Lazarus, and his two sisters, Mary and Martha. They lived in Bethany, a small town on the outskirts of Jerusalem. Once when Jesus was a guest in their home, Martha had busied herself with dinner preparations while Mary sat quietly by Jesus, listening to his every word. Back in the kitchen, Martha became cross because her sister was offering her no help. She came into the room where Mary and Jesus sat and demanded: "Lord, don't you see that my sister has left me to do all the work? Insist that she come and help me."

But Jesus answered, "Martha, Martha! You are too worried about unimportant matters. Mary, on the other hand, has chosen to spend her time with things of more value."

Months later, Lazarus became very sick, and these two sisters were distraught. They sent a message to Jesus, who, at that time, was preaching in an area just across the Jordan River. "Come quickly, Lord," they begged. "Lazarus, whom you love, is sick."

Jesus did not seem worried when he received the news. "This sickness will not lead to death," he told his disciples, "but to the glory of God and his

Son." Then he proceeded to remain two more days in that place. Finally, on the third day, he began the journey to Bethany.

Some of the disciples were worried about Jesus' returning to the area around Jerusalem, for many of the priests and Pharisees there despised him. "Master, do you think it wise to go so near to Jerusalem?" they asked.

"Our friend Lazarus has fallen asleep," Jesus replied, "and I am going to awaken him."

"Well, if he is just asleep," they said, "he will get well without your coming."

Then Jesus spoke to them plainly: "Lazarus is dead."

The disciples looked from one to another, not knowing what to think. How did Jesus know that Lazarus was dead? Why had he not gone to Bethany in time to heal him? Why was he risking his life to go now when nothing could be done? They could not answer these questions, but they still believed in their Lord.

"Come, let us go with him," Thomas said to the others. So they went to Bethany. The trip took several days, and when they arrived, they found that Lazarus had already been buried for four days. The house was full of friends from Jerusalem who had come to try to comfort Mary and Martha.

When word came that Jesus had come at last, Martha ran out to meet him at the edge of town. Her eyes were full of tears. "Lord," she said, "if you had only been here, my brother would not have died."

Jesus answered her: "Your brother will rise again."

"I know he will rise again at the resurrection, on the last day," Martha said.

Then Jesus looked straight into her eyes. "I am the resurrection and the life. He who believes on me will live even if he dies. Do you believe this?"

"Yes, Lord," Martha replied. "I believe that you are the Christ, the One who was promised of God."

Finally Jesus and Martha reached the home where Mary and the others were waiting. When Jesus caught sight of them, he, too, began to weep. Some Jews from Jerusalem who were present noticed it and said, "Look how much he loved Lazarus." But others among them commented, "He healed others. Why didn't he keep Lazarus from dying?"

Then Jesus asked to see the place where Lazarus was buried. The family led him to a cave whose entrance was covered by a huge stone. "He lies within," they explained.

"Take away the stone," Jesus said.

Martha looked up, surprised. "Lord, he has been dead four days!"

"Did I not tell you that if you believed in me, you would see the glory of God?" Jesus reminded her.

So the stone was rolled away. When it lay at one side, Jesus looked up and prayed: "Father, thank you for hearing me. I am aware that you always hear me; but I have said it at this time, so that everyone present will know that it is true." Then he looked into the tomb and shouted, "Lazarus, come forth!"

Out walked Lazarus, still wrapped in his burial clothes.

"Take off those wrappings, and let him go," Jesus said.

Eagerly the sisters tore away the cloth that bound Lazarus' hands and feet. They threw their arms about their brother and then backed away to look again. Yes, it was he! Lazarus was alive! *Luke 10:38–42; John 11:1–44*

TWO FROM JERICHO

From the story of Lazarus we note that Jesus had moved southward from Galilee to Judea and the provinces across the Jordan River. His final destination was Jerusalem, for Passover time was near. In the meantime, he passed through small surrounding villages proclaiming the word of the kingdom. The crowd with him increased each day as others going up to Jerusalem for the annual celebration joined him. Rumors of his work had spread far and wide, and many still hoped that he would declare himself King when he reached Jerusalem.

As Jesus and the multitudes neared the city of Jericho, they passed a blind man, begging outside the gates. His name was Bartimaeus, and he inquired what the noise of the passing crowd meant. When he heard that Jesus of Nazareth was among them, he began to cry out, "Jesus, son of David, help me!"

"Hush! You're making too much noise," some from the group rebuked him. But it only made him shout the louder, "Jesus, son of David, help me!"

By this time Jesus had heard the cries of Bartimaeus, and he stopped. "Tell that man to come here," he said.

"Jesus wants you. Get up and go to him," the crowd now insisted. So the blind beggar started off in the direction in which they pushed him.

"What would you like for me to do for you?" Jesus asked when Bartimaeus reached his side.

"Oh, Teacher, let me see."

"It is done," Jesus replied. "Your faith in me has made it possible." And from that moment on, the man was no longer blind. Singing praises to God, he joined the crowd that was walking along with Jesus.

Within the city walls, another man waited beside the road. He was Zacchaeus, a very small man who was the chief tax collector of Jericho. He had heard that Jesus was coming; and although he was not a believer, he wanted to get a glimpse of Jesus, so he had perched up in a sycamore tree. Otherwise, he could not have seen over the heads of those in the crowd.

Soon Zacchaeus could tell that the crowd was approaching. Then he recognized Jesus among those who walked along. His plan had succeeded. Then something he had not counted on occurred: Jesus stopped beside the tree and looked straight up at him. Zacchaeus could not move from surprise. He thought he had been well-hidden!

But this was only the first surprise. Next, the Nazarene spoke: "Zacchaeus, hurry and come down. I'm coming home with you today."

So Zacchaeus scrambled down and proudly led the way to his house, a taller man than ever before. Some in the crowd, however, were not so pleased. "Why did Jesus choose to visit Zacchaeus, the tax collector?" they asked. "He's known to be a sinner."

Zacchaeus, overhearing them, turned to Jesus and said: "Lord, I am going to donate half of all my goods to the poor. I also promise to repay anyone that I have cheated during my term of office."

"Today you have learned what it means to become part of my kingdom," Jesus replied with pleasure. And turning to his critics, he explained: "This fulfills my very purpose here—to seek for and save those who were lost without me." *Matthew 20:29–34; Mark 10:46–52; Luke 18:35–43; 19:1–10*

QUESTIONS: 1. *What is a parable?* 2. *How was the kingdom of God like a mustard seed? How was it like yeast in dough?* 3. *In what way were the disciples to be like children?* 4. *Why was the king angry when the debtor failed to forgive his friend?* 5. *In what way was the Samaritan a good neighbor? Who failed to be?* 6. *Who was called the Good Shepherd? Why?* 7. *What was the reaction of the man who found the lost sheep and the woman with the lost coin?* 8. *How did the father react when his lost son returned home?* 9. *How did the righteous older brother feel?* 10. *What did Jesus tell the rich young man that he yet lacked? Why did this make the young man sad?* 11. *What will be the reward of those who pay the high cost of discipleship?* 12. *Why did Martha urge Jesus to reprimand Mary?* 13. *In what condition did Jesus find Lazarus? What did he do about it?* 14. *Who was Bartimaeus?* 15. *Who was Zacchaeus?* 16. *What was the purpose of Jesus' ministry?*

The King Reigns

ENTER THE KING

A number of Jews from Jerusalem were among those present when Jesus raised Lazarus from the dead. Naturally this—the most dramatic of his miracles—convinced many of them that within him lay the hope of Israel. At the same time, the stir caused by the event made the Jewish leaders look upon Jesus with even more disfavor than before. They were afraid the whole affair would be brought to the attention of the Romans. They were even more afraid of losing their control over the Jewish nation.

"It is better that he die than our whole nation be led astray," Caiaphas, the high priest, declared. So from that time on, they planned how they might put him to death.

Thus the fears of Thomas and the other apostles regarding Jesus' return to Jerusalem were not unfounded. Nevertheless Jesus himself seemed to feel that his future had been decided—that the time had come for him to offer mankind a hope of salvation, regardless of the consequences. So, like other faithful Jews, he "set his face toward Jerusalem" in order to celebrate Passover.

It was about a week before the feast day when Jesus arrived at Bethany, located on the outskirts of the city. Here he was warmly greeted by Lazarus, Mary, and Martha. The four of them, in fact, attended a dinner together at the home of Simon, a man Jesus had cured of leprosy. At the dinner party, Lazarus and Jesus were honored with important seats, and Martha helped serve the food.

During the meal, Mary, the other sister, tiptoed shyly into the room and came and stood beside Jesus. Her heart was overflowing with love and gratitude for his bringing her brother back to life. His example and teaching had given new meaning to her life. In trying to express these things to him, she had bought a very expensive box of sweet perfume. As she stood near her Lord, she let some of the perfume fall on his head. Then she poured some onto his feet and wiped them with her beautiful, long hair.

The smell of the perfume filled the room, and the others at the dinner stopped talking and looked at Mary with surprise. "Now, why did she do that?" asked Judas, one of the apostles. "That perfume was very expensive. It could have been sold and the money given to the poor."

"Let her alone," Jesus told Judas. "Why are you bothering her? She has done a good thing. There are always going to be poor people for you to help, but I am not going to be with you much longer. I shall have to die, and she has prepared my body for burial with this perfume. I tell you the truth, when the gospel is preached all over the world, the story of Mary's anointing will be told, in memory of her."

Word spread in Jerusalem that Jesus was in Bethany with Lazarus, and many citizens decided to walk out to Bethany and meet him there. At the same time, Jesus sent two of his disciples to a nearby village with these instructions: "You will find a colt tied to its mother. Unfasten the colt and bring him to me. If anyone asks why you are taking him, just say that the Lord needs him."

The disciples found things just as he said. As they were untying the colt, the owner came up and asked, "Why are you taking my animal?"

"Our Lord needs him," they replied, and no more questions were asked.

When they returned with the colt, they laid coats of their own across his back and Jesus mounted the young animal. This was a meaningful act, as both Jesus and the Jews were familiar with the prophecy that read:

> Tell ye the people of Jerusalem
> Behold, thy King cometh unto thee
> Meek, and riding upon a colt.

Therefore, when Jesus neared the city, a joyous celebration began. The crowd that met him grew wild with joy, thinking he had come at last to set up his kingdom in Jerusalem. Many took off their coats and spread them in the road to make a carpet for Jesus to ride on. Others cut branches from palm trees and laid them on the ground. Then they walked before him and shouted, "Bless this son of David! Bless this One who comes from God! Bless his great kingdom! God bless our King!"

When the shouting crowd reached the city, others heard the commotion and asked, "Who is this person?"

"Jesus of Nazareth," came the answer.

The priests and leading Pharisees tried to quiet the crowd, but met with no success. "You cannot change anything by keeping the people quiet," Jesus warned them. "If they were still, the rocks would cry out that I am God's Son."

So the Jewish leaders had to step back and let the parade pass on.

Matthew 21:1–17; 26:6–13; Mark 11:1–11; 14:3–9; Luke 19:29–44; John 11:55–12:19

CLEANING THE TEMPLE

Once Jesus reached Jerusalem, he quite naturally went to the Temple. Here he met with an apalling sight, one that demonstrated what had really become of the religion of God's people. The courts of the house of worship had become nothing less than a market place! Money changers had booths where they changed ordinary coins into the kind allowed in the Temple. Sellers were hawking their wares—mostly birds to be used for offerings. Each man tried to do more business than the others; some had gotten their positions by paying a portion of their earnings to the priests.

In the face of all this confusion and greed, Jesus grew indignant. He began upsetting the tables belonging to the money changers. Then, with his anger still burning, he turned on the cheap businessmen themselves, driving them out, their birds and their money with them.

"Wasn't this meant to be a house of prayer?" he demanded. "You've made it a den of robbers!"

Those Jewish leaders who had been disturbed by his triumphal entry were even more angered by this display. "What right has he to do these things?" they asked. The priests had power over the Temple and its affairs, they felt, and Jesus had implied that they were not handling things well. With even more vigor, the men looked for a way to destroy him.

This situation brought on several days of conflict and argument between Jesus and the Jewish authorities. With questions designed to trap him, the Jews sought to make Jesus look foolish before the crowds. In answer Jesus spoke several parables designed to show that the Jews had rejected God, whom they pretended to serve.

One of the parables likened the priests and leaders to wicked tenants whom the landlord had put in charge of his carefully-tended vineyard. Every year when the landlord sent servants to reap the fruit, the tenants killed them. Finally, the owner sent his own son, thinking they would honor him. But with more wickedness than he had supposed, the tenants killed the son also.

"What will the owner of the vineyard do?" asked Jesus. "He will come and destroy the tenants, and give the vineyard to others." Then he added,

"Have you not read from the *Psalms:* 'The stone which the builders rejected, the same has now become the cornerstone'?"

And the priests and leaders, realizing what he had said about them, would have killed him at the time, had they not feared the multitudes who believed on him. *Matthew 21:12–22:14; Mark 11:15–12:12; Luke 19:45–20:19*

A NEW FEAST

At this point, circumstances brought together a discontented member of Jesus' own group and the Jewish rulers who had vowed to destroy this threat to their authority. The betrayer was Judas Iscariot, one of the twelve. Now none of the apostles were men without faults and they all had an imperfect understanding of the kingdom of God, but Judas was the only one who lost his faith in Jesus and rejected him as ruler over his life. He had been given the responsibility of keeping the funds with which the apostles bought food, and there came a time when he began to dip into this money for his own use without telling anyone. You will recall the hypocritical displeasure he showed when Mary anointed Jesus with the expensive ointment.

After Jesus spoke sharply to him on that occasion, Judas went secretly to the chief priests and asked, "What will you give me for delivering Jesus to you?" Thirty pieces of silver was the price agreed upon, an amount which satisfied Judas. "I will let you know when the time is best for you to take him," he told his fellow-conspirators. Then he returned to the other apostles with no mention of what had occurred.

Soon thereafter, the evening of the Passover feast arrived, and Jesus observed the occasion with the twelve in an upper room in Jerusalem. Like other Jews had done for many centuries, they remembered the time the death angel passed over the Israelites in Egypt. During the meal a sadness seemed to hover over the group, something no one could explain. In the midst of it, Jesus knelt and washed the feet of each one there as an example of the humility he wanted them to display.

Later, after the ceremonial lamb had been eaten, Jesus looked around at the men present and made a startling statement: "One of you here with me is going to betray me and give me up to be killed."

A hush fell over the group. "Is it I?" each one asked in disbelief.

"It is one of you eating from this same dish with me," he answered. Then he added a warning: "He would be better off if he had never been born."

Finally Judas made his feeble protest, "Is it I, Lord?" Jesus dipped some bread into the dish of sauce and handed it to him, meeting his gaze. "You have said it, Judas. What you must do, do quickly."

Immediately Judas left the room and went out into the night.

Afterward, Jesus took bread and wine from the Passover fare, gave thanks for it, and served it to his apostles. He called the bread his "body" and the wine, his "blood." Thus he instituted a new feast, one that was to be observed by members of God's kingdom. Thereafter, as often as they partook of the Lord's Supper, as the bread and the wine came to be called, these men—as well as the followers of Christ in every age—remembered their Lord and his suffering.

Then Jesus gave his apostles their final lesson. "Do not be worried," was his message. "You believe in God; believe also in me. I am going to my Father now, where I will prepare a place for you. When it is ready, I will come again and take you there to be with me.

"Now I give you a new commandment: love one another as I have loved you."

And after prayer and the singing of a Passover hymn, they all went out into the night.

Matthew 26:14–29; Mark 14:10–25; Luke 22:3–20

JUDAS' KISS

From the upper room, Jesus and his apostles walked through the dark Jerusalem streets to the Mount of Olives. Here, at the base of the mountain, there was a garden called Gethsemane where Jesus had come before to meditate and pray. On this occasion, more than ever before, he felt the need of communion with his Father. "Wait here while I go and pray," he asked the disciples when they had reached the edge of the garden. Then, taking only Peter, James and John with him, he went a little further into the garden.

"My heart is almost breaking," he confided to these three, who were his closest friends. "Stay here and watch with me." Then he went off a short distance by himself and fell on the ground. Alone with God, he could admit that the suffering that lay before him was almost more than he could bear. But he promised that he would submit to it if it were God's will.

After praying earnestly for a while, Jesus came back to his friends and found them all asleep. "Why are you sleeping?" Jesus asked Peter. "Could you not watch with me just one hour?"

Then a second time he went away and prayed to his Father for help. When he came back, the three apostles had drifted off to sleep again. They were ashamed of themselves, but still could not manage to remain alert to the needs of their Master. The third time that Jesus went away to pray alone, he agonized with "sweat like drops of blood," yet God sent an angel to wipe his brow and to comfort him sufficiently to meet the demands of the following day.

Once more Jesus came and stood by the drowsy apostles. "Go ahead and sleep," he said as he looked at them. "The time has already come when I am going to be given over to my enemies."

At that, torches lit the garden. The loud shouts of an angry mob broke the silence of the night. Into sight came Judas, leading a band of armed soldiers. "Stay behind until I show you which man is Jesus," Judas whispered to the officers. "He will be the one that I kiss."

Then he stepped forward and came face to face with Jesus. "Master," he said with mock affection, as he leaned forward and kissed Jesus.

The Lord gave Judas a long look of pity. "Do you mean that you would betray me with a kiss?" he asked. Then he turned to the officers and said, "For whom are you seeking?"

"Jesus of Nazareth," they replied.

"I am he. You will not need your swords to take me."

Now Peter had seen all these proceedings and could not stand by any longer. He drew out his sword and cut off the ear of the high priest's servant. "Put your sword away," Jesus told his loyal friend. "Don't you realize that my Father could send angels to save me if I asked him? But this must be done in order to fulfill his will." Then he restored the servant's ear.

Finally, he turned to the soldiers and said, "Why did you come to get me with your swords as though I were a criminal? I have not tried to hide, but have been teaching openly in the Temple." Then he gave himself up and allowed them to lead him away. Confused and terrified, his followers fled, leaving him to face his betrayers alone.

Matthew 26:36–56; Mark 14:32–52; Luke 22:39–53; John 18:2–12

TRIAL

From Gethsemane, the guards led Jesus to the house of Caiaphas, the high priest, where the Jewish council had hastily gathered. Immediately these officials set about to question Jesus in order to find evidence of his law-breaking. One by one, witnesses were called in to testify against him, but no two of them told the same story. Through it all, Jesus stood quietly.

Finally, Caiaphas turned to him and said, "What do you have to say for yourself?"

No answer came.

Then Caiaphas asked, point-blank: "Are you the Christ, the Son of God?"

"I am," Jesus said, breaking his silence. "And one day you will see me sitting on God's own throne and coming in clouds of glory."

Caiaphas turned pale with anger. He turned to the rest of the court. "Did you hear what this man said? We need no more witnesses. He has convicted himself! Do you agree?"

"Agreed! He is guilty of blasphemy!" came the answer. "Surely a man of Nazareth blasphemes against God when he claims to be his son. He deserves to be killed!"

At this, the servants holding Jesus turned to him and began spitting on him. Some of them blindfolded him and hit him; then they asked him to prophesy and tell which one had done it.

In the courtyard outside Caiaphas' house, Peter waited with a crowd to see what would happen to Jesus. Because it was a chilly night, he was standing next to a fire, warming his hands, when a maid came up and looked at him strangely.

"Are you a friend of this man Jesus?" she asked.

"I don't know him at all," Peter claimed, ducking his head and trying to move away from her.

Later on, another maid saw him and said the same thing, "You were with Jesus!"

"I don't know what you're talking about," Peter hotly denied.

Then a third time, someone approached him and said, "You must be a follower of that man—both you and he talk like Galileans."

At this, Peter began to curse and swear. And in the distance a rooster began to crow, for morning was breaking. The sound of it brought a painful memory to Peter's mind: he recalled that Jesus had told him, "Before the rooster crows, you will deny me three times." And just a few hours before, he had promised that he would go to prison or die before he would deny that Jesus was his Lord.

Peter could not remain in the courtyard another minute. He ran outside and fell to the ground, weeping as though his heart would break.

Once Jesus admitted to being the Son of God, Caiaphas had no difficulty in persuading the Jewish council to consent to his death. The formality was quickly dispensed with and he was declared guilty. Still, before any punishment could take place, permission had to be obtained from the Roman authority in the area—in this case, Pontius Pilate, governor of Judea.

Now Caiaphas had been high priest long enough to realize that Pilate would not be interested in Jesus' claims to be the Jewish Messiah, so he pictured him as a rebellious citizen instead. "He is trying to declare himself king in place of Caesar," was the report Caiaphas gave to Pilate.

When Pilate heard this, he took Jesus away privately to question him, but he could not find any evidence that the claim was true. He went back out and reported this to the Jewish council, but they quickly found another charge. "He has stirred up the people in Galilee," they reminded Pilate.

"Well, then," Pilate said, "He is not really under my jurisdiction. Herod, the governor of Galilee, happens to be in Jerusalem. Take him to Herod."

But Herod kept Jesus only a short time. Then he sent him back to Pilate, claiming that he could find no cause for Jesus to be put to death.

By this time, Pilate had become concerned about the decision the Jewish authorities were pressing him to make. He was convinced Jesus had done nothing worthy of death. Even Pilate's wife had sent a message, saying, "Let this Jesus go free—there is something strange about the whole case. This very night I suffered in a dream that had to do with him."

So in desperation, Pilate grasped at his last chance to save Jesus. According to custom, the Romans released one prisoner at the Jewish festival time. "Let me release Jesus this year," he suggested.

But the crowd would have nothing to do with it. "No! Let us have Barabbas!" they shouted, referring to a notorious prisoner being held at that time.

"Then what shall I do with Jesus, who is called the Christ?" asked Pilate.

"Crucify him! Crucify him!" chanted the mob.

Pilate bowed in resignation. "Go ahead and crucify him," he told the Jews. "But I want no part in it. I wash my hands of the whole matter."

"Let his blood be upon us," shouted the crowd. So Jesus was led away to be beaten and crucified, and the murderer Barabbas was released in his place. *Matthew 26:57–27:26; Mark 14:53–15:15; Luke 22:54–23:25; John 18:24–19:16*

"IT IS FINISHED"

The order for Jesus' crucifixion was given by Pilate early on a Friday morning after the evening of the Passover celebration. Afterward, soldiers took Jesus away for a scourging; then, for their amusement, they dressed him like a king, with a scarlet robe and a crown of thorns. In his hand they placed a reed to serve as his scepter. "Hail, O King," they mocked, and then they spit on him.

Without a word Jesus stood, calm and composed in the midst of a howling, angry mob. But the beating had left him exhausted. When they gave him his heavy cross to drag to the place of crucifixion, he stumbled under its weight. A guard grabbed a man named Simon to help Jesus bear it. Out of the city and up a hill called Calvary, the "Place of the Skull," marched Jesus, Simon, two criminals who were also being crucified, the Roman soldiers in charge of the execution, Jewish leaders, and a crowd of onlookers.

By this time, the day's activities were beginning throughout the city, and word spread that the Jewish council had convicted Jesus during the night. When they heard it, those who believed in Jesus also hurried out to Calvary. With horror they saw three crosses already lying on the ground and the soldiers digging the holes to set them in.

Once the holes were sufficiently deep, the Roman soldiers stretched Jesus out upon his cross and nailed him to its wooden beams, driving heavy spikes into his hands and feet. Across the top they fastened a sign that read, "Jesus of Nazareth, the King of the Jews." Then they stood the cross upright and dropped it into the hole they had prepared. There Jesus hung, dying slowly like the thieves on either side of him. With blood pouring from his wounds, Jesus looked down on his executioners and said, "Father, forgive them; they do not realize what they are doing."

While Jesus prayed for those who had nailed him to the cross, the Roman soldiers stood beneath him, dividing his clothes. But the disciples who had gathered there clung to each other and wept. Among them was Jesus' own mother, Mary, and John, the apostle. When Jesus looked down into their sad faces, he said, "John, take care of my mother for me." And to Mary he said, "John will be like a son to you."

Some in the crowd curled their lips in disgust at the sight of the sorrowing disciples. These were the Jewish priests and Pharisees who were responsible for Jesus' conviction. They merely looked up at him and said, "You saved others. Why don't you save yourself now?"

One of the thieves hanging beside him joined in, "Yes, why don't you save yourself and us if you are really God's Son?" But the other thief said to him, "How can you speak this way, knowing you are about to die? You and I deserve to be here, but this man has done no wrong."

Then he turned to Jesus and said, "Lord, remember me when you come into your kingdom."

With the great love he still possessed, Jesus answered, "This day you will be with me in Paradise."

At noon, the sun disappeared from sight and God caused an awful darkness to cover the earth for about three hours. During this time Jesus' pain became more and more dreadful. In the garden the night before, he had committed himself to the purposes of his Father. Still, the agony of the cross and the sins of mankind that he, as God's perfect Son, bore, caused Jesus to cry, "My God, my God, why have you forsaken me?" A short while later, about three o'clock in the afternoon, he whispered his last words, "It is finished. Father, into your hands I give my spirit." And he died.

At that moment, the curtain of the Temple that separated the Holy Place from the Holy of Holies was torn from top to bottom. The ground shook and trembled as during an earthquake. The Roman captain in charge of Jesus' death looked at his noble prisoner and kneeled before the cross. "Truly this *was* the Son of God," he said.

Matthew 27:27–56; Mark 15:16–41; Luke 23:26–49; John 19:16–30

A RISEN LORD

On the same afternoon that Jesus died, one of the few Jewish rulers who had believed on him went to Pilate and asked for the body so that he might bury it. Pilate checked with the captain in charge of the crucifixion; and when he found that Jesus was already dead, he gave the man, whose name was Joseph, permission to take the body away. Joseph wrapped it with fine linen and lay with it the spices another disciple had given. Then he and the small company of faithful followers placed it in a tomb Joseph had bought for himself. It was the kind of tomb common in those days—a hollowed place, carved out of a ledge of rock and covered with a stone.

The next day was Saturday, the Sabbath, and the Jewish authorities met to celebrate the death of Jesus. One of them said, "I remember Jesus' saying something about rising from the dead in three days. Perhaps we had better seal his tomb carefully or one of his followers will come, steal the body, and say that he is risen." So they went to Pilate, who gave them permission to seal the tomb and to keep soldiers there on constant guard.

The apostles and the women who had followed Jesus returned to the upper room where they had eaten the Passover. For three years they had given their lives to a man whom they loved above everything else. Now nothing was left of him or of their hopes and dreams—nothing except a body in Joseph's tomb. Their future king was gone before he had gotten to reign. His glorious kingdom had failed. Jesus was dead.

Early the next morning, Mary Magdalene and some other women went to the tomb to take more spices to lay with Jesus' body. On the way, they wondered how they would move the stone that covered the entrance to the grave. But when they came within sight of the tomb, they saw that the stone was already rolled away. Earlier that morning, an angel of God had felled the soldiers on guard with his dazzling presence and moved the stone away. The soldiers later recovered their senses and ran to tell the priests what had occurred. Rather than have it spread to the people, the priests paid the soldiers to say that the apostles had stolen the body during the night.

When the women reached the tomb, they peered inside. In the place where Jesus' body had lain, stood two angels in shining white clothes. "Do not be afraid," said the angels. "You are looking for Jesus of Nazareth, who was crucified. He is no longer here; he has risen. Go and tell this to the disciples. Tell them that Jesus had gone to Galilee and will meet them there."

The women hurried to relate what they had seen and heard. When Peter and John heard it, they set out running for the tomb. John reached it first, went within and found the linen cloth in which the body had been wrapped. Peter went in even farther and recovered the cloth that had been tied around his face. Then they left, believing that Mary and the others had reported the truth.

By this time, Mary Magdalene had returned to the garden alone with second thoughts about the body's being stolen or hidden. She stood by the empty tomb crying when Jesus himself stood suddenly at her side. "Mary," he said softly. When she looked and saw that it was he, she could hardly believe it was true. "Master!" she said; and her tears turned to ones of joy as she ran into the city to tell the others that she had seen their Lord alive.

Matthew 27:57–28:8; Mark 15:42–16:11; Luke 23:50–24:12; John 19:31–20:18

RETURN TO GLORY

On the evening of the day when Jesus was seen by Mary, two disciples were walking from Jerusalem to the village of Emmaus. As they traveled along, talking about the recent events in Jerusalem, they were joined by a third person.

"What are you talking about?" asked the stranger, whom the men failed to recognize as Jesus.

"You must be the only one in Jerusalem who doesn't know what has been happening," the men declared.

"What *has* occurred?"

"Well, it all had to do with Jesus of Nazareth," they explained. "He was a mighty prophet, sent from God. The people looked to him for salvation, but our leaders condemned him to death.

"It has been three days now since he was killed, yet some women who went to the tomb this morning amazed us with reports that his tomb is empty. In place of his body there are angels who claim he is alive."

Then Jesus began to speak: "You are so slow to grasp what the prophets said were true! Don't you see that Christ had to die in order to reign in glory?" And as they walked along, he explained further how the Old Testament scriptures had prophesied his coming.

By this time, the three had reached Emmaus. Jesus prepared to leave the two men, but it was late and they persuaded him to remain with them. When they sat down together to eat, Jesus picked up some bread and gave thanks for it. Then he broke it and handed a portion to each man. Instantly they knew who he was, but as they recognized him, he was gone.

"Why didn't we know from the first?" they asked each other. "Weren't our hearts burning within us when he spoke with us on the road?"

And they hurried back in to Jerusalem to report to the apostles what had occurred. "Jesus was with us this evening! We recognized him when he broke bread and passed it."

While they were gathered, talking about the experience, Jesus appeared before the whole group. They were all terrified until he spoke, "Peace unto you." Then he showed them the marks on his hands and feet to prove that it was really he.

Thomas was the only apostle absent on the occasion, and he found it difficult to believe when the others told him they had seen Jesus. "I will have to see and touch for myself," he said. So on another day Jesus showed himself to Thomas, that he might be sure.

For forty days Jesus made appearances to his followers, both in Jerusalem and Galilee. He explained to them how he had fulfilled the promises and prophecies of the Old Testament when he died and rose again. At one time he appeared to a large group of five hundred; another time he visited with his brother James alone. It was on a mountain in Galilee that he commissioned them to carry on his work when he returned to the Father. "You are to go and tell all nations of me," he said. "Those who believe in me are to be baptized, and their sins will be forgiven. Then you are to teach them to live lives worthy of the kingdom."

Finally, Jesus led the faithful little band back to Jerusalem. They walked out the familiar road to Bethany, toward the Mount of Olives, and Gethsemane. Jesus' time on earth had come to an end.

"You are to stay here in Jerusalem until the Spirit of God comes upon you," he told his disciples on that day. "When you receive this Spirit, you will have the power to tell about me here in Jerusalem, and in Judea, Samaria, and even to the far corners of the world." Then, as they stood there on the mountain, Jesus raised his hand to bless the disciples and began rising, higher and higher, until at last a bright cloud hid him from sight.

While the disciples were still looking wordlessly into the sky, two angels appeared beside them. "Why are you looking into the heavens?" the angels asked. "This same Jesus, who has returned to glory, is going to come again to earth in the same way that you saw him leave."

Indeed Jesus will come again. And when he does, he will receive not only those first disciples, but all whose life was changed by the story of the risen Lord.

Matthew 28; Mark 16; Luke 24; John 20, 21

QUESTIONS: 1. *What act of love did Mary perform for Jesus?* 2. *Who disapproved of her generosity?* 3. *Why was Jesus' entry on a colt significant?* 4. *Describe the condition of the Temple when Jesus found it.* 5. *Why were the rulers angry when Jesus took charge of the Temple?* 6. *Who betrayed Jesus? For what sum?* 7. *Where did Jesus and the apostles eat the Passover?* 8. *What elements of the Passover meal were brought over into the new feast? What did they represent?* 9. *What did Jesus do in the garden? How did the apostles spend their time?* 10. *How did Judas indicate which of the men was Jesus?* 11. *What "blasphemous" statement convinced the Jewish council of Jesus' guilt?* 12. *Why was Jesus taken to Pilate?* 13. *Who was Barabbas?* 14. *Where was Jesus crucified?* 15. *What did he say while on the cross?* 16. *Who watched the crucifixion and with what attitude?* 17. *Where was Jesus buried?* 18. *Why did the Jews place guards at the tomb?* 19. *What did the women find in the empty tomb?* 20. *To whom did Jesus appear after the resurrection?* 21. *What task did he commission the disciples to undertake?* 22. *How did he return to the Father?*

The Coming of the Spirit

AN UNUSUAL PENTECOST

After Jesus had returned to heaven to be with his Father, the eleven apostles went back to Jerusalem, just as he had told them to do. There they met daily in a little room with some women who knew Jesus well and with his family. Together they studied and prayed while they waited for Jesus to send them the assistance he had promised. They chose a man named Matthias to replace Judas as an apostle. And, because they were faithful Jews, they prepared for the celebration of Pentecost, a feast day following fifty days after Passover.

When the day of Pentecost arrived, the little band of disciples crowded into the Temple area early in the morning along with thousands of other Jewish pilgrims to celebrate in the customary manner. No one suspected that the day would be out of the ordinary. Then suddenly, from high above, there came the sound of a strong, rushing wind; and to their surprise, something resembling a small flame sat above the head of each apostle. From that moment on, they were filled with Jesus' spirit, the sustaining power that would enable them to carry out the mission he had assigned to them. As evidence that they had received the gift, they spoke, and foreigners standing near them were able to understand every word in their own language.

"Aren't these men from Galilee?" someone asked. "Surely they are not educated. How is it that they are able to speak in foreign tongues?"

A few even mocked the twelve and suggested that they were drunk.

Then Peter stood up, now a different man than the one who had denied Jesus on the night of his trial. This time he spoke boldly, gaining the attention of the huge assembly.

"Listen to me, people of Judea," he began. "We are not drunk, as some of you think. We are here to tell you that the words of your prophets have come true, and we have been given the Spirit of God to enable us to do so. Listen carefully to my words: You have crucified and killed Jesus of Nazareth, whose miracles and works you saw. You thought death would put an end to him, but God has freed him from its bonds.

"King David, long ago, foresaw this victory over death," Peter continued, quoting a verse from David's writings with which they were familiar. "We know it is true because we have seen him alive. Now he has been raised to the presence of God, to reign as Lord and Christ!"

The apostle's stirring message awakened the conscience of many of the people there. Some realized how wrong they had been in killing Jesus. In their anguish of heart, they cried out, "What can we do now?"

"Repent of your sins and be baptized in the name of Jesus," came Peter's answer. "You will receive forgiveness of sin, and God will send his Spirit to dwell in you."

That day about three thousand people responded to Peter's message and were baptized. They became members of Christ's church, the great kingdom of which he had spoken; and they were devoted to Jesus and to one another. In the first few days after Pentecost, they met together often to hear the teaching of the apostles; and they practiced sharing among themselves. Daily their number grew as Jesus added to the church those that were being saved.

Acts 1:12–2:47

AT THE BEAUTIFUL GATE

From its first day, the Jerusalem church had three thousand members, and the number continued to grow day after day. Some had known Jesus and had believed he was the Messiah while he was on earth. Others had not and had put him to death, but now they saw that they had been wrong.

Even though these first members of the church met in private homes for meals and prayer, they continued to assemble at the Temple regularly, as well. One day Peter and John were going there at the afternoon hour of prayer, about three o'clock. As they came to the main gate, called the Beautiful Gate, they saw a crippled man sitting on the ground. He had never been able to walk or support himself with a job. Every day his friends carried him to this place in the hope that those entering the Temple might pity him and give him alms, or a gift of charity.

Peter and John stopped in front of the man, and Peter said kindly, "Look at us."

The lame man looked eagerly at the two, hoping that they had some money to give him.

Peter said, "I have no money for you, but I will give you what I have." Then he grasped the man's hand and exclaimed, "In the name of Jesus Christ of Nazareth, rise and walk!"

Immediately the man felt his legs and ankles grow strong. He jumped to his feet and went joyfully into the Temple with the two apostles, praising God all the while. Many of the worshippers inside immediately recognized him as the familiar figure that begged by the gate. They gathered around him in a curious group, asking, "How did this happen? Who healed you?"

Peter stood up among them, anxious to use every opportunity to spread his message. "Why do you stare at us as though we had some great power

Loran Raymond Jones

THE LOST COIN FOUND

Luke 15:8–10

Loran Raymond Jones

THE PRODIGAL SON

Luke 15:11:32

Loran Raymond Jones

JESUS AND THE LITTLE CHILDREN

Matthew 19:13–15

Loran Raymond Jones

BLIND MAN (BARTIMAEUS) CURED AT JERICHO

Mark 10:46–52

Loran Raymond Jones

TRIUMPHAL ENTRY INTO JERUSALEM

Matthew 21:1–11

Loran Raymond Jones

TRADERS CAST FROM THE TEMPLE

John 2:13–17

Loran Raymond Jones

THE LAST SUPPER

Mark 14:12–25

Loran Raymond Jones

JESUS IN THE GARDEN OF GETHSEMANE

Matthew 26:36–56

of our own?" he asked. "In this healing God has glorified not us, but his son Jesus—the very man you disowned even when Pilate wanted to let him go. You demanded that a murderer be released instead and crucified Jesus in his place! But now God has raised him from the dead. We saw him ourselves! And it is through his name that we have made this crippled man well."

Then Peter's voice lost some of its harshness and he said more gently, "I am sure you didn't realize what you were doing. But God has actually made the words of the prophets come true by sending Jesus. Repent of your sins and God will forget them; some day, when his purposes have been accomplished, he will send Jesus again. He will bless you now if you turn away from your wickedness."

But the priests of the Temple had overheard Peter, and they were very displeased to hear him say that the one they had killed was alive. They seized him and John and put them in jail for the night. In spite of these actions, more and more people accepted these words about Jesus as the truth; and the number of believers grew to about five thousand.

The next morning Peter and John were tried before the chief priest and rulers, the same officials who had condemned Jesus to die. "Where did you get the power to heal this man?" they asked.

Peter, filled with the Holy Spirit, spoke up boldly. "If you are questioning us about the good deed we did yesterday, we tell you plainly that it was done in the name of Jesus of Nazareth, the man whom you killed and God raised from the dead."

When the priests heard this they were astonished. They knew that Peter and John were provincial fishermen, yet they had spoken with the boldness of educated men. And there was no denying that they had been present when the lame man was healed. What was the next step for the Jewish officials to take?

Finally they sent Peter and John out of the room while they talked the matter over. Rather than harm the two, they decided to charge them not to spread their teaching regarding Jesus any further.

"What do you mean?" Peter said, when he heard the decision. "Do you think we can obey you rather than God? Why, we cannot help but talk about these things."

Since the people had come to believe the apostles, the rulers were afraid to harm them; so they merely threatened them and let them go. As soon as the two were released, they gathered with a group of believers to pray to God, thanking him for power he had given them. After that they continued to preach with even more courage. *Acts 3:1–4:31*

ALL THINGS IN COMMON

Many of the earliest converts to Christ were foreigners who had come to Jerusalem for the celebration of Pentecost. Because of their new relationship to Christ and to other believers, they remained in Jerusalem longer than they had planned. In order to take care of them, those of the group who lived in Jerusalem opened their homes. Soon they grew to hold many things "in common"—their problems and joys, as well as meals and homes.

Next, their enthusiasm led them to sell property and bring the money to the apostles to be divided among those who needed it. This was what a man named Ananias and his wife Sapphira did. But these two were not filled with a spirit of love as the others were. They wanted only to appear generous without giving up what they owned, so they sold their land and gave Peter only part of what they earned to share with the others. Then they did wrong by telling him that the money they gave him was all they had made.

Peter, however, was filled with the Spirit, and he knew when Ananias brought the offering and told his story that it was a lie. He said sternly,

"Ananias, why have you lied to me about keeping back part of your earnings? You didn't have to sell your land at all. Once you did, you could have kept all the money for yourself if you had wanted to. But you chose to try to deceive us. It is God you are lying to, not us."

As Peter spoke these words, Ananias fell dead at his feet, punished by God for his lie. Some young men carried him out to bury him.

About three hours later, Sapphira came in, unaware of what had happened. Peter asked her, "Did you sell your land for the amount that your husband brought us?"

"Yes, we did," she replied. "It was just that amount."

Peter spoke sharply to her, "Why did you and your husband agree to tell this lie? The young men who just buried your husband will bury you, too!"

And at these words Sapphira died as suddenly as her husband had.

It was a terrible thing that evil had come into the church of Jesus through members who lied. God's punishment had shown the people that he knew their hearts and that they were not to take their membership in his kingdom lightly. *Acts 4:32–5:11*

LOCKED DOORS

Every day the apostles preached and did more good works in Jesus' name. The people who heard of their healing brought out sick friends on beds and pallets as they had brought them to Jesus. They laid them in the streets so that Peter's shadow might pass over them as he walked by, for with this contact, they became well.

The apostles were not held in such favor throughout all Jerusalem, however. Most of the Jewish leaders remained as unwilling as ever to confess that Jesus was the Son of God, the promised Messiah. They still pictured him as a disturber and a criminal. When they heard the twelve claim that Jesus was now alive and reigning at God's right hand, they took it for blasphemy of the worst sort. Therefore, it is not hard to believe that the apostles were often arrested for their public proclaiming of the gospel.

On one such occasion God's angel opened the doors and let the men out of prison. He brought a message from God which was, "Go back to the Temple and tell the people about Jesus." So, as daybreak came, the twelve were back in the Temple, talking to the people. They were not at all afraid; they knew that God was taking care of them.

The doors of the prison were found locked that morning and the guards were standing at their posts, but inside was no sign of the prisoners.

"How could they have escaped through locked doors?" the astonished men exclaimed. "How could they get out without being seen?" The Temple officials were quite perplexed.

Then someone came in with this exciting message: "Those men you put in prison last night are back in the Temple, teaching!"

Immediately some officers went out and arrested the men again, but they were careful not to harm them for fear of making the people angry.

When the apostles came to trial before the council, the high priest demanded, "Didn't we tell you never again to teach in the name of Jesus? The whole city has heard your teaching. Now they blame us for killing that man."

The apostles answered, "We must obey God, not men. You killed Jesus, but God has raised him and placed him at his right hand. He is the Leader and Savior who will give forgiveness of sins to Israel. We know these things are true, and God has given us his Spirit so that we might proclaim them."

The rulers were furious, and some wanted to kill the apostles right away. But one of them, a wise man named Gamaliel, stood and said, "Take these men out for a moment." Then he told the others, "We must be very careful how we treat these men. We have seen other men before who gathered followers and pretended to have a very important message, and they have all died and their groups have scattered. Leave these men alone. If their message is from men, it will fail. But if it should be from God, we surely cannot stop them! We must not risk opposing God!"

The group took this wise advice but ordered that the apostles be beaten before they were released. Even this made them joyful—happy that they were permitted to suffer for the cause they loved. And even more than ever they continued to preach and teach about Jesus. *Acts 5:12–42*

LIFE OR DEATH FOR JESUS

In the young church there were many widows and other poor people who were unable to work and earn money for themselves. Every day the apostles gave them money and food that the other believers had brought to share with them. But there were so many that the apostles did not have time to distribute food and teach other people about Jesus, too.

"We must give our time to the preaching of the gospel," they told the people. "Choose seven of your best men and we will appoint them to do this work."

The members were pleased with this idea and they chose seven good men who were to serve the unfortunate. One of the men was Stephen, a great man so filled with the Holy Spirit that he was able to perform wonderful miracles. But his forceful preaching made him one of the prime targets of those Jews who fought the church. They began to lie about him and tell the people he had spoken against Moses and God. Their ugly rumors won many to their side, and they succeeded in finally capturing Stephen and beinging him before the council.

"This man talks about a Jesus of Nazareth who will destroy this place. He speaks against Moses and God!" they charged angrily.

The council looked at Stephen, whose face had the calm and glory of an angel's. "Is this true?" asked the high priest.

"Brethren and fathers," began Stephen, "listen to me. You know how God helped Abraham and made great promises to him. God also rescued Joseph from his troubles and blessed him and his family. He raised up Moses when the Egyptians were persecuting the Israelites and delivered them from danger. Still, in spite of all this help, the people would not obey him. They turned away and worshipped idols, and they killed the prophets he sent to tell of Christ's coming. Now you have killed this very Christ; you reject God just as your fathers did!"

The rulers and the mob became more and more enraged as they heard these words. Then, to make matters worse, Stephen looked upward and said, "I see the heavens opened and Jesus standing at the right hand of God."

At this the furious crowd rushed toward Stephen and drove him from the city. They began to throw stones at him, taking off their coats and giving them to a young man named Saul, who was part of their group.

Stephen, realizing that he was about to die, looked toward heaven and prayed, "Lord Jesus, receive my spirit." Then he cried loudly, "Lord, do not hold this sin against them!" And he died. *Acts 6–7*

SIMON, THE MAGICIAN

Stephen's death brought out-and-out war against the new church. The believers were so mistreated that many fled from Jerusalem in a great hurry to avoid being dragged into the streets and thrown into prison. Saul, the same young man who had helped in the stoning of Stephen, was one of the most heartless of those who persecuted the church.

Many of those who left the city found themselves in places that were strange and foreign to them. They might have been discouraged or angry after being forced to leave their homes and friends, but they were not. These brave people taught about Jesus wherever they went and were happy to be able to serve him.

Philip, one of the seven ministers that had been chosen, went to preach in the city of Samaria where he healed a number of sick people. Many of the people in the city had known Jesus when he had visited there and talked with the woman at the well. Now they were glad to hear Philip's message. One of those baptized was a man named Simon. Simon had been a magician; he had even pretended to be sent by God. Now he could see that Philip's miracles were much greater than his tricks and magic.

When news reached Jerusalem that there were believers in Samaria, Peter and John came to help strengthen the new group. They laid their hands on each one of the new followers of Christ so that they might receive the Holy Spirit. Simon the magician watched all this with interest. He saw something he wanted.

"Give me this power," he begged Peter. "I want to be able to put my hands on people and give them the Holy Spirit. See—here is my money. I'll pay you well."

Peter became angry. "May your money perish with you, Simon!" he said indignantly. "You can never purchase the gift of God that way."

Simon grew alarmed when he realized how foolish he had been. "Pray for me," he begged the two apostles.

Acts 8:2–24

AN AFRICAN CONVERT

After Philip had done this good work in Samaria, he thought he would return to Jerusalem with Peter and John. But an angel of the Lord brought this message: "Go south to the road between Jerusalem and Gaza."

Philip immediately left for this hot desert country, not knowing what the purpose of his journey was. But soon he discovered why God had wanted him in this place. Down the road he saw the dust raised by a chariot; and drawing nearer, he saw that the chariot carried a black man from Ethiopia, an African country. The man was the queen's treasurer, so he was very important among his people. He had been to Jerusalem to worship in the Temple; now, on his way back, he was reading from a parchment containing Old Testament writings.

The Spirit in the heart of Philip told him to go up close to the chariot; and as he did so, he heard the words the man was reading. He asked, "Do you understand what you are reading?"

The Ethiopian turned in surprise. "How can I," he replied, "unless someone guides me?" And he invited Philip to sit with him in the chariot, hoping to receive some help.

The words this man was reading were from the prophet Isaiah: "As a sheep led to the slaughter or a lamb before its shearer is dumb, so he opens not his mouth."

"I don't understand that," said the black man in a puzzled way. "Was the prophet talking about himself or another man?"

So Philip began to tell the good news of Jesus, how he had been mistreated and unfairly killed, yet how he had risen from the grave after death. As he explained that Jesus Christ could save men—that every day he saved those who accepted him, the Ethiopian came to believe.

Just then the chariot approached a pool of water in the desert. "Look, here is water!" said the black man. "Why can't I be baptized now?"

"You can, if you believe."

"I believe that Jesus is God's own Son."

So another convert was made; and an African returned to his country with the precious truth that had never before penetrated its borders. The gospel was spreading. *Acts 8:25–40*

WELCOME TO THE GENTILES

Peter continued to travel all about Judea and Samaria, preaching and doing good works among the people. In the city of Joppa, where he stayed for some time, he even raised a good woman from the dead. But wherever he went, he never taught about Jesus to the Greeks or Romans, only to the Jews, who had been God's chosen people.

In the city of Caesarea, not far away from Jerusalem, there lived a man named Cornelius, who was not a Jew, but a soldier of high rank in the Roman army. Still, he and his family believed in God and lived righteous lives, praying daily and giving to the poor.

As he was praying one afternoon about three o'clock, Cornelius had a vision which startled him. An angel appeared and called his name.

"What is it, Lord?" asked the frightened man.

"God has heard your prayers and seen your good works," came the answer. "Send messengers to Joppa for a man named Simon Peter who is staying there; you must hear what he has to say."

Then the angel vanished. Immediately Cornelius summoned three of his servants, told them what had happened, and sent them to Joppa.

About noon the next day, as the messengers were approaching Joppa, Peter was praying on the flat roof of the house where he was staying. He became very hungry as he smelled food cooking, but he fell into a deep sleep before it was ready.

He, too, had a vision. He saw a large sheet let down by its four corners from the sky. In the sheet were many animals of all kinds, snakes, reptiles, and birds. Peter heard a voice saying "Get up; kill and eat."

These words surprised Peter, because he knew that the Jewish laws did not allow him to eat these animals which were labeled "unclean" or "not holy." He replied earnestly, "Oh, no, Lord; for I have never eaten any of these common animals!"

The voice spoke again. "What I have made clean, you must not call unclean."

Three times the voice came to Peter, demanding that he eat; and three times he refused. Then the sheet was taken back up into heaven.

Peter was terribly puzzled about what had happened. He did not want to disobey God, but he knew that eating the animals would have broken an ancient Jewish law. As he pondered the meaning of the vision, he did not hear voices at the gate below calling him by name. The Spirit in his heart spoke to him again, "Outside at the gate three men are looking for you. Go down and join them, because I have sent them."

So Peter went down to the gate and said to the men, "I am the man you are looking for. What do you want?"

They replied, "We are sent by Cornelius, a captain in the Roman army who is a God-fearing man and is respected even by all the Jews. He wants to hear what you have to say."

Peter asked the men in to eat and rest for the night, and the next morning they left for Caesarea. When they arrived, they found Cornelius waiting with all his relatives and close friends. He fell down and bowed to Peter but the apostle immediately grasped his arm and pulled him up.

"Stand up," he said to the good soldier. "I am only a man like you."

Then Peter began to talk with the large group that had gathered. "You know as well as I do how it has been against the law for Jews to associate with Gentiles, but God has shown me now that I can no longer call any man 'common' or 'unclean.' That is why I came without hesitation. Now, why did you send for me?"

Cornelius explained about the vision he had had four days before, instructing him to send for Peter and to hear what he had to say.

With that Peter began to teach the good news. "I see now," he began, "that God no longer favors any nation but will accept any person who does what is right." Then he told them how Jesus had died for all men.

While Peter talked the Holy Spirit came into the hearts of all his listeners and they began to speak in other languages as the apostles had done on the day of Pentecost. Seeing this, Peter knew that they believed and that God wanted them to be saved; and immediately he baptized them.

After Peter returned to Jerusalem, the other disciples demanded to know why he had associated with Gentiles while in Caesarea. Once he explained the vision and all that had happened, they could not deny that Jesus had come to save *all* men. The implications of this truth were immeasurable. What an immensely large job they had! They needed to preach about Jesus, not just to the Jews, but to men all over the world!

It was about this time that the disciples of Christ began to be called "Christians."

Acts 9:32–11:18

A MIRACULOUS ESCAPE

The church of Jesus Christ was growing and growing, especially now that Gentiles were being baptized. The Jews who did not believe began persecuting the Christians again and even King Herod began to help them. He arrested James the brother of John and had him killed. When he saw how much the Jews liked this, he arrested Peter, too.

Peter was thrown roughly into prison and four groups of soldiers were stationed there to guard him and to be certain that he did not escape again. The time of the Jewish Passover had come again, and Herod intended to keep Peter in jail until it was over. Meanwhile, the church members in the city kept up constant prayer for him, praying that he would not be killed as James had been.

The night before Herod was to bring Peter out of prison, and probably kill him, the apostle was sleeping between two guards, bound with two heavy chains. All of a sudden a light pierced the gloom of the dingy cell and an angel of God appeared. He touched Peter to awaken him. "Get up quickly!" he whispered.

Peter looked around, but the guards did not move; they seemed unaware of what was happening. The heavy chains slipped easily off Peter's hands and he stood up. "Dress yourself and put on your sandals," directed the angel. Peter moved slowly, still not fully awake. "Now put on your coat and follow me," he was told.

Peter followed the angel out but he felt as though he were dreaming or seeing a vision. Surely one of the guards would sense his absence or one of the sentries at the door would hear them pass! But they passed the first, then the second sentry, finally reaching the great iron gate which opened into the street. No one saw or heard them. Then Peter saw the gate open by itself, as though an unseen hand pushed back the large, heavy bars.

The next thing he knew, Peter was standing in the street alone. Looking about at the dark city and feeling the cool night air, Peter realized that what had happened to him had not been a dream. "The Lord sent an angel to rescue me," he thought, "so that Herod could not kill me."

Where would Peter go in the middle of this dark night to find shelter? He paused only a moment before hurrying toward the house of Mary and her son Mark. He knew he would be welcome in the home of these Christians, and perhaps he even knew of the group that had gathered there to pray.

When he reached the house and knocked at the door, a young girl named Rhoda came to answer. She immediately recognized Peter's voice, and in her great joy she forgot to let him in. Instead she ran into the room where the group was praying and called excitedly, "Peter is at the door!"

"He can't be," everyone said. "Peter is in prison. You must be crazy."

But Rhoda insisted, "It is Peter! I know it is!"

"Maybe it is his spirit," they replied.

Still Peter stood at the door, knocking again and again. Finally someone answered the knock; and surely enough, there stood Peter! The crowd could hardly believe it. They all began talking at once, but Peter held up his hand to silence them; then he told them the miraculous story of how God had brought him out of prison.

Peter could only stay a short time with this group, because he knew Herod would send soldiers to look for him when his cell was found empty. He left to find another place to hide.

In the morning there was a great stir in the prison. Herod was enraged at the guards, who could tell him nothing about what had happened in the night, and he ordered that they should be put to death.

Not long afterward, this wicked king made a speech to some of his subjects and pretended that he was a god instead of an ordinary man. God was displeased that Herod claimed so much glory for himself and he struck Herod with a horrible disease so that he died.

A great enemy of the Christians was gone, but they continued day by day to grow in numbers and strength. God was blessing the young church as its members worshipped him and told about Jesus wherever they went.

Acts 12

QUESTIONS: 1. *What did the apostles do between Jesus' ascension and Pentecost?* 2. *What signs showed that the Spirit had come?* 3. *What were the results of Peter's sermon on Pentecost?* 4. *What happened at the Beautiful Gate?* 5. *Why was it necessary for the first converts to share with one another?* 6. *What was the sin of Ananias and Sapphira?* 7. *For what cause were Peter and John put in prison?* 8. *What man per-*

suaded the council to release the apostles? How? 9. *Why were seven men given a special appointment in the early church?* 10. *Why was Stephen killed? How did he react to danger?* 11. *What reaction did Stephen's death bring about?* 12. *What did Simon the magician want to buy? What was Peter's answer to him?* 13. *What was the African's response to Philip's sermon?* 14. *How did God show Peter that it was safe to welcome Gentiles into the kingdom?* 15. *How did the Jewish Christians in Jerusalem react to the conversion of Cornelius?* 16. *How did Peter escape from prison a second time?*

A Light to the Gentiles

ON THE ROAD TO DAMASCUS

One of the most vigorous of the Jews who persecuted the church was a young man named Saul. He was a member of the Pharisees, the sect of religious Jewish men who had been criticized by Jesus for making a show of their goodness and pretending to be better than other men. Most of the Pharisees who heard the preaching of the gospel rejected it as they had rejected Jesus during his lifetime.

Saul, the young man who had held the coats of the men who stoned Stephen and who had ordered soldiers in Jerusalem to throw the followers of Jesus into prison, was a sincere Pharisee. He had received a good education in Jerusalem, where he had been taught by Gamaliel, the wise teacher who had advised the priests and rulers to let the Christians alone. He hated Christians because he thought they were teaching something that was contrary to God's will. He thought God wanted him to persecute and even kill them. Saul was so convinced that they were wrong and should be punished that he traveled to other cities besides Jerusalem to destroy them.

"We must overthrow these people who work against God!" Saul told the high priest. "If you will give me letters of permission, I will travel to Damascus, where some of them are hiding. If I find any who claim to follow this Jesus, I will bring them back in chains to be thrown into prison."

The high priest granted him permission, and Saul set out on his journey. About noon several days later, he was approaching the city of Damascus when suddenly, a brilliant, blinding light from heaven, even brighter than the sun, flooded the area around him and his companions. They were so startled and frightened that they all fell immediately to the ground.

The young man heard a voice from heaven speaking to him. "Saul, Saul, why do you persecute me?"

Saul was very frightened. "Who is speaking to me?" he asked.

"I am Jesus of Nazareth, the one you are fighting," the voice replied.

Saul hardly knew what to think. He had been so sure that this Jesus was a false teacher and that his followers should be punished. And now to find out that Jesus was not dead—that he was alive, speaking from heaven! All the time, Saul had been the one fighting against God!

"What do you want me to do?" he asked humbly.

"Get up and go into Damascus, and there you will be told what to do," came the answer.

The bright light faded until only normal daylight remained, and the voice from heaven spoke no more. But as he tried to get to his feet to go into the city, Saul found that he could not see; the brightness of the vision had made him blind!

The men who were with Saul had seen the light and had heard the voices, but they had been unable to understand what was happening. Now that the brilliance was gone, their sight was restored, so they led Saul by the hand into Damascus. They took him to the home of a man named Judas who lived on what was called "Straight Street." There Saul remained for three days, unable to see and refusing to eat or drink or talk. He spent the time alone, praying to God and feeling a deep sorrow for the harm he had done to the church which he now knew was proclaiming the truth.

A follower of Christ named Ananias lived in Damascus. On the third day after Saul had arrived in that city, the Lord spoke to Ananias in a vision, telling him to go to Saul and restore his sight.

Ananias became afraid when he heard this command. "Lord, many people have told me of the wrong this man did to the believers in Jerusalem," he protested. "I have heard that the reason he has come to Damascus is to arrest Christ's followers here!"

"You and the other Christians do not need to be afraid of him any longer," the Lord assured him. "I have chosen him to be a great worker for me. He will speak of me to Jews, to Gentiles, and to kings; and he will have to suffer a great deal for my sake."

When Ananias heard these words he went straight to the house where Saul was staying. He told Saul who he was and that he had been sent by God to cure his blindness. Placing his hands on Saul's eyes, he restored their vision.

"God has chosen you to know his will and to tell all men what you have seen and heard," Ananias said kindly. "And now why do you wait? Rise and be baptized in the name of Jesus so that your sins will be forgiven."

So Saul was baptized, becoming a part of the very group he had come to arrest. He was given some food so that he might regain the strength, and immediately he was ready to go out and proclaim that Jesus was the Son of God.

Acts 9:1–20; 22:6–21; 26:4–18

A CHANGE OF HEART

In the morning a new figure was seen in the synagogue, boldly speaking of Jesus and saying, "He is the Son of God!" The Christians who listened were almost afraid to believe what they saw.

"Isn't this Saul, the man who attacked all the believers in Jerusalem? Hasn't he come here to arrest us?" they asked one another.

The Jews who heard him speak were just as surprised, for they had been waiting for him to come and help them launch an attack on the Christians in their city. The impact of his conversion led some of them to believe in Jesus themselves, but the majority were irate. They felt, as Saul once had, that the Christian message was false and opposed to God's will as expressed in Judaism. Therefore, it is no wonder that a group of them devised a plot to kill Saul soon after he began preaching. Night and day they kept a close guard on the gates of the city, planning to capture him as he attempted to escape. But the disciples in Damascus, now convinced of Saul's sincerity, learned of the scheme and devised a way to save him. On a dark night they took him to an unguarded place in the city wall, far from the gate. Here they let him down over the way in a basket, and he returned to Jerusalem unharmed.

In Jerusalem Saul found that the Christians there were not nearly so eager to see him as he was to meet them. They remembered him as a persecutor of believers. They had heard nothing of his vision on the road to Damascus, or his baptism, or his good works in that city. But a disciple named Barnabas, who did know of these experiences, explained to them the change that had come into Saul's life. Once they heard the story of what had happened to Saul, the Jerusalem Christians were overjoyed to receive him as a believer.

Saul wasted no time in beginning to preach in the capital city. If anything, he proclaimed the truth about Jesus with even more enthusiasm than he had shown when he was persecuting Christians. But again the Jews became angry when they heard his teaching; and, like those at Damascus, they plotted to kill him.

Finally, it was recognized that Saul could not remain in Jerusalem with any degree of safety; and friends helped him escape to Tarsus, the city of his birth.

Acts 9:21–31

CALLED BY THE SPIRIT

A great number of the Christians who had been scattered from Jerusalem in the days of the persecution that followed the death of Stephen settled in the city of Antioch, located in Syria. They established a church that grew quite active under the leadership of a man named Barnabas. When the work grew so heavy that Barnabas had to find help, he called on Saul, still in Tarsus, to come and share the ministry with him. It was with this church that foreign mission work had its beginning.

Saul and Barnabas had been in Antioch over a year when the Holy Spirit spoke to the group, saying, "You must do without these two men, for I have a special work for them." The mission was that of preaching in foreign lands, so the church prayed and blessed Saul and Barnabas and sent them on their way.

They, along with Barnabas' young cousin, John Mark, journeyed to the seacoast and sailed for the island of Cyprus. There they walked from the city of Salamis at one end of the island to Paphos at the other end, preaching about Jesus all the way. At Paphos they taught the good news to a man named Sergius Paulus, who was the Roman proconsul (or governor) of the island. He was eager to receive their message, but a wicked Jewish magician named Elymas turned him away.

Saul, who had now begun to use his Gentile name, Paul, seemed to assume the leadership of the group at this point. Greatly annoyed by the intrusion of Elymas, he burst out, "You son of the devil and enemy of righteousness! You are full of wickedness and deceit. You must stop trying to oppose the will of God. His hand is on you now, and you will be unable to see for a while."

Elymas found immediately that he was blind, and he stumbled about, trying to find someone to lead him. This act succeeded in convincing Sergius Paulus that Paul was sent from God and he accepted the message concerning the Christ.

Leaving the island of Cyprus, the missionaries traveled northward to the mainland of Asia Minor and the city of Perga. There an unfortunate thing happened. John Mark, who seemed to have become discouraged either by homesickness or by the hardships of the journey, left the group and returned to his home in Jerusalem. Paul was very disappointed in him, as we shall see later.

Now alone, Paul and Barnabas passed on to another city named Antioch, this one in the province of Pisidia. There Paul was invited to speak in the synagogue when the people gathered on the Sabbath Day. Since there were many Jews in the audience, he began by talking about their history and the Old Testament prophecies about Jesus. He told them that Jesus was the Messiah they had been waiting for, that he had risen from the dead, and that he was now saving men from their sins.

The audience was so impressed by this message that many, both Jews and Gentiles, believed and begged Paul to teach them more. On the next Sabbath, practically everyone in the city gathered to hear him. As usual, a group of Jews grew jealous when they saw all these people eagerly listening to the new teaching. They contradicted what Paul and Barnabas said and spread rumors about them.

"It was God's will that you Jews be given the first opportunity to accept Jesus," the missionaries warned; "but if you reject him, we will preach to the Gentiles instead!"

And that was what they did. They found the Gentiles a most receptive group; in fact, many of them became Christians. Naturally, this made the Jews even angrier, and they stirred up a large group of people who drove Paul and Barnabas from the city.

Acts 13

GODS OR MEN?

Iconium was the next stop for the two disciples. There their success was much the same as before. A few listened and accepted their message, but the unbelieving Jews made things so difficult for them that they had to leave town in danger of their lives.

The escape from Iconium led to Lystra, where they met a crippled man who had not been able to stand or walk since his birth. He listened to Paul's teaching with great faith; and Paul, recognizing this, said to him, "Stand up on your feet." Immediately the man rose and began walking about.

When the crowd that had gathered in the street saw this, they realized that men who could do such a thing had unusual power. They decided that Paul and Barnabas must be gods who had come to earth as men. "Jupiter and Mercury are here with us!" they shouted, using the familiar names of the Roman gods they worshipped. They even began to gather wreaths and animals to offer as sacrifices to the two men. This led Paul and Barnabas to hurriedly explain, "We are not gods. We are men just as you are." And seizing the opportunity, they added, "We have come to bring you good news and to tell you not to worship these idols and Roman gods any longer. There is really only one God, the one who made heaven and earth and everything in them, and he is the one you should worship."

About this time a group of Jews from Antioch and Iconium, who had been unsuccessful in trying to kill Paul and Barnabas when they had visited their cities, arrived in Lystra to try again. The people of Lystra, who had just been disappointed in their attempt to worship the men, were persuaded by these Jews to turn against Paul and Barnabas. They even stoned Paul until they thought he was dead and dragged him outside the city.

When Barnabas and the people who had believed the gospel came to get Paul's body, they discovered, to their great relief, that he was not dead but only bruised and hurt. They brought him back into the city for a night of rest, after which he and Barnabas left for the city of Derbe.

After preaching in Derbe and establishing another small group of believers, the disciples decided to return over the route they had covered and head back toward Antioch of Syria, the city from which they had come. In each place where they had taught, they had started a church; and now as they returned they appointed elders in each of these churches. The task of the elders would be to help guide the activities of the new Christians.

When they arrived in Antioch, the disciples called the Christians together and told them about their journey and about the many Gentiles who had believed in Jesus. They remained there in Antioch for a long time, leading that great church in its work.

Acts 14

A SECOND JOURNEY

After some time, Paul and Barnabas decided to return to the cities where they had established churches and encourage the Christians there. The two friends were enthusiastically preparing for the journey when they had a disagreement about taking John Mark along with them. Paul did not think it would be wise to allow the young man to go when he had been such a disappointment before, and the two argued so sharply that they finally separated, Barnabas taking John Mark with him to Cyprus. Paul asked Silas to accompany him, and these two left to visit the churches that had been started on the mainland.

The two went first through Derbe and Lystra, strengthening the believers. At Lystra Paul found, to his great joy, that the young man Timothy, whom he had converted on his first trip to the city, had made great progress as a Christian and was loved by all the believers in the area. Timothy's father was a Greek, but his mother and grandmother were Jews. They were good women who had taught him the scriptures since he had been a small child. Paul loved Timothy as if he were his own son, and he invited the young man to accompany him and Silas as they continued their journey.

After the three had visited the churches in Iconium and Antioch in Pisidia, the Holy Spirit directed them on toward Troas. There Paul had a dream as he slept one night. He saw a man saying to him, "Come over into Macedonia and help us." Paul knew that this meant God wanted him to travel into a new area, the continent of Europe, and take the good news to people who had never heard of Jesus.

A new figure joined the missionaries as they left Troas by sea and traveled toward Philippi, in Macedonia. He was Luke, the good doctor who later wrote a book about the life of Jesus. Luke kept a careful account of all that happened as he traveled with Paul and he also wrote about Paul's other journeys from what he was told. Later he used these accounts to write the book of Acts.

When the group arrived at the large city of Philippi, they found it a city filled with heathen people who worshipped idols. The very few Jews who lived there were accustomed to gathering at the riverside to worship and pray, since they did not have a synagogue. On the Sabbath day Paul and his company met them there and spoke to them. One true worshiper of God, a business woman named Lydia, heard their words about Jesus and believed. She rejoiced as the disciples baptized her and insisted that they stay in her home while they were in Philippi. *Acts 15:36–16:15*

IN A PHILIPPIAN JAIL

In the city of Philippi there was a poor slave girl. Her masters were greedy men who made a great deal of money by making her tell fortunes.

This poor girl followed Paul and the others through the streets, crying loudly, "These men are servants of the true God, and they come to tell you the way to be saved."

Many people laughed at this, because they knew the girl had an evil spirit in her that caused her to say peculiar things. Paul did not think it was good to have her following them and shouting, so he turned to her and spoke to the evil spirit inside her: "In the name of Jesus Christ, I tell you to come out of her!"

At that moment the spirit left the girl. She was now in her right mind, but she was also unable to tell fortunes any longer. This made her masters furious. It did not matter to them that the girl was well and happy; they cared only for the money she could make them.

Dragging Paul and Silas before the rulers of the city, they shouted angrily, "These men are Jews, and they are disturbing our city! They tell us to practice customs that are against the law." They aroused the people in the market place and before long they were attacking the missionaries. Rulers of the city ordered that Paul and his company be stripped of their clothes, beaten, and then thrown into prison. In the jail the bleeding men were put into stocks, which locked their hands and feet in place and kept them from moving or changing their position. The jailer was told to keep them locked up at all costs.

As the cell grew darker and darker and midnight approached, the disciples sat in pain in the uncomfortable position forced on them by the stocks. They were unable to sleep, but they did not feel sorry for themselves or think about their misery; instead, they rejoiced that they could suffer for Christ and prayed and sang praises to God, while the other prisoners listened.

Then suddenly, a strange thing happened. An earthquake began to shake the prison from its foundations so that the walls quivered, the doors were flung wide open, and the chains and stocks fell apart and released the prisoners. They were free!

The jailer was awakened from his sleep by the noise and the movement of the earthquake as it rocked the prison; and when he saw that the doors were open, he immediately drew his sword to kill himself. He thought the prisoners had escaped and was afraid that the rulers would hold him responsible. But when Paul saw the jailer about to take his own life, he shouted, "Don't kill yourself; we are all here!"

Trembling with amazement and fear, the jailer called for a light and ran into the cell where Paul and Silas stood. Surely these men were from God—they had not even run away when they had been given a chance! He begged them to come out and go with him to his house, and he asked them, "Sirs, what must I do to be saved?" He felt sure they knew the truth and could answer the question for him.

"Believe in the Lord Jesus and you will be saved," answered Paul.

The jailer took the men to his house where the disciples talked to him and all of his household about Jesus. These people did not even know who Jesus was or anything about his life on earth. When they heard the wonderful story of how Christ had been raised to heaven and how he would save them from their sins, they gladly believed the teaching of the disciples. As soon as the jailer had washed and soothed the burning wounds of the missionaries, he and his family were baptized. Then the hungry and tired disciples were fed a warm meal and given a place to rest.

In the morning the rulers sent word to the house of the jailer to let the men go. Most prisoners would have been happy to leave, but Paul and Silas were not. They were Roman citizens, which meant that the Roman government was supposed to grant them certain privileges. For one thing, no Roman citizen could be thrown into jail unless he had first been tried and found guilty.

So when the jailer brought the message from the rulers, Paul replied, "They beat us in public when we had not been tried and condemned, though we are Roman citizens; and they cast us into prison. Do they think they can make us leave quietly and secretly now? No! They have broken the law, and if they want us to leave they can come and bring us out publicly."

The rulers grew afraid when they heard the message and learned that the men were Romans. They hurried to Paul and Silas and apologized to them, asking them more kindly now to leave.

Before they left Philippi the disciples went to the house of Lydia and talked with a group of new Christians who had gathered there. Then they went on to preach in other cities.

In Thessalonica many people were glad to hear the news of Jesus and a church was begun, but the opposition of the Jews was so great that Paul and Silas were not safe and had to leave the city. Going on to Berea, they found a group of people eager to hear what they taught. These people not only listened intently to what was said, but searched the scriptures to see if the prophets really had told of Jesus. Before long, however, the angry Jews from Thessalonica caught up with the preachers and started an uprising.

Because they feared for his life, Paul's friends persuaded him to go on to another city.

Acts 16:16–17:15

IN ATHENS AND CORINTH

Paul went next to Athens, the great city of Greece, and there he waited anxiously for his friends to join him. While he waited, he walked about the city, looking at the large and beautiful temples where the Greeks worshiped their gods. Inside the temples and all around the city he saw idols, for these people knew nothing about the true God and worshiped statues of the gods they had invented.

Paul wanted to tell the people of Athens about God and his Son, and he thought he could find an audience who would listen to him in the Jewish synagogue. So he began to go there every day and talk, and some of the people who happened to be in the market place would come in and listen to him. The Athenians were interested in new ideas and enjoyed talking about many different things; soon a large group of them decided they would like to hear all of Paul's story.

"What is this new teaching we hear?" they asked. "Are you talking about some foreign gods of whom we have not heard? We want to know what it's all about." They took Paul to a meeting place called the Aveopagus; there they asked him to speak to them.

"Men of Athens," he began, "I can see that in every way you are very religious. Everywhere I have gone in your city I have seen objects that you worship and I see that you serve many gods. But in one place I found an altar with a sign that read, 'To the Unknown God.' You are worshiping a god of whom you know nothing, and this is the one I have come to tell you about."

Paul felt that these people were convinced that the false gods they worshiped were real. They were afraid that somehow they might have missed one when they made their statues and idols, so they had built an altar to this "Unknown God" to keep him from being displeased. If Paul had begun by telling the men of Athens that none of their gods were true, they might have been so irritated that they would not have listened to him at all. But by using his knowledge about their "Unknown God," he was able to get their attention. They were eager to hear what he would say.

He spoke boldly: "The God who made the whole world and everything in it is the God of whom I speak. For this reason he does not need to live in any man-made temple. He does not need any of the things you offer as sacrifices; in fact, he needs nothing from us because he is the one who made us all and gives us life and everything else that we have! But this God is a loving God who wants us to seek for him and find him. If we seek him, we will find him not far from us.

"Some of your poets have said, 'We are God's children.' If this is true—if we *are* God's children—how could we think that he could be made by men from gold or silver or stone, as your idols are? In the past you did not know this, and God overlooked your ignorance. But now he wants all men, wherever they are, to repent of their sins. Jesus Christ has been chosen by God to judge all the world on a great day that will come, and God has raised him from the dead to assure you that this is true."

At these words many of the men in the audience began to laugh, because they did not believe that anyone who died could become alive again. But some felt that Paul had spoken wisely, and these asked to talk with him again. Despite all his efforts, only a few conversions were made.

Next Paul traveled on to the city of Corinth, where he began to live with a Christian man named Aquila and his wife Priscilla. After some time he was joined by Timothy and Silas, who found him working with Aquila and Priscilla at the trade of tentmaking. In his spare time, he preached in the synagogue. For a year and a half Paul stayed in this city; and during that time many people believed and were baptized, most of them Gentiles.

From Corinth Paul took Aquila and Priscilla and went to Ephesus. Aquila and Priscilla remained there, but Paul wanted to visit some of the young churches he had started and report back to the church at Antioch. He left by boat, promising to return if it were God's will. *Acts 17:16–18:22*

REVOLT OF THE SILVERSMITHS

After spending some time in Antioch and then visiting a number of other cities, Paul kept his promise and returned to Ephesus. He remained there for more than two years, preaching, healing the sick, and casting out evil spirits. Some of the Ephesians, even many of those in the church, tried to perform miracles like those of Paul; but without the power of God. When Paul showed them the evil of performing their magic and glorifying themselves, they repented and burned all their magic books in a great fire.

In the city of Ephesus there was a magnificent temple to the goddess Diana, whom the Greeks worshiped as the goddess of hunting. Inside the temple was a huge statue of Diana, and the silver craftsmen of the city made little images of this statue to sell to the people of the city and to those who visited the temple. The Ephesians felt that Diana was especially favorable to them because of the great temple in their city, and they all thought that they should have an image of her in their homes to show their appreciation for her favor. They bought so many images that the silversmiths became rich.

But because of Paul's teaching about the one true God, fewer people came to worship at the temple and not as many silver images were sold. Demetrius, one of the silver workmen, became alarmed and called his fellow silversmiths together.

"Men," he said, "you know that we make our money by selling these images. This Paul has turned away many people here and all over Asia by telling them that our handmade images are not gods at all. If he continues to do this, not only will our business be ruined, but the temple which has brought recognition to our city will be forgotten."

The silversmiths became angry at the thought that this might happen, and they began to cry out, "Great is Diana of the Ephesians!" They grew louder and louder and caused so much commotion that the entire city joined in the uproar. A mob formed which grabbed two of the disciples who were with Paul and dragged them into the theater. Paul wanted to go with them and try to talk to the people, but a group of the Christians were afraid he might be hurt and kept him from the rioting throng.

In the theater the great mob that had been attracted by the noise and excitement continued to create confusion and disorder, but they were not really sure why they had come together at all. Some of them were shouting one thing and some another. A man named Alexander tried to quiet them, but they began to cry out in unison, "Great is Diana of the Ephesians!" and no one could be heard above the uproar.

For two hours the crowd kept up the same shout until they were tired and hoarse. Finally the town clerk managed to get them quiet and he spoke to them reasonably. "Men of Ephesus," he said, "we all know that our city holds the great temple and statue of Diana, and there is no cause for us to be alarmed. These men you have brought in have done nothing wrong. If Demetrius has anything against them he should take the matter into court rather than cause a riot. We are in danger of being put in prison for this disgraceful commotion."

At last the noise died down and the crowd began to leave. When all the confusion was over, Paul decided it was time to end his long stay in Ephesus. He called together the Christians he had baptized, told them goodbye, and set out once again on his journey for Jesus. *Acts 19*

ARREST IN JERUSALEM

After Paul had journeyed to many other cities, strengthening the Christians and establishing new churches, he arrived at last in Jerusalem. Many of his Christian friends had not wanted him to go to that city because they feared he might be imprisoned. But Paul felt it was God's will that he visit the believers in Jerusalem. The Christians in the holy city were happy to see him and listened gladly to his report of his journeys.

Many of the Jews of the city, however, were jealous of Paul's attention to the Gentiles, and they stirred up an angry crowd by saying that he had made the temple unholy by bringing in foreigners. Though Paul had not taken any Gentiles into the temple, many of the people believed the story and became so angry that they rushed at Paul and dragged him from the temple.

"Kill him! Kill him!" they shouted wildly.

Just then some soldiers whose captain had heard of the disturbance rushed upon the scene. Seeing them, the people moved back and stopped beating Paul. But still they were furious and they began to shout at the captain as he was binding Paul with chains. The captain asked who the man was and what he had done, but the people were screaming so loudly, some one thing and some another, that he could learn nothing. So he ordered his soldiers to take Paul back to the barracks as the people cried, "Away with him! Kill him!"

As he was being taken away on the shoulders of the soldiers so that the rioting mob could not harm him, Paul spoke to the captain in Greek. The captain was amazed, for he had thought Paul was an Egyptian who had stirred up some people earlier.

"I am not an Egyptian, I am a Jew;" replied Paul, "and I beg you to let me speak to the people."

So the captain gave permission, and Paul stood on the steps and began to speak to the people in Hebrew. When they heard him speaking in their own language, they finally quieted down.

Paul carefully explained to the crowd, which just a few minutes before had been trying to kill him, that he had been born a Jew just as they. He told how he had hated the Christians and how he had killed some and put others in prison. Then he told them about his trip to Damascus. He explained that he had planned to go to that city and arrest Christians there. And he told them how the Lord had spoken to him on the road and caused him to realize his error.

After listening for a short time, the people decided they wanted to hear no more, and they began to shout again, "Away with him! This man is not fit to live!" They became so violent that they threw dirt into the air and waved their clothing about. The captain ordered that Paul be taken to the barracks and beaten until he admitted the crime he had committed.

Carrying out their orders, the soldiers began to tie Paul's hands and feet for his beating. Then Paul turned to one of them and asked, "Is it lawful to beat a man who is a Roman?"

These words surprised the soldier, who knew it was against the law to arrest or beat a Roman citizen unless he had already been tried and condemned in court. He went immediately to his captain and asked, "Do you know what you are doing? This man is a Roman citizen!"

The captain was alarmed, because he knew he could be punished for so treating a Roman. He released Paul immediately; but because he was still curious about what it was that Paul had done, he called together the council in the morning and took Paul before them. There the priests got into an argument among themselves when Paul was testifying; and seeing that they were becoming angry, the captain had to take Paul to the barracks again for safety. He still had no more idea about what Paul had done wrong.

That night the Lord spoke to Paul, saying, "Take courage. You will not be killed here in Jerusalem, for I plan to send you to Rome to preach about me there." Surely these words were of great comfort to Paul during the days that followed, for many times it seemed as though the Jews would cause his death. When the captain saw the great danger, he finally arranged to have Paul sent to Caesarea where he could be tried safely. *Acts 20–23*

BEFORE GOVERNORS AND KINGS

A few days after Paul arrived in Caesarea he was brought before Governor Felix to be tried. The Jews had sent a spokesman to present their case,

Loran Raymond Jones

JESUS BEARING THE CROSS

John 19:16–42

Loran Raymond Jones

THE RESURRECTION

Matthew 28:1–10

Loran Raymond Jones

THE STRANGER AT EMMAUS

Luke 24:13–35

Loran Raymond Jones

PHILIP AND THE ETHIOPIAN

Acts 8:26–40

Loran Raymond Jones

PETER AND THE ROMAN CENTURIAN

Acts 10:1–33

Loran Raymond Jones

SAUL'S CONVERSION

Acts 9:1–22

Loran Raymond Jones

PAUL AND SILAS AT PHILIPPI

Acts 16:25–26

Loran Raymond Jones

JOHN, THE APOSTLE, AT PATMOS

Revelation

and he spoke to Felix in polite and fine speech, explaining that the Jews had found Paul to be a troublemaker.

When it was Paul's turn to speak, he also addressed Felix politely and spoke well, for he was an educated man. Paul said that he had not made trouble in the city and that the men could not prove their charges. "But it is true that I do believe in Jesus," he said firmly, "and I also believe what has been said by the law and the prophets. These men cannot accuse me of anything except that while I was among them I said that I believe in the resurrection of the dead."

Felix could find nothing wrong in anything that Paul had said. But not wishing to offend those who opposed Paul, he decided to hold him in Caesarea anyway. One soldier was chosen to guard Paul as a prisoner, though he was given some liberty and his friends were allowed to visit him. For two years Paul was forced to remain in Caesarea. Several times he talked with Felix and his wife about Jesus and about the group called "Christians." Although Paul's words about the Judgment Day frightened Felix, he never became a Christian.

After two years another man, Festus, took Felix's place as governor. The Jews in Jerusalem, who still remembered Paul and wished to be rid of him, asked Festus to allow Paul to return to Jerusalem for trial. They had plotted together to have some of their men waiting on the road to ambush Paul and kill him.

When Festus called Paul before him, he asked the great apostle if he wished to go to Jerusalem to be tried. Paul knew of the plots that been laid for his life before, and he felt sure that the Jews were planning to kill him this time, too.

"I have done no wrong, as you well know," he told Festus. "If there is not truth in their charges against me, I do not deserve to die. I will not go to Jerusalem; I appeal to Caesar!"

Since Paul, as a Roman citizen with all the rights guaranteed to citizens, had asked to have his case tried by Caesar, Festus had no choice but to agree to take him to Rome. For years Paul had wanted to go to this great city, and God had said that he would; but Paul had not realized that he would go as a prisoner!

During his last days in Caesarea, while he waited to leave for Rome, Paul had a chance to speak about his beliefs to Agrippa, another ruler who had come to visit Festus. He described in detail the experience on the road to Damascus which had led him to his present situation.

"O King Agrippa," concluded Paul, "I did as the vision told me and began to preach in Damascus, then Jerusalem, then in all Judea, and even to the Gentiles. I told the people they must repent and turn to God. This is the only reason the Jews seized me in the temple and tried to kill me. But God has been with me at all times, and I will continue to tell what Moses and the Jewish prophets said would happen: that Jesus Christ suffered and rose from the dead to save all men, both Jews and Gentiles!"

Agrippa was moved by Paul's words, and he said, "Paul, you almost convince me to become a Christian." Then he left the room; and when he was alone with Festus, he said, "This man has done nothing wrong. He might have been set free if he had not appealed to Caesar." *Acts 24–26*

SHIPWRECK

The trip from Caesarea to Rome was long and had to be made by sea. Luke, the doctor who was to write a story of Jesus' life and that of Paul's, as well, was Paul's traveling companion on the journey. Paul was put in the care of a centurion named Julius, an officer with one hundred men under him. Julius was kind to Paul and allowed him to see his friends in cities along the way.

As the ship carrying the men sailed along the coast of an island named Crete, it began to have trouble. The wind was blowing in the wrong direction, and since ships in those days had to depend completely on the wind for their power, the boat traveled with great difficulty. At last they arrived at a place called Fair Havens, but by now they had lost so much time that the good season for sailing was almost over. The weather began to get worse and worse.

Paul said to the soldiers, "I am afraid if we go on now we may lose our ship and all its cargo; perhaps even our lives. We should not try to cross the Great Sea until the winter is over."

But the owner of the ship and the captain did not want to spend the winter in Fair Havens, and they convinced Julius that they should try to move farther up the coast. In a few days the wind did become more gentle, and the ship left the port and sailed along the coast of the island. Not long afterward, the wind suddenly shifted and began to blow fiercely from a northeasterly direction. The captain soon found himself caught in such a terrible storm that he lost control of the ship altogether and was forced to let it be driven about by the wind and waves.

The next day the storm had not lessened at all: the wind howled, the rain was pouring down as lightning streaked the sky, and the waves continued to crash against the ship. The men began to throw overboard the ship's cargo or equipment in order to lighten the load, but still it seemed that the ship would not stand much more of the terrible beating the storm was giving it. The sky was completely black for several days and nights except for the flashes of lightning which continued to accompany the noise of the storm, and the crew gave up any hope of escaping with their lives.

Then Paul stood up and said to all present: "You should have listened to me when I warned you earlier not to sail. We can do nothing about that now, but I tell you to take heart anyway. Last night an angel of the God I worship spoke to me and said that although our ship will run ashore on an island and be destroyed, none of our lives will be lost."

The storm raged for two weeks before the sailors began to suspect that the ship was nearing land. When they churned, their instruments indicated the depth of the water was less than before. Anchors were lowered to keep the ship from crashing on the rocks near the coast. While the men aboard waited and hoped that daybreak would come, Paul urged them to eat.

"You have been too fearful to sit down and eat for fourteen days now," he told them, "but you are going to need strength for what is coming. You must take some food and quit worrying that you will be killed." When the men saw Paul's bravery they were encouraged and ate with him. Then the remaining food was thrown overboard to lighten the ship.

As the sun came up, land finally came into view; but none of them could recognize the coastline. It looked as though they would be able to land the ship on a beach not far away, so the anchors were taken up. The waves and the wind, still strong and forceful, began to drive the ship closer to the shore. When it looked as though they might make the beach, the front of the ship suddenly struck a huge shoal and ran aground. The back end was broken to pieces by the pounding of the storm.

"Swim for your lives!" shouted Julius to all those on board. Though the soldiers usually killed the prisoners in such a situation to keep them from escaping, Julius let them all have the chance to save themselves because he wanted Paul to live.

Some of the men jumped overboard and began to swim desperately for the shore. Others grabbed floating boards or other objects loosened from the back of the ship. And just as God had said, they all reached land safely; not one life was lost.

When the islanders told the men where they were, they discovered that the storm had driven them much farther than they had thought and that they were not far from their destination. They set out again when the winter was over, and at last they reached the end of their journey, the city of Rome.

The last chapter of *Acts* tells us that Paul had to wait in Rome for two years before Caesar would hear his case, but during this time he was not forced to stay in a jail. He rented a house for himself where only one soldier stayed to guard him; and he spent his time as he had for so many years, preaching to all who would listen. He also wrote letters to the Christians in many of the cities he had visited, and these letters are now part of our New Testament.

This is all that the Bible tells us about Paul, and we know nothing more except that his courageous life ended in death for the cause of Jesus Christ. He had suffered many times because of his love for Jesus. He was beaten, shipwrecked, imprisoned, mocked, and stoned. But his life was beautiful because he lived so close to God.

Acts 27–28

QUESTIONS: 1. *Why had Saul gone to Damascus?* 2. *What happened to him on the way?* 3. *What Christian came to teach Saul in Damascus?* 4. *When Saul first preached Christ, what was the reaction of other Christians? What was the reaction of other Jews?* 5. *Why did Saul go to Antioch?* 6. *Why did Saul and Barnabas leave Antioch?* 7. *Who was John Mark? How did he figure in the first missionary tour?* 8. *What events took place on the island of Cyprus?* 9. *What was the general reaction of the people in the cities visited on the journey?* 10. *Why did Paul and Barnabas turn to the Gentiles?* 11. *What Roman gods did the people of Lystra mistake the missionaries for?* 12. *Why did Paul and Barnabas part company before the second journey?* 13. *Who accompanied Paul on his journey? Who went with Barnabas?* 14. *Who was Timothy?* 15. *Why did Paul cross into the continent of Europe?* 16. *Who was Luke?* 17. *Why were Paul and Silas put into jail at Philippi?* 18. *What was the result of the earthquake?* 19.

Where did Paul speak while in Athens? What was the point of his sermon? 20. *With whom did Paul live while in Corinth?* 21. *What was the great tourist attraction in Ephesus?* 22. *Why did the silversmiths revolt?* 23. *What happened when Paul returned to Jerusalem?* 24. *Why was he transferred to Caesarea?* 25. *To what officials did Paul speak while in Caesarea? What was their reaction to his message?* 26. *Describe Paul's hazardous journey to Rome.*

The Kingdom Established

LETTERS TO YOUNG CHURCHES

By the end of Paul's life, the apostles had fulfilled Jesus' command and had spread the good news of his death and resurrection throughout the world of their time. As a result, churches had been established in Asia, Europe, and Africa. Prominent congregations met in Jerusalem, Antioch, Ephesus, Corinth, Rome, and Alexandria, as well as other leading cities. Guided by the Holy Spirit, these groups, rather than Israel, now qualified as "God's chosen people," the community of faith bound to him by a new covenant in Christ.

Most of the congregations were begun either by a missionary, such as Paul, or by Christians forced to leave Jerusalem during times of persecution. The members' new roles as sons of God were often explained to them from a distance by Spirit-led men; many of the letters which they wrote form part of our New Testament. The majority were written by Paul to churches he established on his missionary journeys. Others were written by apostles, such as Peter and John, or by church leaders like Jude and James. Since the gospels were just being written during this period, and there were no other Scriptures besides Jewish history and prophecy, these letters were an invaluable guide.

The New Testament writers dealt with many problems the inexperienced Christians faced. One of the most prominent of these was reconciling Christianity and Judaism. Some of the believers were Jews and they questioned whether or not they still had to maintain the Jewish laws. They also had very uncertain feelings about the Gentile converts who formed a majority in many congregations. What status did these non-Jews hold? the Jewish Christians wondered. Should they obey God's law as delivered to Moses as well as the one given through Christ? The books of *Romans*, *Galatians*, and *Hebrews* speak directly to this problem.

Difficult situations arose which involved everyday Christian living. Those who tried to pattern their lives after the teaching of Jesus found themselves out of step with their neighbors. They were reminded that Christ, as a human being, had also suffered and been tempted; therefore, he was able to help them in their time of trouble. And they were comforted in knowing that when one suffers as a Christian, he is blessed by God and is not to be ashamed. The epistles of *James*, *Peter*, *John*, and *Jude* are written to, and give us our best picture of, the "average" Christian of the first century.

THE BODY OF CHRIST

Paul powerfully described the groups of Christians who met throughout the world as the "body of Christ." As his body, they were to fulfill Christ's ministry in the world. Each person did this by using his own talents and abilities as a response to God's grace.

One of the personal gifts that was utilized early in the history of the church was that of leadership. Originally, the twelve apostles proclaimed the gospel to the world, but it wasn't long until they had to appoint seven men to assist them in dealing with the poor and distressed in the Jerusalem church. The pattern that seemed to follow in the congregations Paul established was an organization led by "elders" or "bishops," and their assistants, known as "deacons," all of whom were responsible to Christ. Another important role was filled by the evangelists and teachers. These are all discussed in Paul's letters to *Timothy* and *Titus*.

Christian worship in New Testament times was centered around preaching, baptism, and the Lord's Supper. They also borrowed worship forms from Judaism—scripture reading, singing of psalms, and prayer. Weekly worship services were held on Sunday, the day Christ rose from the dead, which came to be known as the "Lord's Day." These services were climaxed in the celebration of the Lord's Supper, the memorial feast instituted by Christ on the night before he died. Prayer was considered a communion with God, based on the intercession of Christ. Baptism was the point at which one began this communion by burying his own life of sin and acquiring the righteousness of Christ.

As an extension of the public worship services, the early Christian also engaged in private devotions, including prayer and fasting. He accepted the leadership of the Spirit in his personal affairs, as did the apostles, elders, and deacons in their leadership of the group as a whole. Thus they acknowledged that while Christ was head of the church, he ruled it through his Spirit.

A NEW JERUSALEM

One of the most exciting concerns of the first century Christians was their anticipation of Christ's return to earth in glory and power. Their fervent hope for his arrival is best expressed in *The Revelation of John*, which contains the old apostle's vision of the time when Christ will forever crush the powers of evil and reign throughout eternity with his own. The book served as a great source of comfort and encouragement to those who were faced with Roman persecution and perhaps martyrdom.

As the last living apostle, John was exiled because of his preaching. Banished on the lonely island of Patmos, he received a vision of hope that he recorded and sent to his distant Christian friends. In it he pictures a glorious Christ, reigning over a new heaven and a new earth.

"I saw a holy city, a new Jerusalem," he wrote, "coming down out of heaven from God." God's own royal throne was contained within, and the company that stood around it were the faithful of all time. They served God, living with him in perfect peace, for there was no more death or pain or suffering. God himself was present to wipe every tear from their eyes.

The holy city was a splendid thing, made of gold. Its walls were made of jewels and the city gates of pearl. Through its borders passed the river of the water of life; and beside its banks grew the tree of life, whose leaves were for the healing of nations.

There was no need for sun or moon in that city, for the glory of God was the light. This light would shine a welcoming beam to all the pure—to those written in the "Lamb's book of life." No darkness nor evil would ever mar the perfect light of God's presence.

The gates of God's love stood open wide. "Come," Christ issued the invitation to enter, while behind him the hosts of the redeemed praised with a loud voice,

> Worthy is the Lamb who was slain
> To receive power and wealth and wisdom and might
> and honor and glory and blessing!
> To him who sits upon the throne
> And to the Lamb be blessing and honor and glory
> and might for ever and ever! Amen!

The Revelation of John